THE TAX-FREE EXCHANGE LOOPHOLE

THE TAX-FREE EXCHANGE LOOPHOLE

How Real Investors Can Profit from the 1031 Exchange

JACK CUMMINGS

WILEY

John Wiley & Sons, Inc.

Published by John Wiley & Sons, Inc., Hoboken, New Jersey.
Published simultaneously in Canada.

For general information on our other products and services please contact our Customer
Care Department within the U.S. at (800) 762-2974, outside the United States at
(317) 572-3993 or fax (317) 572-4002.

Wiley also publishes its books in a variety of electronic formats. Some content that
appears in print may not be available in electronic books. For more information about
Wiley products, visit our web site at www.Wiley.com.

Library of Congress Cataloging-in-Publication Data:

Cummings, Jack, 1940–
    The tax-free exchange loophole : how real estate investors can profit from the 1031
exchange / Jack Cummings.
        p. cm.
    Includes index.
    ISBN 0-471-69578-5 (cloth)
    1. Real estate investment—United States.   2. Real property, Exchange
of—Taxation—United States.   3. Capital gains tax—United States.   I. Title.
    HD1382.5.C855 2004
    336.24'16—dc22

                                                                2004059085

Printed in the United States of America.

10   9   8   7   6   5   4   3   2   1

To Kassandra and Sebastian,
United in the Search of World Peace

CONTENTS

CONTENTS

Contents

CONTENTS

Contents

CONTENTS

Contents

CONTENTS

Contents

Tax-free exchanges offer a passage to greater wealth that is open to everyone in the United States, but is used only by those who know it exists, and how to take advantage of it.

The greatest real estate investment tool known to mankind is called a "tax-free exchange." In the Internal Revenue Code it is simply called IRC Section 1031. It works its magic in such a way that, when properly used, an investor need never pay capital gains tax on his or her real estate investment profits. That's right. Roll the capital right back into another investment without paying capital gains tax—ever. And you can roll it over and over again.

A tax-free exchange, as IRC Section 1031 is called, is, in essence, a loan to you that you don't pay any interest on and which you never have to repay (if you play your cards correctly). This book not only shows you how to play those cards properly, but it demonstrates to you in easy-to-follow steps how to multiply the effect of the tax-free exchange over and over. Best of all, this book uncovers the secrets that the insiders keep to themselves; it shows you how you can legally use this loophole to make a sale and not pay any capital gains tax at all, ever, no matter how much you actually make—exchange or not.

Financial Independence
Is Just around the Corner

This book will give your journey toward financial independence a tremendous boost. By elevating you into the ranks of real estate insiders, it gives you a working knowledge of not only IRC Section 1031 tax-free exchanges, but also how the technique of real estate exchanging can give you the edge in real estate investing no matter whether the market is hot or has grown cold. Investment potential at its greatest level is attained by using all the tax and legal advantages the laws allow.

Of all the investments you can make, the most productive commodity is real estate. Ask Donald Trump, Warren Buffett, and even George W. Bush if you have any doubts about this. Real estate is it—simply it. You can't add it to a sold-out subdivision, you can't create it on the already built-up oceanfront of Miami, or Saint-Tropez, or wherever people want to be. Best of all, real estate is an item that you can easily control and master. It is local, so much so that perhaps it is the office building or hotel just down the street from where you live that supports your family with jobs, wages, and a financially independent life. Real estate can ensure that you are in control of your future.

Real estate is a solid investment that is not volatile or subject to the whims of the stock market, and, thanks to the current financial market, it is affordable and can be acquired with a down payment that is just a fraction of its real value. Sometimes it can be purchased with nothing more than a promise to pay. Take these benefits and tie them to the greatest investment tool known to mankind and your financial future will take off like a rocket to the moon. Or even further.

There's Magic in Real Estate

All real estate insiders know that there is much that is magical about real estate. From a wealth-building point of view, real estate receives special treatment by the IRS that, if you know the loopholes, gives the real estate investor the edge over everyone else.

That's right, there are several great loopholes that the IRS hands out to real estate investors, only not all these investors are standing in line to receive them. Not everyone knows all the loopholes that exist, or how to use them to their maximum potential. And sadly, many investors, lawyers, and accountants are shy about using the real estate investment tool known as the tax-free exchange. Why? Because they don't fully understand the rules. When lawyers or accountants do not fully understand something, do you think they will advise their clients to use it? Absolutely not. That's bad news for you, if you are their client. The good news is this book and the greatest real estate tool it exposes.

This book tackles this subject in an easy-to-follow way. It is filled with my own personal portfolio examples, my own painful experiences (to save you from those pitfalls), and many rewards that just keep on giving. Easy-to-follow and smart-to-use checklists turn the IRC 1031 into a good friend—that is, a good moneymaking friend.

The book builds your knowledge as you go. Each chapter opens with the goals of that chapter, and is followed by a section titled "Terms and Concepts You Need to Know." These are the building blocks of each chapter and set the stage for the walls and roof of that structure to follow.

Through the many real-life examples you can discover what you need to do to avoid making mistakes in using this tool.

I invite you to share your exchange potentials and questions with me via e-mail at jwcre@aol.com.

CHAPTER 1

How to Use This Book to Maximize Your Real Estate Investment Profits

The goal of this chapter is:

To Set the Stage So You Get the Most from This Book

This book is written in a building-blocks style. Each element will not only help you understand the information, but also enable you to use one set of data to better understand the next to follow. This will help you in many other ways, too.

First, this building-block method speeds up the whole process of becoming a real estate insider. Second, it gives you the terms and concepts that insiders use, and enables you to quickly begin to use those terms. Third, you will see concepts that most of the professional people in real estate, including some accountants and lawyers, only vaguely understand and therefore tend to shy away from. The worst part of that scenario is that when accountants or lawyers are not comfortable with a concept, they rarely want to acknowledge that fact, and instead of owning up to their lack of knowledge they might just say, "You had better stay away from that."

Each chapter of this book begins with the goal to which the chapter is dedicated. That does not mean that is the end of the involvement with that subject; it is simply the main goal of that chapter. Once the goal has been stated, each chapter follows with a heading "Terms and Concepts You Need to Know." You may already know many or even most of them, but do not rush through the text that defines and discusses them. Why? Simply this, the terms and concepts take you into other areas of real estate investing that may be new to you. You may know the term in an entirely different context, and not realize its significance as it pertains to Internal Revenue Code (IRC) Section 1031 exchanges or other features of the tax code that this book will introduce to you.

The goal of this **book** is:

To Improve Your Real Estate Investing Opportunities
    through Exchanging

This easy-to-read book deals with the various forms of real estate exchanges. You will discover the mechanics of creative financing and insider techniques of how to successfully complete many types of exchanges. Some of these techniques will save you money you would have had to pay to Uncle Sam (the IRS). Other techniques show you how to buy or sell real estate more profitably by putting the word *exchange* into the equation. Still others will help you fine-tune your ability to expand your knowledge of the Starker exchange and other tax-free kinds of exchanges that have become some of the biggest events in the real estate world.

Terms and Concepts You Need to Know

Pretax Investment Value
Boot Paid or Received
Tax Basis
Net Operating Income
Amortization
Balloon Mortgage
Estate Taxes
Planning and Zoning
Comfort Zone

Let's review each of these terms or concepts in detail.

Pretax Investment Value

The concept of pretax investment value is simple enough. In the context of real estate investing it is the value of the assets you give up when you purchase a property. In essence, if you use cash and/or other assets, what will that cash and/or other assets cost you at the end of the year in the way of tax? If there is no added cost in the transaction, the amount you spend (the pretax cost) will equal the after-tax cost. If, however, you have to reach into your pocket and pay an additional sum of money in tax, the after-tax cost will exceed the pretax cost.

The tax in question is the tax on any gain to you at the time of a sale. Keep in mind that I am talking about a gain as a result of a sale as calculated by the Internal Revenue Service (IRS). You will soon discover that if you take depreciation on a property, the amount of the depreciation taken is recovered as a gain when you sell. So, it is possible to sell at the same price you paid for a property and still have a taxable gain. Here is an example of what I mean:

Brad's Transaction

Brad is a manager of a local department store. He makes good money, which is a combination of his salary and annual bonus for exceeding his

3

projected level of sales. Let's say that at the end of the year he sees that he will receive an unexpected annual bonus of $50,000. He wants to invest that as a down payment on a small apartment building he has had his eye on for several months. It is for sale at a bargain price of $220,000 with the seller holding all the financing. The apartment building is in need of repair and cosmetics, which Brad feels he will be able to do working weekends over the next 18 months at a cost of around $30,000 for the material (he will do all the labor). His total price, he figures, will be $250,000. But Brad has forgotten that he will have to pay income tax on the $50,000 bonus, which at his (overall) 20 percent bracket would cost him another $10,000 and bring his overall cost to $260,000.

But wait, Brad owns a residential lot in North Carolina that is worth $60,000. He thinks about it, and decides that as he is never going to build on the lot, why not see if he can put it into a deal with the owner of the apartment building? If he offered the seller of the apartment building the $60,000 lot and all cash for the balance, he would owe $160,000 ($220,000 less the lot's value of $60,000). The seller might be motivated enough, now that he is getting a big block of cash, to take the lot and perhaps even lower the price on the apartment building. Now Brad can take his cash, even as much as $40,000 of his $50,000 bonus, and plug it into the building by hiring a contractor to do the needed work right after closing, so that he can get the benefits of the work right away. If the work was mostly repair and fix-up, Brad may be able to take advantage of a tax write-off of the expense and end up having a much lower tax base, and now a year-end income tax on only $10,000 (his $50,000 of earnings less $40,000 repair expense). This reduction in his taxable income for that year may have an added bonus by lowering his income to a level that would also reduce his overall tax rate.

However, the nicest part of this transaction is yet to come. He ties up the property with a firm contract that gives him access to the property prior to the closing to do the fix-up work. If properly structured, the contract to acquire the building creates several win-win benefits for both parties. The owner of the apartments would like the fact that Brad is spending money on a building he doesn't own yet, while at the same time it speeds up Brad's overall process to improve the building so that he can raise rents the moment he takes title. Perhaps best of all, the added improvements and newly projected rents will increase the value of the property and boost the lending value to the extent that a new lender will see the building in a new light. It will no longer be a fixer-upper; it will be an apartment building with a fresh new look, with fresh new rents predictable. The value of the newly fixed up building might be $285,000 or even more. Using this new value Brad should be able to borrow as much as $228,000 as that would represent only 80 percent of the new value.

What does Brad's deal look like now? Well, his total investment cost is the $220,000 price on the apartment building (unless he could now get it for less due to the cash paid to the seller), plus the cost of the work that goes into the building of $40,000. So we can say that his cost is $260,000. What does he actually pay from his pocket? Well, he borrows $228,000, which might cost him $3,000 in loan costs so he nets out $225,000. As he has to give the seller only $160,000 of that (plus his $60,000 lot), he still has $65,000 left. Brad pays for the work to the building with his earnings, because remember, that work is done prior to closing on the apartment building. But he adds the leftover $65,000 from the loan to the remaining $10,000 in the bank. Of the $75,000 now in the bank, only the $10,000 left over from the repair cost is taxable.

Recap of Brad's Deal So Far

Price of apartments	$220,000	
Repair and fix-up cost	40,000	(Paid for by Brad prior to closing)
Total Brad will have invested	$260,000	
Brad gives owner North Carolina lot	$ 60,000	(This occurs at the closing)
	$200,000	
Less repair and fix-up cost	40,000	(Already paid by Brad)
Cash Brad owes the owner	$160,000	
Brad borrows	$228,000	
Less cost of mortgage	3,000	
Net proceeds of loan	$225,000	
Less what Brad still owes	160,000	
Tax-free cash left over	$ 65,000	

Plus cash still in bank   <u>10,000</u>   ($50,000 less repairs of $40,000)

New bank balance $75,000

How did Brad end up with $65,000 tax-free cash? Because $65,000 he borrowed is not taxable at this time, if ever. Brad started out with only $50,000 and an unproductive lot in North Carolina. He ends up with $75,000 cash in the bank and is the proud owner of a freshly fixed up apartment building. As the North Carolina lot was owned as a long-term investment, he didn't have to pay any capital gains tax on the transfer of that lot to the seller of the apartments. Brad can start looking for another real estate investment because he took a hard look at what his real cost would be (the after-tax cost), and by applying some creative techniques he leveraged his assets to greatly improve his situation.

Brad's transaction is a simple example of using the exchange process to improve his overall situation. He has accomplished several positive steps in maximizing his investment potential. He has gotten rid of an asset that was not doing much, if anything, for his investment future; maximized his new loan opportunity by borrowing on a building already fixed up; and took advantage of bringing in tax-free capital from the proceeds of the loan. This is just one way in which the tax code can benefit you just as it did Brad. As we move further into exchanging, and in particular using the IRC Section 1031 tax-free exchange, you should keep focused on the fact that not all exchanges involve a one-on-one exchange like the one accomplished by Brad. Also, exchanges can include other elements besides real estate. When a non–real estate or a nonqualified type of real estate is used in the exchange, that part of the deal may become taxable to the party receiving it. These elements are called boot.

Boot Paid or Received

Although the term *boot* does not show up in the tax code, its use is accepted to mean cash or other assets that do not qualify for Section 1031 status. In essence, if you give me real estate worth $100,000 and I give you real estate worth $80,000 and to sweeten the deal I throw in $5,000 cash, a diamond ring worth $5,000, and a personal note to pay you the balance of $10,000, then you have received $20,000 of boot. In this example that entire amount of $20,000 in value is subject to being taxed, provided that your gain was at least $20,000.

In many real estate exchanges both sides may give and take non-qualifying values in the exchange. Here is what a deal might look like.

You Get from Me	You Give Me
A condominium worth $80,000	A vacant lot worth $100,000
A sailboat worth $30,000	Cash in the amount of $10,000

The net effect for you in the boot transfer is $20,000. You took from me a sailboat worth $30,000 but had to pay me $10,000 to balance the equities. Still, if your gain equals $20,000 then that becomes taxable. If your gain (in the lot) is only $15,000 you will owe tax only on that amount.

Many real estate exchanges include the transfer of some cash and/or other nonqualifying assets. These assets can be other real estate that would not meet the test for 1031 treatment (say, real estate that is not in the United States or an investment that would become inventory for resale or is clearly not a like-kind property according to the IRS). All of these assets would be taxable by the party that receives them up to the extent of the gain that is present on the property given up by that person.

In the closing of the exchange, boot is a netted-out factor. By this I mean that the IRS allows a party to receive boot in the transaction, but if that party pays (or gives) to the other party boot, the two amounts can cancel each other out. In some situations each party receives taxable boot, and if one party has received more boot than he or she has given to the other party, there could be a tax due on that overage. But in no event will the taxable boot be greater than the actual gain on which the taxpayer would have had to pay tax in the first instance. If one party receives excess boot but that party has no taxable gain, then the question of tax to that party is moot and a nonissue.

Eight Causes of Boot

In the calculations of boot, there are a number of factors to take into consideration. Overlooking any of these elements can result in a surprising tax consequence at the closing when none was anticipated. Let's look at the eight most obvious causes for boot.

Cash Received: If money changes hands, then this is boot. To the extent that all boot that is given and received is added up and netted between the parties, the act of giving or receiving boot is not the final determination of whether there is a tax to be paid, and if so which side will be obliged to pay it. In the netting of boot, several factors must be considered.

1. Cash boot that is paid always offsets cash boot received.
2. Cash boot paid to the owner of the replacement property also offsets mortgage relief given up by the owner of the exchanged property.
3. Net cash received from the replacement owner is not offset by debt assumed (on the replacement property). Any net cash to the taxpayer taking the replacement property will be taxable (if there is a taxable gain).

Net Debt Relief: As the IRS considers that if you are relieved of a debt obligation in the deal, such as a mortgage against the property you are giving up, then that is treated as though you have been given cash in the amount of the mortgage you no longer have to pay. Remember, you got the benefit of that mortgage at the time you purchased the property, or you received cash when you refinanced the mortgage some time ago. Now you may have to pay the piper (Uncle Sam). But as boot is netted out between the parties, if you are relieved of a mortgage, say $500,000 in the property you give up, but assume a $501,000 (or larger) mortgage on the property you get and there are no other boot items to upset this balance, you are clear of tax on the boot issue. The extra amount that you are obligated to, in this case $1,000 (or more), will increase your tax basis by that amount. But let's not get ahead of ourselves.

Closing Service Cost: If the closing agent dips into the 1031 escrowed funds to cover certain costs that would not be qualified acquisition costs, such as cost of a survey or title insurance, those funds could be treated as boot. This should not be a problem, and one way to ensure that does not happen is to question every debit and credit on the closing statement. If there is any doubt about the ultimate netting of boot, have cash (or your checkbook) and pay those fees outside of the escrowed funds.

Closing Prorations: When there are debits and credits in a closing that have nothing to do with the values of the actual transaction, such as rent prorations, utility escrows, real estate tax prorations, tenant deposits and advance rent payments, and the like, these can be classified as boot by the IRS. Again, question each item and have them separated from the monetary transfers of the deal and paid separately rather than simply debited or credited to the appropriate party.

New Financing Cost or Assumption Charges on Existing Mortgages: Although the amount of debt that one party becomes obligated to (secured by the replacement property) or becomes relieved of (secured by the exchanged property) is important in calculating the net boot situation, any cost attributed to those mortgages may be challenged by the IRS as being boot. If there is doubt about this, pay them separately and not out of the escrowed funds.

Non-Like-Kind Property: This can be tricky. If the seller of the relinquished property takes a promissory note from the buyer as a part of that transaction, the promissory note will likely be treated as boot. Any non-like-kind property, either real or personal, is considered boot.

New Financing or Refinancing from a Third Party: When the rules that govern financing are followed there may be no problem, but the IRS looks very closely at certain elements. Did the taxpayer end up with tax-free cash by overfinancing the deal? This would happen if the taxpayer was, say, $30,000 short of giving the replacement property owner sufficient equity to make the exchange, so the taxpayer put $50,000 in new financing on the property and walked out of the closing with $20,000 cash. Mind you, courts have sided with the taxpayer on this issue, taking the position that this is no different from when someone purchases a property and ends up with cash from a greater than 100 percent new debt being placed on the property. But this issue can wave a red flag and it is never a good idea to do that. Watch for some additional comments from the IRS on this issue in the future.

Seller-Held Financing: The idea of a seller of the exchanged property holding financing in an IRC Section 1031 transaction is contrary to meeting the like-kind property criteria. Because the mortgage would be an asset received by the taxpayer in the transaction, which does not meet the like-kind test, this kind of transaction would most likely fail to qualify in the event of an IRS audit.

I have seen methods that appear to get around the seller-held financing situation. Some of the suggestions may actually work—that is, until the IRS audits that transaction. None of the suggested ways I have seen are covered by any current IRS rulings or regulations and do not appear to be protected by current safe-harbor provisions. However, you should keep in mind that safe-harbor provisions are not meant to be absolute requirements as it is possible to argue that your situation is so unique that you should be allowed to slide past the absence of a distinct ruling. There is risk in doing this, so I will end my comments on this subject right now.

If the only way your would-be exchange can fly is by added financing, seek it from a third party, and make sure your facilitator and your lawyer checks the most current IRS rulings on this factor.

Tax Basis

The tax basis of any real estate is the original cost, plus any capital improvements, less any deductions from value. A capital improvement is any improvement to your property that would not be considered repair and/or general maintenance. If you add a new building, that is a capital improvement, but merely painting your old building is a repair or maintenance expense. If the property is an investment property such as an apartment building, then the expenses for repairs or maintenance can be deducted from annual income. Paint your home (in which you are living) and you cannot deduct that cost as a business or investment expense. So, capital improvements add to your tax basis.

Let's look at the three factors making up tax basis. The original cost is what you paid for the property when you acquired it. Of course, it might be that you didn't pay anything at all because you made an exchange in that first instance, as was the case with Brad when he exchanged the North Carolina lot as a part of the apartment building deal described earlier in this chapter. Sure, he actually reached into his pocket and paid some cash for fix-up, but at the completion of the transaction he ended up with more cash than he had when he started. We'll see how that gets sorted out in a second. The key to understanding tax basis is to think of it as the book value of your property.

We all know about the book value of a car. The day you buy it the value begins to depreciate. While real estate may not actually depreciate, the IRS gives you the right to write off, or in this case to take a tax deduction each year, the supposed depreciation of the capital improvements made to the real estate. In Brad's case, there are no improvements to his lot, so no depreciation is possible.

Let's start with the tax basis of Brad's lot in North Carolina. Assume he paid $5,000 for it and did nothing to add or take away value. If he had spent $60,000 on the construction of a log cabin, that would have added that much value to the lot, thereby increasing his tax basis from $5,000 to $65,000. However, as he started with a tax basis of $5,000 and did nothing to improve it, the tax basis remains at that original cost of $5,000.

To add value you must make additional capital investments to the property. A capital investment or capital expenditure will increase your tax basis no matter what it is. It could be a new building, adding to an existing building, or making other improvements to the property. Remember, repairs and maintenance, no matter when they are done, do not count as a capital improvement, and those costs do not increase your tax basis.

To decrease your tax basis, you can take an amount each year as depreciation if the property qualifies as an investment property or one used in your business. Of the overall cost of that investment or business property, only the improvements can be depreciated. Land is not a depreciable item.

Depreciation is, in essence, the deduction of a cost of a capital improvement over a period of time. Just as paying for janitorial services to your office building is a business operational expense and as such is a deduction from your gross revenue, depreciation is treated the same way. The big difference is you have already paid for that $500,000 building, and the IRS allows only a fraction of that cost to be deducted as depreciation expense. There are several methods of taking depreciation, but let's not get into them right now. Just remember that you do have an option as to the period of time during which you can write down the value of the capital improvements to best fit the investment profile you have established. As depreciation is a tax write-off, say you take $5,000 in depreciation one year (if that amount is allowed on your improvement); that is a direct tax deduction from your otherwise taxable income. In essence, you can put $5,000 into your pocket without paying tax on it that year. The flip side of that story is that when you sell the property at a profit over what you paid, you will now have an additional $5,000 of capital gain, all of which would be taxable income, at a capital gain rate.

Your edge in this game is that you have converted earned income, at a potentially higher tax rate, into capital gains income that is, as I write this chapter, at a maximum of 15 percent tax. Some parts of an exchange, however, may be taxed at a higher rate. This can happen when the party making the exchange has a "recapture of depreciation." Recapture of depreciation occurs when a depreciable real property asset (called Section 1250 property, which would be a building or other improvement and never the land itself) has been depreciated at an IRS-approved rate that allows a faster write-off than the maximum straight-line term offered. The importance of this is that if you take advantage of a faster write-off of the improvements on a property you give up in an exchange and take a vacant tract of land with no 1250 property on it, it is possible to incur a taxable event, even though there was no net boot in your pocket at the end of the exchange. The amount of depreciation of 1250 property (what is depreciable and not land) that exceeds straight-line depreciation and is recognized (taxable) and will be taxed at a rate that as of this writing exceeds the capital gains rate of 15 percent as it is treated as earned income at a 25 percent rate.

Another deduction to your tax basis comes in the way of depletion. This is a mining or timber or fruit tree grove sort of thing and has to do with the estimated value of minerals or timber or food-bearing trees on the property when you purchase it. As those items are mined or cut down or become barren, the value of the remaining property is affected, and the tax basis is reduced accordingly. This is a complex situation, and if you think you will be impacted by mining of minerals or timber being cut on your property, then be sure to check out the latest IRS rules on those subjects with your accountant.

Depreciation is the element that most real estate investors come to know very well because it puts more spendable cash in their pockets and converts earned income into capital gains income, which would likely be taxed at a lower tax rate, if taxed at all. If investors use the IRS rules to their advantage, when it comes time to sell they can avoid capital gains tax on the sale. The downside of that statement is predicated on using the rules to their advantage. It is easy to make a mistake in deciding when to sell a property, or to attempt to make a tax-free exchange (which is really a tax-deferral exchange) and then to fail to meet the final test of rules. Much of this book is dedicated to helping you use the rules properly and avoid the mistakes that can rear up and bite you where it will hurt most— your pocketbook.

The following is a simple but effective checklist to use to ensure you keep up on your tax basis. My suggestion is you fill this out once a year right up to the time that you either sell or exchange your real estate. Have one of these for each property you own.

Tax Basis Checklist for 20__

Original purchase price or last year's tax basis $ _____

(Always start a new year with the previous year's tax basis)

Plus capital improvements _____

_____

_____

_____

Total capital improvements $ _____

Original cost plus improvements $ _____

Less depreciation taken for the year $ _____

Tax basis ending the year $ _____

You should keep one of these checklists filled out each year for your home. If you have an office in your home and have elected to take depreciation of that part of the home, then be sure to include the depreciation taken. But keep in mind that just because the IRS allows you to take depreciation, that does not mean you must do so—although as long as you pay income tax on your earnings at a greater tax rate than that for capital gains, you likely will come out ahead by taking depreciation. However, a sale of a home qualifies for an exclusion of $250,000 per husband and wife, or $500,000 total in gain if you have lived in the home two years out of the past five years, so you will most likely escape most of the capital gains tax that might have come back to you from depreciating your home office.

Net Operating Income

Most income-producing property values are controlled by the net operating income (NOI). This is gross rents less refunds and operating expenses. The only accounting factors that should not be a part of the overall financial operation of any income-producing property are debt service and capital expenditures.

Debt service is the cost to repay debt that is secured by the property, in essence the interest charge on the debt. Although interest on the debt is a deductible expense for investment and business properties, that cost should not be a deduction from the income collected to arrive at the net operating income amount. NOI is always treated as if the property were free and clear (F&C) of any debt.

Capital expenditures occur when a new asset is acquired. This happens when a piece of machinery used in the business is acquired, or a new building or addition to an existing one is built. The easiest way to distinguish a capital expense from an operational expense is this. If the item acquired remains after the end of the year, it is a capital expense: Repairs to or maintenance of any capital item previously purchased is an operational expense.

Remember that not all accountants use the same terminology, nor do they produce income and expense statements in the same format. It should not, therefore, surprise you to see different forms with other items excluded from the operating expenses of a property. You may need to adjust any income and expense statement that contains deductions for expenses that are directly related to debt or the acquisition of a capital item. However, those items should be shown as deductions from the NOI to arrive at the actual cash flow from the business. Because capital expenses generally have a long-term benefit to a business or operation, the lack of cash flow due to large capital expenditures during any given year should be closely reviewed to ascertain if that cost would result in new revenue. Sometimes a large capital expenditure is a result of prior poor maintenance of equipment that must be replaced earlier than its normal operating life. Because the maintenance of capital items can be one of the first places cuts are made by a management posture intent on showing growth in the NOI, the actual condition of the physical part of real estate should be closely inspected.

Net operating income is very important because it allows you to judge and compare different but similar properties when attempting to choose one or the other as an investment. So all the apples should be where they are supposed to be. Just remember, if the property is debt free there will be no interest charge, so 100 percent of the expenses of a property will be operating expenses.

What about an accounting charge or the cost to build a 50,000-square-foot addition to your shopping center? Where does that cost go? Well, all of the cost that is allocated as a capital expenditure will simply not show up on the income and expense sheet at all, although a notation might be made to explain what happened to cause a reduction of $500,000 or whatever the cost was from the company's bank account. Yet any qualified expense that can be an operational expense that was attributed to the new addition can be put back into the operational expenses.

Assume that you are an investor with $500,000 to spend and you want to earn a minimum of 10 percent on that investment. That would mean that at the end of the year you would expect to pocket at least $50,000 as a return of 10 percent on the invested cash. If the total price of the investment was only $500,000 then your NOI is your absolute bottom line as there would be no fixed charges. The only other expense to be considered would be the income tax on those earnings.

However, few investors buy debt-free property and keep it that way. The concept of using other people's money is an integral part of savvy real estate investing. If you can obtain leverage by obtaining financing at a cost that is less than the NOI return on your investment, then you can parlay your investment capital into millions quicker than you think if that is what you want to do. Here is an example.

Charlene's Deal

Charlene has $100,000 to invest. She likes the idea of finding a fixer-upper apartment building where she can use her decorating talents to increase the property's appeal for would-be tenants and therefore increase the NOI of the property. She wants to net before taxes at least $10,000 on her investment. She finds a six-unit property that happens to be on a lot that is zoned for eight units. This zoning factor is important to what is going to happen, and is one of the real insider secrets to getting more out of a property than a previous owner did. As it was, the seller reported that the apartments were bringing in close to $55,000 per year in gross rents.

The seller wants a fair $300,000 for the property. Charlene has already done her homework and is sure she can get the gross rents up above $60,000 within a year, so she offers $290,000 with $55,000 down. She asks the seller to hold a second mortgage of $45,000 at 7 percent interest, with no principal paid until the balloon (final payment) in 10 years. This mortgage is to be subordinated (other debt allowed to be ahead of it) to no more than $190,000 in new first-mortgage money. Charlene knew that a lender might balk at having a second mortgage on the property, and if that happened she was ready to switch the seller into holding a second mortgage with her own home as the security.

With a relatively low loan-to-value (LTV) ratio for the first mortgage lender, Charlene was counting on getting a low interest rate. In fact, the lender was so pleased with her business plan and intended improvements, which she already had the cash to pay for stuck in the bank ($45,000), that she got a 30-year term for her needed $190,000 at a 5.5 percent fixed mortgage rate. Here is how her investment turns out.

Recap of Charlene's Results

Total purchase price	$290,000	
Cash down	55,000	
Balance owed	$235,000	
First mortgage	$190,000	(30 years at 5.5% interest)
Second mortgage	45,000	(10 years at 7% interest)
Total debt	$235,000	

As a part of the fix-up she manages to convert part of the building so that instead of three two-bedroom apartments and three one-bedroom apartments she ends up with eight one-bedroom apartments. With a little hard work and spending most, but not all, of her budgeted $45,000, by the end of the first year she was taking in an average of $700 per month for the eight units. This income totaled $67,200 for the year. Her operating expenses were 40 percent of that amount, which left her with $40,320 at the NOI level.

Charlene's Eight Units Income and Expense Statement

Gross rents		$67,200.00
Less total operating expenses		26,880.00
Net operating income before depreciation		$40,320.00
Less fixed charges:		
Interest on first mortgage	$10,661.75	
Interest on second mortgage	3,850.00	
Total fixed charges	$14,511.75	
Profit before taxes and depreciation	$25,808.25	

Remember that Charlene invested just under $100,000 in this property ($55,000 down and about $40,000 for fix-up). A good part of that would likely be deductible fix-up expenses, too, but those expenses have not been included in the operational expenses of the property. If she had actually spent $25,000 of deductible expenses that year she would have more than enough tax credit (don't forget the depreciation) to shelter the entire gross profit for that year. Her return would be substantially above the goal of 10 percent return.

Keep in mind that we have not shown any principal repayment on the two loans. If they have a principal payment that would amortize the loans in full during their terms, the principal payment for both mortgages would be at most $6,333 for the first mortgage (a simple $190,000 divided by 30 years would equal this) and $4,500 for the second mortgage as it would be spread over 10 years. A total of $10,833 in principal still leaves Charlene with a cash flow of $14,975.25 for the year. If she had that kind of debt amortization, her interest total would drop each year as the principal was paid off so her cash flow would increase even if she never increased the rent for the next 30 years. Her yield with these numbers is seen in the following chart:

Charlene's Yield on Her Investment

Gross profit before taxes and depreciation	$25,808.25
Principal payments on debt	10,833.00
Cash flow	$14,975.25
Invested capital	$95,000.00
Cash-on-cash return	15.76%

To find your cash-on-cash yield (percentage return on your invested cash) what you want to know is what percent of your cash invested is $14,975.25. To do this you divide the cash flow by the amount invested (divide $14,975.25 by $95,000). Then move the decimal point two places to the right to get your yield. In an economic environment where it is hard to find a place to earn even 4 percent, 15.76 percent is rather refreshing.

Charlene leveraged her investment well above the desired 10 percent yield that she wanted. Part of the $40,000 she spent on making changes to the apartments will clearly be capital cost, which will add to her tax basis. Assume that $25,000 of those funds went into new walls to reconfigure the former two-bedroom apartments into a greater number of one-bedroom apartments. Here is what her new tax basis would look like at the end of the year. Assume that her total depreciation taken during the year (as set up by her accountant) was $9,000. Remember that only the amount of capital improvements can be depreciated. The value of the land under the buildings and improvements cannot be depreciated.

Charlene's Tax Basis Checklist

Original purchase price		$290,000.00
Plus capital improvements:		
Remodeling cost	$25,000.00	
Total capital improvements		$ 25,000.00
Original cost plus improvements		$315,000.00
Less depreciation taken for the year		9,000.00
Tax basis ending the year		$306,000.00

Let's go back and adjust Charlene's NOI to reflect depreciation.

Charlene's Taxable Income

Gross profit before taxes and depreciation	$25,808.25
Deduct the amount of depreciation taken	9,000.00
Actual taxable income	$16,808.25

If Charlene, due to other sources of income, is in a 20 percent tax bracket, she would have to pay $2,951.65 in income tax allocated to the income from the apartments. However, see how the noncash deduction of depreciation as a business expense affects her cash flow.

Charlene's Cash Flow

Income left after all expenses except taxes and depreciation	$25,808.25
Less depreciation	9,000.00
Taxable income	$16,808.25
Less tax at 20% rate (due to other income and expenses not shown)	3,361.65
Subtotal	$13,446.60
Add back the noncash deduction of depreciation	9,000.00
Adjusted spendable cash flow after taxes and depreciation	$22,446.60

Taking into account all of these assumptions, Charlene has $22,446.60 of earnings after taxes and depreciation on an investment of less than $100,000, which can now be added to her growing bank account.

Amortization

The concept of amortization of a mortgage is a multifaceted event. In many parts of the world, mortgages are very different from what we in the United States are accustomed to. You have already seen one example in this chapter. Remember Charlene's two mortgages? The first mortgage was originally a $190,000 mortgage over 30 years at 5.5 percent fixed interest. The second mortgage was $45,000 at 7 percent interest only for 10 years with a balloon (final payment) at the end of that term.

In the example showing Charlene's cash flow, I assumed a fixed amortization of the debt. In other words, I took the total debt, $190,000, and divided it by the term of years (30) and came up with a schedule of debt reduction. I did the same thing with the second mortgage of $45,000 due over 10 years. These two examples were given as a simple approach to the real approach to debt reduction. That kind of amortization would be called "equal principal reduction each year plus interest on the balance owed." This is not a common approach to setting an amortization schedule for investors in the United States and Canada; however, it is used in many parts of the world. I want to stress the point that in real estate investing jargon, the same term can often be applied with considerably different end results. Amortization is no exception to this rule. Let's see several other ways mortgages and debt can be set up to be amortized.

Interest-Only Payments with Final Payoff at Future Date

These mortgages would have a contract rate, which is the applicable interest rate paid without any principal reduction of the amount owed. In this situation the amount borrowed (principal owed) remains the same until it is eventually paid off or otherwise reduced.

Zero Principal with Discounted Interest Paid

This mortgage, as with the interest-only form, has no principal reduction until specific periods. Those periods might be annually, every five years, or only at the final payment. Because the interest payment is discounted, the amount owed will grow in between the principal reduction payments. For example, a loan for $100,000 with 10 annual payments at 7 percent interest discounted to an actual payment of only 4 percent, with a single payment at the end of the term to bring everything current, would look like this for the first three years of the term:

Zero Principal with Discounted Interest Paid

	Year 1	Year 2	Year 3
Amount owed at start of year	$100,000	$103,000	$106,090
Interest due at 7%	7,000	7,210	7,426.30
Interest paid at 4%	4,000	4,120	4,243.60
Unpaid interest added to principal	3,000	3,090	3,182.70

You can see that this method of payment will have a positive effect on the cash flow in the early years of its schedule.

Reverse Mortgage

This is a mortgage that pays you money from day one and continues doing that until a predetermined date in the contract when it comes due and payable or you start paying it off over a predetermined term. For example, the lender agrees to pay you $1,000 a month using your home as security for the debt until a future date when the principal amount paid to you, plus interest on that growing balance, equals $200,000. Naturally these amounts will depend on the value of the property and the terms you negotiate with the lender. As the principal balance grows its growth rate increases as the annual contract rate is accruing. Generally there is a provision that will allow you to pay off the loan early without a penalty.

In the illustration, this reverse mortgage pays the homeowner $1,000 a month for 10 years. At the end of the 10 years the amount paid, plus accrued interest, becomes the principal owed on the mortgage. This principal would then be either paid off in full or refinanced by the homeowner with some form of repayment. The usual provision for a reverse mortgage would require it to be paid off if the property was sold prior to the end of the term—in this example, before the end of 10 years. Assume interest in this example is 7 percent per year.

Reverse Mortgage Calculation

Annual amount paid to homeowner at start of loan	$12,000.00
Interest owed for year at 7%	840.00
Principal owed by homeowner at end of first year	$12,840.00
Payment to homeowner at start of year 2	12,000.00
Total owed by homeowner at end of year 2	$24,840.00
Plus interest on new total owed at 7%	1,738.80
Principal owed by homeowner at start of year 3	$26,578.80
Payment to homeowner at start of year 3	12,000.00
Total owed by homeowner at end of year 3	$38,578.80
Plus interest on new total owed at 7%	2,700.52
Principal owed by homeowner at start of year 4	$41,279.32

This would continue until the end of the tenth year, at which time a total of $120,000 would have been paid out to the homeowner ($12,000 × 10 years = $120,000). Interest would have continued to compound on the increasing debt. The interest portion of the amount at the end of the tenth year would be $33,797.38, so the final amount owed by the homeowner (principal paid plus interest compounded and now due) would be $153,797.38.

Equal Payments of Principal and Interest Combined

This is the more standard form of bank loan. Here there is generally a monthly payment, but the actual term can be any agreed-to method of payout. This form of payment takes into account the interest due plus a certain amount of principal so that the periodic payment remains fixed for the term. We tend to take this mathematical phenomenon for granted, but it works wonders in mortgage lending. Simple-to-use amortization tables and calculators employ this kind of formula in their calculation of the monthly payments for any loan amount, at any contract rate of interest, and for any specific term of years and method of payment.

This form of mortgage payment may have a number of special features that allow you to adopt a mortgage payment schedule that better
suits the property you are acquiring or refinancing. For example, an adjustable contract rate is where the lender can adjust the interest rate you
pay at specific periods you agree to when you first establish the mortgage. Often the adjustment is tied to a benchmark such as a prime rate or
the London Interbank Offered Rate (LIBOR—an insider term that refers
to the rate large banks charge each other for loans between themselves),
or other such established benchmarks such as different U.S. Treasury
bond rates, or even the price of gold. The key to these benchmarks is that
they be easily identified and universal in their calculation. As long as you
agree to it, any other benchmark can be used. As the loan progresses the
lender applies the adjustments and your payment will change (usually go
up) and remain at that adjusted amount until the next adjustment.

Other Features

Loans are offered in various kinds of packages. For example, they may
have fixed or adjustable rates spread over different terms of years, say,
10, 15, 20, 25 years or more. Some lenders may encourage a longer
amortization period with a shorter call (payoff) date. This kind of loan
could be a 30/15, which indicates a 30-year amortization with a 15-year
payoff date. The early payoff date is called a balloon (discussed in the
next section). However, a longer amortization period reduces the monthly
payment somewhat. The shorter call date, say 15 years, allows the lender
to get paid off early and avoid the risk of being stuck with a lower than
market rate for the full term of 30 years or longer.

One element you need to remember is that all of these methods of
structuring a loan repayment schedule are created with a specific benefit
to both the borrower and the lender. Adjustable mortgages protect the
lender from having its funds committed at a contract rate that is too low
in future years for them to profit from that loan. Borrowers, however, can
often benefit from the lower rate a lender can offer when it has an adjustable protection provision, as long as the rate doesn't go up too much
or too fast.

Balloon Mortgage

The balloon mortgage is one that has one or more dates when all or most of the principal still outstanding comes due. Generally a balloon mortgage has one such payment, for example the 30-year amortization schedule referenced a moment ago, with a call date at the end of 15 years. That payoff amount would be the balloon payment. The term likely comes from the fact that this payment is so much larger than the normal monthly payment. Typically the balloon payment format is used in conjunction with one or more other features. An interest-only mortgage schedule with a final payment is called interest only with a balloon of the total amount of principal.

Creative financing advocates get occasional use out of this technique as well as using a balloon as a "split funded" purchase. In that technique the buyer puts less down at the closing, and the seller holds either a first mortgage for the total balance or secondary financing behind the buyer's bank-financed first mortgage. The part the seller is holding may have one or more short-term balloons. For example, you purchase my property and I hold a second mortgage for $100,000 that calls for interest only for five years, except there is a balloon in the amount of $50,000 at the end of the first year and another $50,000 at the end of the fifth year.

This kind of creative approach can be helpful when the purchased property needs work, which translates to more capital being spent in fix-up and cosmetics. A seller, in that situation, might soften the buyer's down payment by creating a mortgage like the one discussed in the previous paragraph, especially if the buyer is pouring additional capital into the just purchased property.

Estate Taxes

Tax-free exchanges can have a major impact as a strategy for building the value of an estate. Because IRC 1031 provides that when used according to the rules no capital gains tax need be paid, it is possible for an investor to roll one profitable investment over into another for his or her (or their) lifetime. At the time of the investor's death, the property moves into the estate at its present value. No capital gains tax need ever be paid. Depending on the amount of the overall estate, it may be that not even estate tax comes into play. There are many different strategies that a good estate planner can show you that involve real estate. Exchanging, stepped-up basis from a death, or a gift, when accomplished correctly, can make the difference for the heirs between having to sell off an inherited asset just to pay the tax and being able to benefit from the hard work of a relative who has passed away. While I may speak of estate taxes from time to time, and even provide some examples of where good or poor planning have an impact on the parties, this is a very special field and it is a good idea to confer with experts in that field. Start with a good estate lawyer for those matters.

Planning and Zoning

Although we live in one of the most emancipated countries in the world, there is no real estate anywhere in the United States that is so unrestricted that you can do anything you want on, over, or under it. The restrictions that encumber real estate can be some of the most frustrating aspects you will ever encounter in your real estate investing career. These restrictions come in different packages. Some are federal in nature, perhaps a riverfront property that has restrictions from the Army Corps of Engineers, which may exert control over such waterways. Other restrictions are thought of and voted into law by state governments, and sometimes later controlled by local county or city officials. But the biggest block of these restrictions comes from the very local element of the community. The planning and zoning departments, as well as building construction, fire, and health and environmental departments generally work together with regard to rules and regulations. At times, however, minor conflicts develop between their codes. New health and fire codes usually have priority and supersede the building codes. The frustrating part of all of this is that very few communities, even those adjoining each other, have exactly the same language in their codes and apply them equally.

This is the catch-22 of real estate investing. Often you don't find out what you are permitted to do until you make application for a building permit. It is there, as you seek a site plan approval, which is one of the pre–building permit steps for certain types of new construction, that the ugly head of arbitrary decision making becomes your major hurdle.

The plus side of this is that if you get to know all the rules of the community thoroughly, those same frustrating city rules, regulations, and ordinances can become your stepping-stones to success. How so? Because within those rules are also hidden gold mines. The five old homes down the block can be purchased at a bargain price, but it seems no one wants them. Only you know that the zoning under those old homes will allow you to build a 20-unit apartment building, a supermarket, or . . . well, something worth a whole lot more than those five old homes, or five new ones for that matter.

Comfort Zone

From time to time you will see that I am a staunch believer in what I call one's comfort zone. This is a geographic area in which you can easily and quickly become an expert on what is going on, and why. You can learn all the rules, regulations, and ordinances and become familiar with the people who make them up, apply them, and enforce them. The rules of exchanges and creative financing are a part of your need to learn and master real estate insider tools. This book is a good start in that direction.

My latest book, *Commercial Real Estate Investing: Twelve Easy Steps to Getting Started* (Wiley, 2004), provides a detailed step-by-step process for establishing and implementing your comfort zone. With more than 40 years of hands-on experience as a real estate broker and investor, I have found opportunities are always present. The key is to spot them before they become so evident that all the other investors in your area can also see them. That is the moment when the prices go through the roof. Savvy real estate investors are the people who get to the motivated seller before the whole world knows how hot that property really is. The only true way you can do this is to pick an area and a type of property in which to become the absolute expert. You will be surprised how quickly you can do that.

CHAPTER 2

The Real Estate Insider's Bag of Loopholes

The goal of this chapter is:

To Introduce You to Real Estate Investment Alternatives

Easy Access to Information
Toxic Sources of Pollution
Finding the Owner of a Specific Property
Determining the Legal Description of the Property
Discovering the Sales History for the Entire Neighborhood
Tax Appraisals
Size and Shape of a Property
Zoning
Allowed Use
Other Important Factors

Let's review each in detail.

Easy Access to Information

Real estate investors within the United States have it made. Not only is the U.S. real estate industry professionally unsurpassed in the world, but inhabitants of this immense market have one single language with which they can successfully transact their business.

Communications are generally state-of-the-art, and sound information with which good business decisions can be made is readily available, accurate, and cheap. Usually the most critical data you may need is as close as your computer and an Internet connection. The freedom of access to public information is unique in the entire world, which sometimes is not so much of a blessing. But for real estate investors it is a fantastic edge available to those who use it first, and know how to assimilate the data.

There is a wealth of public data that is just sitting out there waiting for you to access it. For the real estate investor this data comes in many forms. Look at the following discussions of just some of the data that you can pinpoint quickly and with a high rate of accuracy. These might be the most important data for an investor to obtain about any property prior to acquiring it.

Toxic Sources of Pollution

The location of sources of toxic or disagreeable pollution is so important, and so often not even considered until a great deal of time and effort has been put into a due diligence period, that I put this at the top of the list. Why would you tend to overlook this? Because if you are new to the area, or have not spent the night in the neighborhood, you can easily overlook smells that come only when the wind blows from a certain direction, or a dozen passing trains and their warning horns that can be heard clearly in the middle of the night even though the rail line is half a mile or so away. Factories, airports, and a dozen or so of other sound- and dirt-producing sources can have major impacts on any property's value.

This goes for existing sources, as well as those that are in the planning stages at the very moment you are thinking of buying a property that can be impacted.

Finding the Owner of a Specific Property

Often the first step in acquiring a property is to know how to contact the present owner. This is critical because some of the best investments in real estate are made by approaching a property owner directly even before a decision has been made to sell it. Once the property is on the market there may be easy access to a listing broker, but that access is openly available to every other investor around. Smart investors try to beat other investors to that source as early as possible.

There are several sources for this information, but generally the best is the county (or city, depending on your area) tax assessor's office. Assuming you know in which county the property is located, drop by the office and learn how to easily access that and much of the other information listed in this chapter. At the tax assessor's office you will find everything from plat maps, which are detailed drawings of all of the real estate in the county. These plat maps are usually matched to actual aerial photos that are taken looking straight down at the property, typically in one-mile-square areas for urban properties, and a larger scale for rural locations. Both the plat maps and the aerials are updated on a regular basis depending on the amount of change that occurs in the area and are available for you to purchase.

Figure 2.1 shows a printout of a Hillsborough County, Florida, tax assessor's office property data sheet. This is the Tampa area of Florida. Shown on this printout is the name of the owner, Royal Palm Tampa LLC, and the legal description (which is in a form called metes and bounds, describing the property by a measurement rather than a subdivision, lot, and block method; this method is long and cumbersome, and takes up 13 lines to fully describe the property). You will also find the present tax appraisals and assessments compared to the previous year. Note the detailed listing of how the taxes are divided among the different county departments. The property records show several sales dates; the most recent sale was in the year 2000 for the amount of $12,100,000. It is

ROB TURNER, CFA
Hillsborough County
Property Appraiser
Online Inquiry System

Internet Site

> *You cannot bookmark this page.* **These results were retrieved from a database - your browser will not read it correctly the next time it is opened. Please print the information you have obtained for your records.**

PIN: A-16-29-18-ZZZ-000005-47590.0
Folio: 110963-0000
PriorPIN: - - - - -.
Prior Folio: 000000-0000

ROYAL PALM TAMPA LLC

SUITE 635
300 71ST ST
MIAMI BEACH, FL 33141-3038

Tax District: TEN TAMPA
DOR Code: 3922 LMTD SERV B
Plat Book/Page: /

Summary - Sales - Land - Extra Features - Trim - Legal - Map - Similar Sales - Tax Records -Tax Estimator

Building 1 2 3 4 5 6 7 8

Sales History

Off. Record		Date		Type Inst	Qualified or Unqualified	Vacant or Improved	Sales Price
Book	Page	Month	Year				
10528	1007	12	2000	WD	Unqualified	Improved	$12,100,000
9020	1825	05	1998	WD	Unqualified	Improved	$7,500,000
7407	0170	05	1994	WD	Unqualified	Improved	$100
6886	0281	02	1993	CT	Unqualified	Improved	$100

Legal Lines

L N	Legal Description
1	A TRACT IN NW 1/4 OF NE 1/4 DESC AS FOLLOWS BEG
2	AT PT OF INTERS OF S BDRY OF NW 1/4 OF NE 1/4 AND
3	W R/W LINE OF DALE MABRY HWY RUN WLY 744.73 FT RUN

Figure 2.1 Tax Sheet—Hillsborough County, Florida

4	N 466. 75 RUN E 94 FT THN N 14.91 MOL RUN THN E
5	651.66 FT TO A PT ON WLY R/W LINE OF DALE MABRY
6	HWY RUN S 479.87 TO POB AND LESS FOLLOWING DESC
7	TRACT FOR POB COM AT INTERS OF S BDRY OF S 1/2 OF
8	NW 1/4 OF NE 1/4 AND W R/W LINE OF DALE MABRY HWY
9	THN N 268 FT THN S 89 DEG 36 MIN 13 SEC W 178.50
10	FT THN S 72 DEG 09 MIN 24 SEC W 48.58 THN S 01
11	DEG 03 MIN 50 SEC W 93.58 THN N 89 DEG 36 MIN 13
12	SEC E 14.34 FT THN S 159.93 THN N 89 DEG 36 MIN
13	13 SEC E ALNG SD S BDRY 212 FT TO POB

Trim Information (2004)

Taxing Authority	Base Taxable Value	Additional Exemptions Granted	Taxable Value	Last Year Property Taxes	Proposed Property Taxes	Rollback Property Taxes
General Revenue	$7,295,600	$0	$7,295,600	72818.59	52351.04	48795.89
By State Law	$7,295,600	$0	$7,295,600	56500.59	40074.73	37863.43
By Local Board	$7,295,600	$0	$7,295,600	27282.78	19581.39	18283.50
Tampa	$7,295,600	$0	$7,295,600	66246.61	47705.93	44833.65
County Library	$7,295,600	$0	$7,295,600	6507.14	4685.96	4358.39
SWFWMD	$7,295,600	$0	$7,295,600	4275.28	3078.74	2835.80
NW Hills Basin	$7,295,600	$0	$7,295,600	2715.11	1955.22	1834.11
Port Authority	$7,295,600	$0	$7,295,600	2937.99	1896.86	1969.08
Children's Board	$7,295,600	$0	$7,295,600	5065.50	3647.80	3394.64
Transit Authority	$7,295,600	$0	$7,295,600	5065.50	3647.80	3393.18
Environmental Lands	$7,295,600	$0	$7,295,600	1058.69	704.03	704.03
School I & SF	$7,295,600	$0	$7,295,600	2127.51	1341.66	1341.66
Totals				252601.29	180671.16	169607.36

	Just Value	Assessed	Exemptions	Taxable
Last Year	$10,131,000	$10,131,000	$0	$10,131,000
Current	$7,295,600	$7,295,600	$0	$7,295,600

Figure 2.1 *(Continued)*

likely that the tax appraiser jumped the appraised amount ($10,131,000) up to reflect the sale price for that year. The current appraisal is $7,295,600, and the proposed property tax total for 2004 is $180,671.16.

Compare the Hillsborough County data with a printout from Broward County. Figure 2.2 presents data for a property that is owned by Andre Raymond Investments Inc. This property data sheet is a bit more comprehensive than the one from Hillsborough County and also shows

THE TAX-FREE EXCHANGE LOOPHOLE

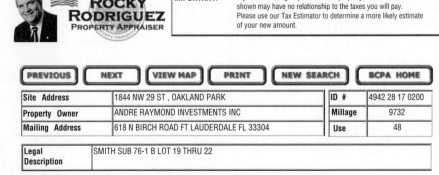

PREVIOUS NEXT VIEW MAP PRINT NEW SEARCH BCPA HOME

Site Address	1844 NW 29 ST , OAKLAND PARK		ID #	4942 28 17 0200
Property Owner	ANDRE RAYMOND INVESTMENTS INC		Millage	9732
Mailing Address	618 N BIRCH ROAD FT LAUDERDALE FL 33304		Use	48

Legal Description	SMITH SUB 76-1 B LOT 19 THRU 22

Property Assessment Values					
Year	Land	Building	Land Value AG	Total	Tax
Current	$ 169,000	$ 602,970		$ 771,970	
2003	$ 143,000	$ 344,390		$ 487,390	$12,630.48
2002	$ 132,600	$ 321,680		$ 454,280	$11,967.17

Save Our Home Value	Exemptions				
	Type	Widow(er)'s/Veteran's/Disability		Homestead	Non-Exempt
					$ 771,970

Sales History						Land Calculations		
Date	Type	Price	Book	Page		Price	Factor	Type
01/04	WD	$ 938,000	36779	227		$6.50	26,000	SF
10/99	WD*	$ 460,000	29995	1199				
05/72	W	$ 40,000	4884	765				
						Adj. Bldg. S.F.		18000

Special Assessments					
Fire	Garbage	Light	Drainage	Improvement	Safe
17					
S					
1					

Please Note: Assessed values shown are **NOT** certified values and are subject to change before final certification for ad valorem tax purposes.

Figure 2.2 Broward County, Florida, Tax Roll

current and former years' assessment values, together with the appropriate tax levied against the property. Other data includes a sales history, indicating that the property first sold (as a vacant lot one would presume) in 1972 for $40,000. Later, in 1999, it sold (as a small industrial building consisting of 18,000 square feet) and then was purchased by the present owner in 2004 for $938,000.

Other Property Owned in a Specific Name

Once you find the name of a property owner, perhaps because you are interested in buying the property or you want to sell to that owner an adjoining property you own, you can now access general information and find out what else that property owner owns. This information can be very important as it can give you a new perspective on the kind of person you may be dealing with.

Ownership History of a Specific Property

The tax data as shown in Figure 2.2 provides an interesting history of the ownership. Sometimes this history is limited to more recent information, but generally it will go back to the time when the property was first platted, or sold by the initial developer. Subsequent sales and tax appraisal data can help an interested party ascertain when the property changed from a vacant tract to an improved property.

Determining the Legal Description of the Property

Every property has a distinctive name, called its *legal description*, that separates it from neighboring properties. This legal description is important for further investigations outside the tax assessor's office if you want to seek other data that would be found within building and zoning offices or the county recording facilities.

This legal name will also enable you to pull up or otherwise locate similar information on the entire area or subdivision in which the property is located. By expanding a property search to an entire area around a property you are interested in, you can quickly obtain a profile of what is going on in that part of town.

When accessing this information on a web site, remember that not all assessors use the same format (and not all tax assessors are Web oriented as yet). It is a good idea to give the tax assessor's office a call and ask how to navigate the web site. Most assessors will be very helpful in this respect. Some of the web sites even have a tutorial or learning program that will help you learn how to make the most of the web site.

Discovering the Sales History for the Entire Neighborhood

One of the ways in which the tax assessor's data can generally be navigated is by subdivision. In so doing you end up pulling up all the data for a specific subdivision. If you do not know the exact name of the subdivision, though, you may end up roaming around the wrong part of town. I find that in a situation where I don't know the exact legal name of the subdivision I can back into it by doing a search using an address for a specific site I know is in the subdivision I want. Once I have found the site by address, I will get the full and exact legal description of that property (even if it is not the one I ultimately want), and within that description will be the legal address. Look at Figure 2.2 and locate the legal description. You will see the description as: SMITH SUB-76-1 B LOT 19 THRU 22. This indicates that this property is in a subdivision called SMITH SUB and is further identified as 76-1B, and that within that subdivision, the subject property consists of lots 19 through 22.

When the subdivision has been found, I can open my search to include all properties within that area. With a subdivision search a detailed history of recent sales can be developed. Direct comparisons of specific properties may reveal a trend of valuation changes in the neighborhood.

Is the overall value of property going up, is it stagnant, or is it even going down? These are important clues to the future of the area.

All Property Listed by Local Realtors

In many areas of the country, a Realtor may have access to special databases that combine information from more than one source. This is the case when the local Realtor listing services interlink with the tax assessor's data. The information that is generated from this kind of computer-driven information source can be far more extensive than just the tax assessor's data. Figure 2.3 shows such a combined report.

The addition of the Realtor data can be very informative. In Figure 2.3 there is a combination of information from the tax rolls as well as listing information from the Realtor database. This is a luxury apartment complex in West Palm Beach, Florida, and its current tax assessment is $177,889.65. The owner is West Palm Beach Villas LLC. By reviewing the printout you can see that the land area on which the apartments are built is 5.88 acres and they were built in 1973. In the sales data, the property sold in 2003 for $8,085,000. A look at the multiple listing service data (not shown) would reveal that the current asking price is $12,000,000.

Keep in mind that all this data is from public records and from the real estate listing information and statistics. The property for sale information and the property sold data are especially important because they indicate the current trend in market conditions when there is sufficient activity in the market. If the data shows a great deal of property on the market and few sales, usually at significantly lower than listed prices, there may be additional investigation necessary to ascertain the reason for this. Do not assume that this indicates a declining neighborhood. There are many reasons a market will dry up for a short period of time, only to come back stronger than ever. One such event would be a major construction project that, when finished, will have a very positive impact on the area, but during the period of construction (often several years) the neighborhood must endure all the downside of traffic detours, construction noise and dirt, and general disruption of businesses and living conditions in the area.

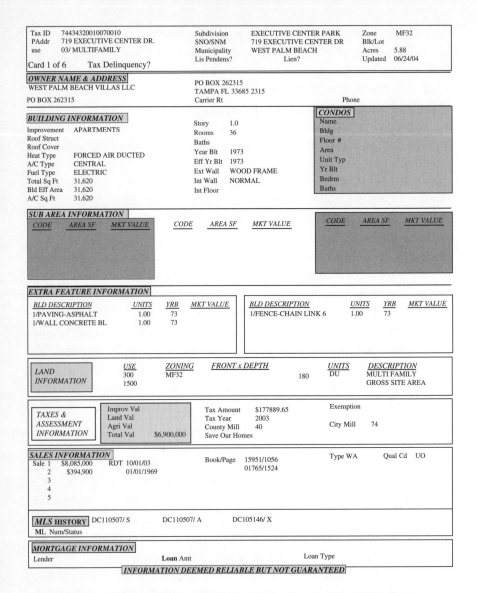

Tax ID	74434320010070010	Subdivision	EXECUTIVE CENTER PARK	Zone	MF32
PAddr	719 EXECUTIVE CENTER DR.	SNO/SNM	719 EXECUTIVE CENTER DR	Blk/Lot	
use	03/ MULTIFAMILY	Municipality	WEST PALM BEACH	Acres	5.88
		Lis Pendens?	Lien?	Updated	06/24/04
Card 1 of 6	Tax Delinquency?				

OWNER NAME & ADDRESS
WEST PALM BEACH VILLAS LLC

PO BOX 262315

PO BOX 262315
TAMPA FL 33685 2315
Carrier Rt   Phone

BUILDING INFORMATION

				CONDOS	
Improvement	APARTMENTS	Story	1.0	Name.	
Roof Struct		Rooms	36	Bldg	
Roof Cover		Baths		Floor #	
Heat Type	FORCED AIR DUCTED	Year Blt	1973	Area	
A/C Type	CENTRAL	Eff Yr Blt	1973	Unit Typ	
Fuel Type	ELECTRIC	Ext Wall	WOOD FRAME	Yr Blt	
Total Sq Ft	31,620	Int Wall	NORMAL	Bedrm	
Bld Eff Area	31,620	Int Floor		Baths	
A/C Sq Ft	31,620				

SUB AREA INFORMATION

CODE	AREA SF	MKT VALUE	CODE	AREA SF	MKT VALUE	CODE	AREA SF	MKT VALUE

EXTRA FEATURE INFORMATION

BLD DESCRIPTION	UNITS	YRB	MKT VALUE	BLD DESCRIPTION	UNITS	YRB	MKT VALUE
1/PAVING-ASPHALT	1.00	73		1/FENCE-CHAIN LINK 6	1.00	73	
1/WALL CONCRETE BL	1.00	73					

LAND INFORMATION

	USE	ZONING	FRONT x DEPTH		UNITS	DESCRIPTION
	300	MF32		180	DU	MULTI FAMILY
	1500					GROSS SITE AREA

TAXES & ASSESSMENT INFORMATION

				Exemption	
Improv Val		Tax Amount	$177889.65		
Land Val		Tax Year	2003		
Agri Val		County Mill	40	City Mill	74
Total Val	$6,900,000	Save Our Homes			

SALES INFORMATION

						Type WA	Qual Cd	UO
Sale 1	$8,085,000	RDT	10/01/03	Book/Page	15951/1056			
2	$394,900		01/01/1969		01765/1524			
3								
4								
5								

MLS HISTORY DC110507/ S   DC110507/ A   DC105146/ X
ML Num/Status

MORTGAGE INFORMATION
Lender   **Loan** Amt   Loan Type

INFORMATION DEEMED RELIABLE BUT NOT GUARANTEED

Figure 2.3 Combined Tax and Multiple Listing Service Data, Palm Beach County, Florida

Tax Appraisals

Tax appraisal of any specific property is an essential piece of information for any investor. The tax assessor's principal job is to uniformly assess the real estate in the county. The assessor's staff uses various methods to accomplish this, and the tax assessor's appraisal of the subject property is the basis on which the various governmental bodies and departments raise their needed capital for the following year. In the vast majority of communities in the United States, all these various entities are combined to end up with a total *millage*, which is the multiple to arrive at an actual tax amount the property owner must pay. This grand total millage can vary considerably for different areas within a state.

One factor that can affect this and must be taken into consideration when reviewing the tax assessment of any given area is whether there are *homestead properties* in the area, and whether this state has limitations on increases in tax appraisal value of a homestead property. Only a property that is a taxpayer's personal residence can be homestead property. Once the property is sold or ceases to be used as the owner's primary residence, the tax authorities are not bound by the limitations on increases in value. The gap between the old owner and the new owner is fair game for the tax assessor to raise the tax. That new value, if increased, will become the base on which future increases are made only if the property becomes the new owner's primary residence. Many states have such a law, and the maximum increase that can be applied yearly to homestead properties is typically 3 percent. When reviewing the tax appraisals of an area of owner-occupied residences (homes, condos, co-op apartments, etc.) keep in mind that it is likely that some of the properties with low tax appraisals may actually be worth more (therefore likely sell for a greater amount) than properties with higher tax appraisals.

If the property has not changed hands for many years, and the property is in an area of town that has not had much (if any) new development, the tax appraisal, and therefore the tax assessment value, will tend to be lower than the cost of the property. This is because the tax assessor's office looks at the price paid when a property sells, and is likely to make an upward adjustment in the tax assessment the year following the purchase. A sudden jump in a tax assessment can wipe out the profit you might have counted on, so be very cautious in these situations.

However, it is possible that a property has been overassessed. Here the tax assessor's office has based its appraisal on a past sale, say several years ago when the property was in full bloom as a major commercial venture. In a few years a lot can happen to cause such a venture to decline. A major employer goes out of business; a new bridge is needed and traffic is diverted and tenants move out. Whatever the case, these things do happen. So you come along and you have a new use for the property. If you can show the tax assessor that you have purchased the site at half what it was appraised at by the assessor, you have a good chance of getting the tax lowered.

Size and Shape of a Property

Physical information about any property is very important. You can never trust your eye when it comes to a visual guess as to the size of any property. This goes for the square footage of buildings as well as the land under them. However, every investor should have some idea about sizes, and I have always recommended that one good way to do this is to find a large vacant tract of land that you can have access to. Get some yellow caution plastic tape (available at any good hardware store), eight wooden stakes, and a 100-foot-long tape measure. Measure a square that is 208.75 feet on each side. Set the wooden stakes at each corner and in the middle of each side, and tie the yellow caution plastic tape to those stakes. You have just made a square that is the exact size of one acre. Walk the line, stand in the middle, and visualize what 43,560 square feet looks like.

Later on, in a large vacant building that is for sale, do the same thing with the yellow tape on the floor and measure 20 feet by 60 feet. It is best to do this, if you can, so that two sides of that rectangle are walls. This is 1,200 square feet, which is often the size of a small strip mall store bay, or a two-bedroom rental apartment, or a warehouse work area.

The overall area of both land and buildings is often available from the tax data and/or the Realtor data. A word of caution, however: Often the real estate data as to square footage of buildings is incorrect. Why? Because the agent that supplied the information may have measured gross area that included balconies and porches and that sort of thing, whereas tax data often is limited to heated or air-conditioned space.

Nothing can fully take the place of viewing an actual survey or building plan, so if the exact area or square footage is critical, wait until you have a certified survey or building plan. Both of these documents may be available through the local building department. Often these documents are extra copies of the real thing that will offer you a wealth of added data. In large communities where the storage of the real survey or building plans would overwhelm a storage facility, the building departments resort to making microfiches of the plans. This requires a special machine to view the documents, and their quality can leave a lot to be desired. These images can be reproduced, generally at a per page fee.

Zoning

While the zoning category may show up on the tax assessor's and/or the Realtor's reports, there is only one place to confirm exactly what the zoning will permit. This is the building and zoning department for that city. Never assume that you have the right data until someone from that department has given you the current information. The rules and regulations of city and county zoning change from time to time, and having the updated information is essential for any decision made about a property.

Zoning is one of the most important factors you will encounter about any real estate, and especially investment realty. It is the zoning category given to real estate that defines what can go on that property. The zoning of any property is very specific to that property in that community. Each entity (city or county) makes up its own terms. Learning the zoning code of the city or cities where you plan to invest will be critical to finding the hidden gems of real estate that less knowledgeable people overlook.

Figure 2.4 is from the Fort Lauderdale, Florida, zoning regulations. It shows the general commercial districts, which are listed as B-1, B-2, B-3, B-4, C-1, CR, and OP. The zoning code shown is Section 39-292 and provides information on some of the commercial zoning allowed in the city of Fort Lauderdale. Within Broward County, there are many cities—Fort Lauderdale, North Lauderdale, Lauderdale Lakes, Lauderdale by the Sea, Pompano Beach, Wilton Manors, Oakland Park, Hollywood, Tamarac, Plantation, and Margate, just to name the larger cities. Each has its

ARTICLE XVII. COMMERCIAL DISTRICTS

Sec. 39-292. Commercial zoning districts.

The following shall constitute commercial zoning districts for the purposes of this Code:

B-1   Limited Commercial Business District

B-2   General Commercial Business District

B-3   Intense Commercial Business District

B-4   Commercial Redevelopment Overlay Districts

C-1   Commercial Warehouse District

CR   Commercial Recreation District

OP   Office Park District

(Ord. No. 1999-23, § 3, 5-11-99; Ord. No. 2000-14, § 1, 4-11-00)

Sec. 39-293. Purpose of districts.

(a)   The B-1 Limited Commercial Business District is intended to meet the personal service needs of the local neighborhood. Such districts are primarily located on a local collector road, contiguous to residentially-zoned properties, rather than a major thoroughfare. All activities of permitted uses are limited to the interior of a building, except as specifically permitted in section 39-300, "Limitations of uses."

(b)   The B-2 General Commercial Business District is intended to meet the shopping and service needs of several residential neighborhoods or a substantial residential area. B-2 districts are primarily located on a major thoroughfare or arterial catering to vehicular traffic. All activities of permitted uses are limited to the interior of a building, except as specifically permitted in section 39-300, "Limitations of uses."

(c)   The B-3 Intense Commercial Business District is intended primarily to accommodate establishments and services catering to the business and industrial community and for services not used by residents on a regular basis. Such districts are not appropriate for locations which are contiguous to residential properties. Due to the size of permissible items which may be sold or maintained, display and storage are permitted outside.

(d)   The B-4 Commercial Redevelopment Overlay Districts are intended to provide incentives for redevelopment of older, commercial areas which have experienced a decline in occupancy, maintenance and economic viability.

(e)   The C-1 Commercial Warehouse District is intended for certain repair and maintenance services, wholesale, storage and warehouse uses, and sales

Figure 2.4   Business/Commercial Zoning—Fort Lauderdale, Florida

or rental of large or heavy machinery and equipment. Such districts serve a regional clientele or nearby industrial areas and do not cater to residential areas or pedestrian traffic.

(f)   The CR Commercial Recreation District is intended to accommodate major public and private commercial recreation facilities which offer opportunities to residents and tourists.

(g)   The OP Office Park District is intended to encourage the location of planned office complexes and corporate headquarters in a campus-like atmosphere with substantial buildings and ample open space, including limited services for employees such as shopping and food service establishments.

(Ord. No. 1999-23, § 3, 5-11-99; Ord. No. 2000-14, § 2, 4-11-00)

Sec. 39-294. General provisions.

(a)   *Alcoholic Beverage Establishments.* Any establishment selling or dispensing alcoholic beverages or allowing on-premises consumption of alcoholic beverages must comply with all requirements of Article XI of this Chapter, "Alcoholic Beverage and Adult Entertainment Establishments."

(b)   *Display of products for sale.* Display of products for sale. In B-1, B-2, B-4, RO and OP districts, all products displayed for sale shall be located within a building, except that produce, plants and lawn and garden equipment may be displayed and stored outside in an area designated on an approved site plan, provided the display and storage is located at least fifty (50) feet from any residentially-zoned plot and is not within any required landscape buffer. Such outside display areas shall be enclosed with a fence at least six (6) feet in height. At least one side of the display and storage area shall be contiguous to the principal building to which it is accessory. Stocking of the produce or plants or pick-up by customers shall be done internally or through a single gate at the designated off-street loading area.

(c)   *Dumpsters and dumpster enclosures.* Dumpsters located on any property in a commercial zoning district as of the effective date of this article and/or constructed subsequent to the effective date of this article shall comply with the following:

(1)   Dumpsters shall be kept within opaque or translucent enclosures and shall be located at least five (5) feet inside any plot line; however, no dumpster or dumpster enclosure shall be located in a required setback or buffer area, unless a street or dedicated alley separates the commercial plot from any adjacent residential property.

(Continued)

Figure 2.4   *(Continued)*

(2)   Dumpsters shall be maintained free of jagged or sharp edges or inside parts which could prevent the free discharge of their contents.

(3)   Dumpsters shall be emptied by a licensed collector at intervals which will preclude overflow. Dumpsters and the area around the dumpster and dumpster enclosure shall not be used for disposal of furniture and major appliances and shall be maintained by the property owner free of overflowing refuse at all times. If a continuous problem of insufficient dumpster capacity is proven to exist, additional or larger capacity dumpsters and enclosures or increased frequency of pick-up shall be required in order to eliminate the overflow problem.

(4)   All dumpster pads shall be at least two (2) feet larger than the dumpster on all sides. Wheel stops or posts shall be permanently affixed to the pad at least one foot inside the perimeter of the pad to prevent the dumpster from striking the enclosure during collection.

(5)   Dumpsters and dumpster enclosures shall be located in a position accessible for collection by the equipment of the collector.

(6)   The dumpster enclosure shall be constructed so as to accommodate recycling bins, if the recycling bins are over forty (40) gallons.

(7)   The gates of the enclosure shall be constructed of a frame with opaque or translucent walls affixed thereto, and both frame and walls shall be of a material of sufficient strength to withstand normal use. Gates shall be attached to metal posts at least three (3) inches in diameter with at least two (2) hinges. Each gate shall have a wheel at the bottom to prevent sagging and shall have drop pins or rods to hold the gates in place in both open and closed positions.

(8)   The base of the enclosure must be poured concrete, in accordance with the requirements of the South Florida Building Code. The base shall extend three (3) feet beyond the front opening of the enclosure as an apron, and all concrete must be level with adjacent asphalt.

(d)   *Landscaping.* All buildings and uses shall provide landscaping in accordance with Article VIII of this Chapter, "Functional Landscaping and Xeriscaping."

(e)   *Off-street parking.* All buildings and uses shall provide off-street parking, loading areas and lighting in accordance with Article XII of this Chapter, "Off-street Parking and Loading," except as provided for B-4 Commercial Redevelopment Overlay Districts.

Figure 2.4   *(Continued)*

(f) *Setbacks and buffers between commercial business and residential districts.*

(1)   Except for CR Commercial Recreation districts, the minimum setback for the construction or erection of any building or structure, except fences and walls, in any commercial zoning district which is contiguous to a residentially-zoned plot in separate ownership, shall be twenty-five (25) feet from such plot line, unless a greater setback is required for a specific use in this article. A landscape buffer as required by Article VIII, Functional Landscaping and Xeriscaping, shall be provided within the setback area, including a visual barrier in the form of a fence, wall or hedge a minimum of six (6) feet in height, constructed or planted and maintained as provided in subsection (7) following.

(2)   Except for CR Commercial Recreation districts, the minimum setback for the construction or erection of any building or structure, except fences and walls, in any commercial zoning district which is separated from a residentially-zoned plot by a street, dedicated alley, canal, water area, railroad right-of-way or public open space, shall be ten (10) feet from any such plot line, unless a greater setback is required for a specific use in this Article. The entire setback area shall be a landscape buffer as required by Article VIII of this Chapter, "Functional Landscaping and Xeriscaping," crossed only by pedestrian walkways and driveways necessary for ingress and egress to and from the plot.

(3)   No building or structure, except fences and walls, shall be erected or maintained in any CR Commercial Recreation district closer than one hundred (100) feet from any plot line.

(4)   No building or structure shall be erected or maintained within twenty-five (25) feet of the intersection of two streets, nor within fifteen (15) feet of the intersection of any driveway and street, except as permitted in subsection (7) following.

(5)   The setback areas in OP Office Park districts shall be double the sizes specified in subsections (1) and (2) above.

(6)   The setbacks required by this section shall also apply to those unincorporated lands which abut a municipal jurisdiction. Such setbacks shall be applied in the same manner as if the municipal lands were unincorporated lands.

(Continued)

Figure 2.4   *(Continued)*

(7)   Fences, walls and hedges may be erected or planted and maintained within the setback to a maximum height of eight (8) feet, except in vehicular use areas. Fences and walls shall be translucent. Hedges used as a required visual barrier shall be a minimum of four (4) feet in height at time of planting and shall be of a species which will reach a height of at least six (6) feet within two years after planting. Open-weave or chain link fences may only be used if appropriate landscape material, in accordance with Article VIII, is planted along such fence, which, after planting, will obscure the fence and provide a translucent barrier within one year after planting. Within twenty-five (25) feet of the intersection of two streets or within fifteen (15) feet of the intersection of a private accessway and a street no fencing may be erected or maintained. The use of barbed wire, razor wire or electrified fencing shall be prohibited.

(g)   *Signs.* All buildings and uses shall be subject to provisions in Article VI, of this Chapter, "Signs," except as specified in Section 39-301(d)(5) of this article.

(h)   *Use of residentially-zoned property for access.* No privately owned land or public or private street upon which residentially-zoned properties directly abut shall be used for driveway or vehicular access purposes to any plot in a commercial district, except where a public street provides the sole access to the commercial property.

(i)   *Use of premises without buildings.* All permitted uses shall be conducted from a building on the plot which building shall be a minimum of one hundred fifty (150) square feet in floor area and which shall contain permanent sanitary facilities.

(j)   *Definitions.* Terms used herein are defined in Article II, "Definitions," of this Chapter.

(k)   *Nonconforming uses and structures.* Nonconforming uses and structures in commercial business districts shall be subject to Article VII, "Nonconforming Uses and Structures," of this Chapter.

(l)   *Property maintenance.* Buildings and properties in commercial business districts shall be maintained in accordance with Article X, "Property Maintenance and Junk and Abandoned Property," of this Chapter.

(m)   *Miscellaneous provisions.* In addition to general provisions herein, commercial business districts shall also be subject to Article IX, "General Provisions," of this Chapter.

(Ord. No. 1999-23, § 3, 5-11-99; Ord. No. 2000-36, § 36, 8-22-00)

Figure 2.4   *(Continued)*

own set of zoning and building ordinances. While there may be some similarity, it would be foolish to assume that each code has the same name. What is B-1 in one city may actually be closer to C-2 in another.

Zoning categories are usually shown in the Realtor data, sometimes in the tax data, but the zoning category for a property should always be verified by finding the property on a recently updated zoning map, which you can purchase from the appropriate city or county building department for your area. Be sure to get the appropriate zoning information that goes along with the map. Keep in mind that zoning is not absolutely fixed and etched into stone. It can sometimes be changed by you to a more favorable use, or changed by the city for various reasons. If a site you like doesn't come with the zoning you need, discuss with the planning and zoning (P&Z) director what you can do to change it. If there is a glimmer of a chance, you might go for it.

Many building departments have all this information on the city web site, so it is a good idea to give them a call and find out how to access it.

Allowed Use

You need to know what is allowed and not allowed on the property. Figure 2.4 is a partial printout of commercial zoning for Fort Lauderdale. It indicates some of the general uses that are allowed in the specific zoning. As you can see, the zoning tends to become more restrictive when there is residential zoning nearby.

The regulations shown in Figure 2.4 outline various criteria for development within that specific zoning, such as setbacks for building walls from property boundaries. There are usually other restrictions that do not show up in the individual zoning category description. These can be what I call "gotcha restrictions," and they come in a variety of packages and are found in other more general sections of the code.

For example, parking codes can require additional parking garages that might eat up the available land area, thereby reducing the overall usable building. Dry area retention for storm water can take away space for parking garages, and codes may prohibit the development of certain uses close to other uses (a school close to a bar or gas station, for example).

Some communities establish the permissible overall volume of a building according to what is called floor area ratio (FAR). This means that multiplying the area of the land by the FAR amount determines the total floor area of a building that can be built. A floor area ratio of 2 would indicate that on a site that consists of 100,000 square feet (just a little more than two acres considering that one acre is 43,560 square feet), you could build a building with 200,000 square feet of usable space. The term *usable space* may not mean the same thing for all communities. You must get the local definition for any FAR-controlled zoning. Be sure to ascertain if the FAR includes parking garage, stairwells, elevator shaft space, and so on. This can make a very big difference in the ultimate usable space that can be developed on the site.

In some instances, the zoning will allow a use but only when a "special exception" has been granted. Gas stations often fall within this category, and even though you might see gas stations on three corners of an intersection, that does not automatically mean that the fourth corner will be an approved location for another gas station. Local political involvement may have put a halt to such development years ago, and the only reason there are three stations is they got there when development was more lax, prior to a change in the zoning rules and regulations. The key here is never assume anything when it comes to real estate. Check it out, and then double-check it.

Other Important Factors

There are many other bits of information that are available to you from the various governmental offices at your disposal. Never be intimidated by the thought that getting information from these departments will be difficult or impossible. If the data is in the hands of a government office, it is generally public information. Here is a list of some of the additional data that you can get from a building and zoning department.

Other Important Information from the Building and Zoning Department
Property violations (if any).
Liens against a property.

Liens against the property owner.

Dates of improvements for which permits have been issued.

Approximate costs of those improvements.

The local department of transportation, which may exist at state, county, and city levels, has a great deal of data available for you. Start at the county level and go from there. Here is some of the data that department will provide.

Important Information from the Department of Transportation

Current traffic flow information.

Future department of transportation plans for the area.

Governmental involvement that will impact the area.

Changes in present infrastructure that will impact the area.

The best place to discover what developers are planning would be at the planning and zoning department or board. The P&Z board is an appointed body of citizens backed up by employed professional staff. The P&Z board has the task of approving much of the new development that takes place in the community. The board has regularly scheduled public meetings with the developers. Depending on the size of the project, there may be several meetings prior to ultimate approval by the board. Some of the projects may be called up or have mandatory review by the city or county commission for final approval prior to development. Most of these meetings must be advertised to the public, or placed in advance agendas that you can obtain.

The P&Z staff conduct development (or design) review committee (DRC) meetings, which are generally the first place the public can discover what a developer is proposing. It is possible to get on the mailing list for agendas to any public meeting, or access the agendas of all government meetings on a web site.

If your community has an industrial development board, they or the local chamber of commerce can help you find access to the names and phone numbers of virtually all people who can have an impact on real estate in the area. They will also have lists of all meetings by governmental departments open to the public, or be able to tell you who does.

The most important aspect about all this data and information is never take it for granted. Few places in the world offer investors such a wealth of information just for the asking.

Why the United States Is Such a Great Place for Real Estate Investments

There are many reasons why the United States is a great place for the real estate investor. Here are just a few of the primary benefits the U.S. real estate insiders have on their side of the game.

Great investment environment.

Capital gains tax treatment.

Residential gain exclusion.

Installment sale treatment.

IRC 1031—Tax-free rollover of investment capital.

Let's review each of these benefits in detail.

Great Investment Environment

The United States is blessed with a financing system that is widespread, and available to almost everyone. For those who have marginal assets to back up their investments, there are governmental programs that give assistance. For those who qualify there is a program for active and former military personnel that is not matched anywhere else in the world. To top that off, the government, including the dreaded IRS, has programs that offer direct assistance through deductions and credits to help the investor buy, sell, or keep the majority of the value gained from those investments.

There is so much going for U.S. real estate investors that it is easy to take it all for granted. To understand the reality of just how good it is in the United States, take an investment tour around the world and you will find a scary place out there that awaits the innocent and trusting American. What will you find on this tour? The most obvious situation will be the real estate industry itself. For the most part once you are outside of the United States, you will discover that there is an absolute absence of a national real estate listing service. We, in the United States, take the real estate industry for granted. The National Association of Realtors and its local boards, plus the non-Realtor franchise agencies that abound around the country, are unique. They serve a great purpose in a country that is on the move. People change homes on a regular basis in the United States, and unlike families in Europe and elsewhere who seldom never migrate very far from their place of birth, people in the United States demand better service from their real estate agents. And they get it, too.

Real estate agents, or estate agents as they are called in England and elsewhere, generally serve very local areas, sometimes only small areas in neighborhoods. There is little or no cooperation among brokers or firms, and to hunt up a property in a city the size of London, Paris, or Rome could spread you among half a dozen companies or more, each of which may show you only the in-house listings. Things get worse if you go to one of the former Soviet countries where it may be next to impossible to find someone who can give you information on where to buy or rent local real estate.

Things get a bit better if you are dealing in very large investment-type properties, but only because there are fewer brokerage firms that deal in those kinds of properties.

Getting data on which to make a decision forces the investor into a long due diligence process with little data offered up front. "Make up your mind, mate?" might be the seller's reaction in many parts of the world.

Governments vary on the amount of help they give would-be real estate investors, even homeowners. Often the financing is handled by the seller or a local lender who wants to see the buyer put down a sizable chunk of cash and then repay the loan at a high interest rate over a much shorter time than is available in the good old United States.

Some argue that tough financing forces a buyer to save up until he or she can make that sizable investment. Advocates of that view point out the problems of excess freedom of credit in the United States, and show statistics of how many Americans overextend themselves in loans, and especially the high-interest credit card debt. I agree with those who caution their children (or even their parents) about running up large credit card balances, which, like smoking cigarettes, is a road to some purgatory that can be otherwise avoided.

Capital Gains Tax Treatment

A capital gain is an amount you receive when you sell or dispose of a property at a value that exceeds your adjusted cost. Later on this chapter deals with what goes into arriving at an adjusted cost, but for the moment, let's see how this would affect Brad.

Brad's Transaction: Brad wants to dispose of a lot in North Carolina by selling it (by virtue of an exchange or outright sale) to an apartment building owner for $60,000. The lot cost Brad $5,000 cash 15 years ago, and he owns it free and clear (F&C) of any debt. He did not build anything on the lot, didn't sell off timber, and did not remove any buildings. It is simply a vacant lot that he looks at once a year, if that. Assume that there would be $500 in closing costs for a lawyer to handle Brad's expenses in a sale of the lot. Following the rules set by the IRS we would use the following illustration:

Brad Sells the Lot in North Carolina

Gross amount of sale	$60,000
Less cost of sale	500
Net to Brad	$59,500
Less Brad's original cost	5,000
Amount of gain realized	$54,500

In an outright sale, Brad would have to pay a capital gains tax on the amount realized. At the 2004 level of 15 percent, his tax would be $8,175. If this were the case, Brad would have had only $51,325 to reinvest ($59,500 less the capital gains tax of $8,175 = $51,325).

Compare the similar example in Chapter 1 where Brad exchanged the lot to the seller of the apartments. He saved himself $8,175 in tax by not having to pay the capital gains tax on the exchange. He would have had to pay the IRS $8,175 plus give the apartment seller another $8,175 to bring the $51,325 up to the needed level of $60,000 to close on the apartments.

Residential Gain Exclusion

The IRS has provided all U.S. taxpayers with a major bonus to encourage people to own their own homes. Many people have taken advantage of the new rule to build their fortunes quickly and safely.

Here is how this works. The IRS allows any taxpayer to exclude a maximum of $250,000 in gain on the sale of one's principal residence if the taxpayer meets the rules of this provision. I will get to the rules in a moment, but first understand that a husband and wife can combine this exclusion, with the result that a $500,000 gain can be excluded from tax. In essence, if you qualify, you will owe *zero* on that gain. This rule replaced an older provision that allowed you to reinvest your gain into a new home with some limitations and avoid payment of tax at that time. Erase that old rule from your mind (if it was there to begin with) and concentrate on the residential gain exclusion rule.

Rules of the Residential Exclusion: At the date of the sale and transfer of the home to another party, a $250,000 exclusion of gain from your taxable income is allowed if you:

- Meet the ownership test.
- Meet the use test.
- Did not exclude gain from the sale of another house during the two-year period ending on the date of the sale.

You can exclude up to $500,000 of the gain on the sale of your home if all four of the following statements are true:

1. You are married and file a joint return for the year.
2. Either you or your spouse meets the ownership test.
3. Both you and your spouse meet the use test.
4. During the two-year period ending on the date of the sale, neither you nor your spouse excluded gain from the sale of another home.

In these circumstances, if one of the married couple does not meet one or more of the tests, but the other one does, then that person is entitled to exclude $250,000 of the gain.

Ownership and Use Tests Defined: To claim the exclusion, you must meet the ownership and use tests. This means that during the five-year period ending on the date of the sale, you must have:

- Owned the home for at least two years (ownership test), and
- Lived in the home as your main home for at least two years (use test).

The two years is counted as a total of 24 months, or 730 days. The time does not have to be continuous, and will count even if you were away for short periods of time and rented out the property in those absences.

The five-year period can itself have suspensions of time. These come in several forms: uniformed services, foreign service member, qualified official extended duty, individuals with a disability, previous homes destroyed or condemned, home transferred from a spouse (by death or divorce), and other circumstances that you may meet.

Even if you do not meet the ownership or use tests, there are other situations that still may allow you to exclude part of the gain from your taxable income. Although these situations require considerable documentation and calculation, which are beyond the scope of this chapter, it is important for you to know that the two-year use out of five years of ownership basis for the rule is more flexible than that statement would suggest. Anytime you must sell because of the following factors, be sure to check with your accountant to see if you qualify for any gains exclusion: a change in place of employment; health problem of you or a relative you care for, and the primary reason for the sale is to obtain, provide, or facilitate the diagnosis, cure, mitigation, or treatment of the health problem; unforeseen circumstance such as death; unemployment; change in employment that reduces your ability to pay for the home; divorce or legal separation; multiple births from the same pregnancy; terrorist attacks; inability to maintain your home due to financial difficulties; the suitability of the property as a home materially changed; and during the time you owned the home it was your home, even if shorter than the five-year ownerships/two-year use rule.

If you meet the full test of ownership and use, and further qualify as indicated, the following example shows how the residential gain exclusion rule will benefit you.

You and your wife purchased a home five years ago for a price of $200,000. You lived in it for exactly 13 months, and moved to another state to go back to college. You stayed away from the home for two years, renting it out during that time. You move back to the home and live there until the end of the fifth year of ownership. You sell the home for $500,000. Assume that you have taken two years of depreciation on the home while it was rented out and that depreciation was not an accelerated form of depreciation—say, $12,000 of total depreciation. Your tax basis in the home would be $200,000 less the depreciation, or $188,000. Your gain is shown in the following calculation:

Calculation for Gain

Sale price		$500,000
Less adjusted basis:		
Original tax basis	$200,000	
Less depreciation taken	12,000	
Adjusted tax basis		$188,000
Gain		$312,000

As you and your wife meet the exclusion test and as $312,000 is less than the total exclusion, you would qualify for a total exemption of $500,000, the entire amount is free of income tax.

The news gets better, since you can take this money and purchase another home; say you spend $400,000. At the end of the next five years you can (if this IRS perk still exists) do the same thing again. This time you could sell the new home for up to $900,000 and not owe any tax on the gain.

Installment Sale Treatment

The IRS has provided another perk to real estate investors in the form of installment sale treatment on the receipt of a gain. Here is how it works.

Assume you sell a property (home or whatever kind of real estate) that would qualify as a capital gain (and not earned income). In any such sale in which you do not receive 100 percent of the sale price during the year of the sale, you may report this sale under the rules of the install- ment sale. When you do this you are allowed to spread the gain over the period of years during which you receive the balance of the sale price.

The benefit of using this tax reporting technique will depend on the amount of the gain and the amount of your other income during the year of the sale. It is possible that you would receive a more favorable tax rate by spreading a large gain over several years.

Installment Sale Example: Fredrick has received an offer to purchase a tract of land he has owned for 20 years. He purchased it at a price of $50,000 and now is being offered $1,300,000 for it. He has kept the land vacant all this time and has made no improvements to it at all. If he were to take cash for the property he would have a gain of $1,250,000 and could expect to pay a substantial tax on that amount. If he could spread the sum over a period of time he could save some money.

He agrees to the price offered provided that he gets $200,000 down and holds a mortgage for the balance over a period of 10 years with an- nual principal payments to him of $110,000 plus interest at the rate of 7 percent per annum on the unpaid balance.

As the IRS knows that each payment received on an installment sale is made up of three elements (interest, return of original investment, and gain) the IRS will tax the payments that Fredrick receives as follows:

Installment Sale Calculation: Find the Ratio of Gain to the Original Basis

1. Selling price	$1,300,000
2. Adjusted basis for sold property	50,000
3. Selling expenses	0
4. Depreciation recapture	0
5. Total adjusted basis for installment sale (add lines 2,3,4)	$ 50,000
6. Gross profit (line 1 less line 5)	$1,250,000
7. Contract price for property (line 1)	$1,300,000
8. Gross profit percentage (line 6 divided by line 7)	96.15%

The gross profit percentage of 96.15 percent indicates that of each dollar of principal paid to the seller, 96.15 percent of it will be treated as gross profit or gain on the sale. For the down payment of $200,000, 96.15 percent gain or a total of $192,307.68, is taxable gain the year of the sale. For each of the $110,000 principal installments, the same percentage of gain, or $105,765 each year, will be treated as taxable gain, while 100 percent of the interest payments each year will be treated as earned income.

The overall advantage of this kind of treatment is questionable, but the option to use it is available to any taxpayer. The alternative option of using the IRC 1031 (tax-free or tax-deferred exchange) would be a possible choice with greater benefits. Each deal, however, has its own circumstances, and as with any IRS rule it is important to seek the best advice possible. This book is not meant to replace the sound advice that your accountant can offer to you.

In the previous example, it is likely that Fredrick would have qualified for treatment under IRC 1031. In that event he could have reinvested the entire $1,300,000 into another qualified property and avoided paying any capital gains tax on the proceeds. The advantage in this is quickly seen in the following illustration.

What If Fredrick Used IRC 1031 to Shelter His Taxable Gain? The IRS allows the reinvestment of a capital gain that is made in an investment property such as what Fredrick owned into another like-kind property. I will get into this thing called "like kind" in much more detail later on (Chapter 3), but for the moment simply trust me that the term has a wide range of options. Fredrick did not have to look for another vacant tract of land. Say he knew of a shopping center that was for sale at a price of $5,000,000. The seller would take $1,300,000 down and hold the balance of the price in a long-term mortgage. It is likely that this would qualify for 1031 treatment and would convert that tract of land into a shopping center that could easily throw off annual revenue of $175,000 while at the same time paying off a $3,700,000 mortgage. The center will likely appreciate and 10 years later Fredrick might sell it for $7,000,000 or so, and reinvest into a larger center or several other income-producing properties and still not pay the capital gains tax. In the final analysis, Fredrick could set this investment portfolio up so that it continued to roll into other qualified assets and so that his estate would inherit the whole thing with no capital gains tax ever paid.

IRC 1031—Tax-Free Rollover of Investment Capital

Most of the balance of this book is dedicated to the use of IRC 1031. It is one of the best ways to invest in real estate and allow the asset to produce both income and appreciation. The income will be taxable, but there is no reason for a real estate investment that qualifies under IRC 1031 to ever be taxed on its appreciation.

This book will slowly build your knowledge in this technique. It is the basis for most real estate exchanging, but, as you will see, it is not the sole reason for using exchanges as an investment tool. There will be times when the situation does not warrant using IRC 1031, or when the parties will not fully qualify to use it.

Do not worry if you seem confused about anything this chapter has dealt with thus far. It will all start to come together as we look at different examples and learn the many different methods where you can use your new skills in investing. The key is to understand how to use this and other IRS rules to your investment advantage.

CHAPTER 3

How to Put the IRS on Your Side for a Change

The goal of this chapter is:

To Get You Ready to Become a World-Class Exchanger

You have already embarked on this journey the moment you decided to read this book. This chapter takes you a bit further into the world of the IRC 1031. It introduces you to some of the bits and pieces of the exchanging puzzle in an attempt to help you to understand the jargon of the real estate investor who uses exchanging, both the 1031 kind as well as barter where the tax consequence is not the principal issue at hand to make the most of his or her assets.

Terms and Concepts You Need to Know

Introduction to IRC 1031
Like-Kind Properties
The 1031 Clock
Replacement Property
Benefits and Burdens
Assumption of Liabilities
Havers and Takers

Let's review each of these terms or concepts in detail.

Introduction to IRC 1031

The Internal Revenue Code is divided into many sections. Here we are discussing IRC Section 1031, which describes the method whereby in qualified exchanges any gain on the exchange can escape all or most of the capital gains tax that would otherwise be applicable and due. The following is the entire text of IRC Section 1031 as published in the year 2004. Over the next several chapters I will break this section down into its important elements.

As you can tell from reading this section, it applies to non–real estate assets as well. There are references in the code of Section 1031 that call attention to Sections 1035(a), 1036(a), and 1037(a), which relate to non–real estate items. Section 1035(a) references insurance policies for endowment or annuity contracts and the like, 1036(a) deals with the exchange of stock in the same corporation, and 1037(a) relates to the exchange or surrender to the United States of obligations of the United States (Treasury bonds and bills) issued under Chapter 31 of Title 31 (of IRS Regulations) for other obligations issued under such chapter.

Choses in action mentioned in paragraph (a)(2)(F) is a very vague term and rarely used to disallow an exchange. A chose in action is the right to recover or receive money or other consideration from another person. Generally, this type of recovery deals with interests of a partnership.

IRC Section 1031

Section 1031, Exchange of property held for productive use or investment.

(a) Nonrecognition of gain or loss from exchanges solely in kind.

    (1) In general. No gain or loss shall be recognized on the exchange of property held for productive use in a trade or business or for investment if such property is exchanged solely for property of like kind which is to be held either for productive use in a trade or business or for investment.

    (2) Exception. This subsection shall not apply to any exchange of—

        (A) stock in trade or other property held primarily for sale,

        (B) stocks, bonds, or notes,

        (C) other securities or evidences of indebtedness or interest,

        (D) interests in a partnership,

        (E) certificates of trust or beneficial interests, or

        (F) choses in action.

        For the purposes of this section, an interest in a partnership which has in effect a valid election under section 761(a) to be excluded from the application of all of subchapter K shall be treated as an interest in each of the assets of such partnership and not as an interest in a partnership.

    (3) Requirement that property be identified and that exchange be completed not more than 180 days after transfer of exchanged property. For purposes of this subsection, any property received by the taxpayer shall be treated as property which is not like-kind if—

        (A) such property is not identified as property to be received in the exchange on or before the day which is 45 days after the date on which the taxpayer transfers the property relinquished in the exchange, or

        (B) such property is received after the earlier of—

            i. the day which is 180 days after the date on which the taxpayer transfers the property in the exchange, or

            ii. the due date (determined with regard to extension) for the transferor's return of the tax imposed by this chapter for the taxable year in which the transfer of the relinquished property occurs.

(b) Gain from exchanges not solely in kind. If an exchange would be within the provisions of subsection (a), of section 1035(a), or of section 1036(a), or of section 1037(a), if it were not for the fact that the property received in exchange consists not only of property permitted by such provisions to be received without the recognition of gain, but also of other property or money, then the gain, if any, to the recipient shall be recognized, but in an amount not in excess of the sum of such money and the fair market value of such other property.

(c) Loss from exchanges not solely in kind. If an exchange would be within the provisions of subsection (a), of section 1035(a), or of section 1036(a) or of section 1037(a), if it were not for the fact that the property received in exchange consists not only of property permitted by such provisions to be received without the recognition of gain or loss, but also of other property, then no loss from the exchange shall be recognized.

(d) Basis. If property was acquired on an exchange described in this section, section 1035(a), section 1036(a), or section 1037(a), then the basis shall be the same as that of the property exchanged, decreased in the amount of any money received by the taxpayer and increased in the amount of gain or decreased in the amount of loss to the taxpayer that was recognized on such exchange. If the property so acquired consisted in part of the type of property permitted by this section, section 1035(a), section 1036(a) or section 1037(a), to be received without the recognition of gain or loss, and in part of other property, the basis provided in this subsection shall be allocated between the properties (other than money) received, and for the purpose of the allocation there shall be assigned to such other properties equivalent to its fair market value at the date of the exchange. For purposes of this section, section 1035(a), and section 1036(a), where as part of the consideration to the taxpayer another party to the exchange assumed (as determined under section 357(d)) a liability of the taxpayer, such assumption shall be considered as money received by the taxpayer on the exchange.

(e) Exchanges of livestock of different sexes. For purposes of this section, livestock of different sexes are not property of a like kind.

(f) Special rules for exchanges between related persons.

    (1) In general. If—

        (A) a taxpayer exchanges property with a related person,

        (B) there is nonrecognition of gain or loss to the taxpayer under this section with respect to the exchange of such property (determined without regard to this subsection), and

        (C) before the date 2 years after the date of the last transfer which was part of such exchange—

            i. the related person disposes of such property, or

            ii. the taxpayer disposes of the property received in the exchange from the related person which was of like kind to the property transferred by the taxpayer, there shall be no nonrecognition of gain or loss under this section to the taxpayer with respect to such exchange: except that any gain or loss recognized by the taxpayer by reason of this subsection shall be taken into account as of the date on which the disposition referred to in subparagraph (C) occurs.

    (2) Certain dispositions not taken into account. For purposes of paragraph (1)(C), there shall not be taken into account any disposition—

        (A) After the earlier of the death of the taxpayer or the death of the related person,

        (B) In a compulsory or involuntary conversion (within the meaning of section 1033) if the exchange occurred before the threat or imminence of such conversion, or

        (C) With respect to which it is established to the satisfaction of the Secretary that neither the exchange nor such disposition had as one of its principal purposes the avoidance of Federal income tax.

    (3) Related person. For purposes of this subsection, the term "related person" means any person bearing a relationship to the taxpayer described in section 267(b) or 707(b)(1).

    (4) Treatment of certain transactions. This section shall not apply to any exchange, which is part of a transaction (or series of transactions) structured to avoid the purposes of this subsection.

(g) Special rule where substantial diminution of risk.
  (1) In general. If paragraph (2) applies to any property for any period, the running of the period set forth in subsection (f)(1)(C) with respect to such property shall be suspended during such period.
  (2) Property to which subsection applies. This paragraph shall apply to any property for any period during which the holder's risk of loss with respect to the property is substantially diminished by—
    (A) the holding of a put with respect to such property,
       the holding by another person of a right to acquire such property, or
    (B) A short sale or any other transaction.
(h) Special rules for foreign real and personal property. For purposes of this section—
  (1) Real property. Real property located in the United States and real property located outside the United States are not property of a like kind.
  (2) Personal property.
    (A) In general. Personal property used predominantly within the United States and personal property used predominantly outside the United States are not property of a like kind.
    (B) Predominant use. Except as provided in subparagraph (C) and (D), the predominant use of any property shall be determined based on—
      i. in the case of the property relinquished in the exchange, the 2-year period ending on the date of such relinquishment, and
      ii. in the case of the property acquired in the exchange, the 2-year period beginning on the date of such acquisition.
    (C) Property held for less than 2 years. Except in the case of an exchange which is part of a transaction (or series of transactions) structured to avoid the purposes of this subsection—
      i. Only the periods the property was held by the person relinquishing the property (or any related person) shall be taken into account under subparagraph (B)(ii).

ii. Only the periods the property was held by the person acquiring the property (or any related person) shall be taken into account under subparagraph (B)(ii).

(D) Special rule for certain property. Property described in any subparagraph of section 168(g)(4) shall be treated as used predominantly in the United States.

I will refer to this section of the Internal Revenue Code as we continue. I suggest you attach a paper clip to the first page of the description of IRC Section 1031 in this chapter.

Like-Kind Properties

One of the most misunderstood concepts of IRC Section 1031 is the idea of like-kind properties. I have heard lawyers and accountants as well as sophisticated real estate investors give conflicting definitions of this very important aspect of 1031 exchanges. The tax code gets into whether one black angus is a cow or a steer or a bull. But we will stay within the scope and goal of this book and concentrate on exchanges of real estate, where the primary factor is this: Is the real estate held as an investment, or is it held for use in a trade or business? Each type will qualify for 1031 treatment, as long as you stay within one category. In essence, you can exchange property held for trade or business with that same kind of property, or investment property (we are focused on real estate here) for other investment property. What does not qualify at all in either category is property held primarily for sale. Real estate developers cannot use IRC 1031 as a way to trade inventory of lots or other property they hold that is considered inventory for sale.

Often the distinguishing factors of these different elements are not easily defined. The IRS may suddenly get tough on certain elements of the definition. If the property you are giving up can be clearly defined as an investment, then you would presume that any replacement that could also meet that definition would be a like-kind property. This would open the door for exchanges of vacant land for shopping centers or other kinds of income-producing properties. However, if there was some question about the property you are giving up being held for investment and not some other use, then things could slide into a gray area and be open for attack by the IRS. Two of the determining factors here would be your past history of real estate ownership and how long you have owned the property you are now giving up in an exchange or selling via a Starker exchange.

It seems that the IRS looks more closely at exchanges that are of properties (real estate and other assets) that are held for "productive use in a trade or business," which can include both real estate and personal property. An example of real estate that would meet this criterion would be a parking lot owned by someone whose business was ownership and operation of parking lots. An exchange of one parking lot for another would clearly be "like kind" as to intent. However, if the intent to make the exchange was to promptly sell the parking lot taken in the exchange, then the taxpayer could have many sleepless nights awaiting the dreaded summons to IRS offices to discuss the pending audit.

Most real estate investors who are not developers, however, will discover that the IRS is somewhat lenient in this respect. But because IRS codes are constantly in a state of flux, no matter what I say in this book, tomorrow the codes could change. Ouch, you say! Well, it is not likely that *everything* I say will change, and some changes may actually be beneficial. My point is that some things might change from time to time, and you need to make sure that the accountant or exchange facilitator you might use, or your lawyer, is up-to-date on what is going on. My sad experience over 40 years as a Realtor and investor has shown me that so-called experts are not always up-to-date.

So what should you do? You can ask for an IRS ruling. This is not always forthcoming in time for you to make a decision (if at all), but if the situation appears to be in one of those gray areas it will establish the fact that you realized that and were trying to get to a conclusion that the IRS agreed with. Tax courts have ruled in favor of taxpayers who have gone that extra mile to try to meet all the rules and tests of IRC Section 1031. Be sure that you do seek advice from a good real estate lawyer who is familiar and up-to-date with IRC 1031. Dealing with one or two exchanges a year may not constitute sufficient experience to properly earn your trust.

The 1031 Clock

The 1031 clock is, oddly enough, one of the simplest aspects of the 1031 test, yet it seems to baffle many astute investors, accountants, and lawyers. It shouldn't be a problem to those who read this chapter and specifically this section.

The IRS has a very specific timetable for identifying replacement properties and making the exchange, to qualify for nonrecognition of the gain. Take note, however: No matter what the code says, some circumstances can extend this time—death, military service, financial ruin, and so on. For the normal exchange situation, here is how the timetable works.

Jake's Exchange

Jake has a small strip shopping center that he has owned and managed for the past 10 years. He now wants to move to be closer to his grandchildren. He purchased this center 10 years earlier for $200,000, and because of the revenue it produces it is now worth $1,000,000. Jake has no debt on this center, and his tax base (purchase price, plus capital improvements less depreciation) is $50,000. A quick look at the finances of this deal suggests that Jake will have a capital gain of $950,000 and even at the 2004 tax rate a capital gains tax of $142,000 (or more). As he plans to move to Santa Fe, he puts an ad in the local newspaper there to see if there is any similar property or other investment property that might be available for exchange.

Jake receives many proposals for one-to-one exchange, but none of them looks attractive to him. Reading up on the essence of the Section 1031 exchange, he discovers that he can actually sell his property outright, put the money from the sale into the hands of an exchange facilitator, and buy a replacement property. This entire transaction, if handled correctly, would pass the test of a correct 1031 exchange (called at this point a Starker exchange), and in the best-case scenario Jake would owe no tax on his capital gain.

Therefore, on January 1 Jake enters into a contract to sell his property for $1,000,000 net to him of all costs of the sale. The closing is set for March 1 of the same year. It is important to note at this point that the timetable to properly qualify for 1031 treatment begins on the day that Jake's property is transferred to the buying entity. The January 1 contract date has no real significance in 1031 treatment. However, as you will discover later, it is a good idea to have more time (if the buyer will allow it) between entering into a firm and binding contract to sell and the actual closing date.

Before the closing, Jake should set up his relationship with an exchange facilitator to handle the different parts of this exchange. The facilitator can be a person or company that specializes in this activity, a title insurance company that is set up to do this work, an independent law firm, one of many national banks that have departments to do this, or other such qualified parties or companies. It is important to remember that there should be no prior relationship with these persons or entities, other than using them within the scope of this kind of transaction. I suggest you never use a related person, your own lawyer, your accountant, or anyone connected with your other business activities.

The Clocks Start Ticking: On March 1, the closing takes place and the IRC Section 1031 clock starts ticking. Following the closing the proceeds from the sale would be deposited into the escrow account of the facilitator. The funds will remain there, where Jake will have no control over them other than to direct the facilitator to acquire one or more of Jake's replacement properties. At that point any profit is paid over to Jake and he must meet the tax obligations that come with that event. All of the things that can go wrong are covered later in this book. However, for the moment, take note that on March 1 both the 45-day and the 180-day timetables have begun to run at this point at the same time. These are what I call the 45-day clock and the 180-day clock.

The 45-Day Clock—Identification Period: The 45-day clock begins March 1 in this transaction. March 2 indicates the passing of one day; March 3 indicates the passing of two days; and so on. It is the "identification of a replacement property" period. What this means is that within the first 45 days after the date of the transfer of the property Jake must have identified his replacement property. Because finding property that will meet Jake's criteria as a good investment and will also qualify for the

1031 treatment is difficult, Jake is well advised to select more than one such potential replacement property. How many can he choose? There is nothing in the code that specifies, but there are some safe-harbor rulings that suggest that three properties is a safe move. Do not worry about that right now.

Jake finds three properties he likes, and each of them would serve to use up all the money from the sale of his shopping center. He identifies them clearly and notifies the facilitator of that selection well within the 45-day period. He now starts whatever due diligence he wants to do on the three properties in hopes that at least one will pass. It might be that the purchase of one or more of the replacement properties requires that a purchase money mortgage be obtained. Clearly, a $3,000,000 shopping center would be more than the proceeds held in Jake's facilitator's escrow account, so financing would be needed to come up with $2,000,000. Jake can add other cash if he has it to make up the needed equity, or he can seek new financing to balance the deal.

Financing generally means an appraisal would be needed, and these are elements that start eating up time. Full property inspections of a large property may require audits (reviews) of dozens of leases, service contracts, and the like if the new property is large and there are many tenants.

The 180-Day Clock—The Period to Close: Jake's deadline to close on one of the three replacement properties is the 180th day following the day he transferred his property to its new owner. As the date of the closing was March 1, Jake has until August 28 of the same year to close. Remember, the day count starts the day after the date of the closing. It is important to know what will be going on the 180th day. Is it a weekend day, holiday, your closing agent's anniversary or preplanned vacation time? The IRS will not be happy if you close on the 183th day because of an excuse that could easily have been avoided. It is a good idea to schedule a closing at least a week early to take into consideration last-minute delays.

The IRS does, however, allow some flexibility in this timetable. Death, military action, and other unavoidable factors can mitigate the need to complete both the 45-day identification and the 180-day closing on the replacement property. These exceptions to the rule are subject to change, so if you discover that you are going to run out of time, check with your accountant early enough to document those exceptions if they pertain to you.

Replacement Property

In a quick review of the 1031 clock just discussed, remember that within the first 45 days following the transfer of the exchange property (also called the relinquished property), the taxpayer making the exchange must identify the replacement property. To qualify as a replacement property it must be of like kind, which has also been discussed. However, the taxpayer is confined to that first 45 days after which no additional properties can be identified, and a failure to close on one or more of the identified properties will cause the exchange to fail. This timetable set up as a confinement to the court's ruling in *Starker vs. Commissioner* that created what is commonly referred to as a Starker exchange or deferred exchange.

Later IRS rulings have created a safe-harbor procedure that suggests that there are three methods of selection of a replacement property. Of these three methods only two are practical, the Three-Property Rule and the 200 Percent Rule. Of these two, the better choice to follow is the Three-Property Rule.

The Three-Property Rule

This rule states that the taxpayer can select any three properties, regardless of their market value. Keep in mind that any of these three could be the sole replacement property, or any combination of them could make up the exchange proceeds. Why three properties? As you will note when we discuss examples of different exchanges, finding a replacement property that can be closed within the time allowed (180 days following the transfer of the relinquished property) can be difficult.

The value of any identified property is in itself not material. However, to maximize the tax-free benefit of 1031 treatment, it is best if the taxpayer take on more debt than is given up and use the total amount of cash that results in the sale of the exchange property. In essence, if your relinquished property was worth $600,000 and had a mortgage on it of $300,000 (which you are going to be relieved of), you would want to take on at least the same value of property and new debt. Ideally you would want to leverage up to, say, a replacement property valued in excess of $600,000 that would have more than $300,000 in debt. Remember, too, that you can add other cash to a deal outside of the exchange proceeds.

The 200 Percent Rule

This is a situation where the IRS says you can select any number of properties as long as the total fair market value of the selected properties does not exceed 200 percent of the relinquished property at the end of the 45-day identification period. This rule is not realistic for most exchanges, but if it fits your current exchange needs then use it.

Benefits and Burdens

Remember that the 1031 exchange clock begins counting the day following the title transfer. The first 45 days lead up to the deadline to identify the replacement property. Following that there are an additional 135 days (45 + 135 = 180 days) to close on the replacement property. It becomes essential that the transfer date be established in accordance with federal tax purposes. According to the IRS it is possible that you have effected a transfer without knowing it, or conversely you might believe you have when, according to the IRS, you haven't.

The IRS takes the position that the date of transfer for income tax purposes is the moment when there has been a transfer of "benefits and burdens." Anytime a party has given up one without the other, it is possible that a federally qualified transfer of title has not taken place. A contract for deed, as an example, may give the buyer right to access the property, but until the contract for deed has been fulfilled there is no actual transfer of title.

This situation need not become a problem for any real estate investor who has properly established the exchange with a qualified facilitator who is aware of all the conditions of the deal.

Assumption of Liabilities

In many real estate exchanges, either qualified 1031 tax-deferred exchanges or otherwise, it is likely that either or both the relinquished property or the replacement property will be encumbered with debt. Consider that anytime you are relieved of a debt (in a sale or exchange) the IRS considers that you have received cash. Also, anytime you take over, assume, or become otherwise obligated to the existing debt on a replacement property, the IRS considers that you have paid cash.

When both properties are encumbered with debt of different amounts, the net debt will be calculated to ascertain which party has been relieved of more debt than he or she took over. For example:

1. I give you a $100,000 property that has a $50,000 mortgage on it.
2. You give me a $300,000 property that has a $250,000 mortgage on it.
3. I have a net mortgage increase of $200,000.
4. You have a net mortgage relief of $200,000.

	I Give You	*You Give Me*
Property valued at	$100,000	$300,000
With a mortgage of	50,000	250,000
Equity	$50,000	$50,000

	My New Debt Status	*Your New Debt Status*
New debt	$250,000	$50,000
Debt relief	– 50,000	– 250,000
Net debt	$200,000	–$200,000

The importance of net debt relief is that when I calculate the new tax basis in the replacement property, the amount of new debt increases my tax basis by that amount (in my case $200,000). Why would you do this kind of a deal? There may be no tax consequences to you, as you purchased the $300,000 property with $50,000 down and the seller holds the first mortgage of $250,000—so you have no capital gain at all.

Havers and Takers

Havers and *takers* are terms that relate to two different sides of an exchange transaction. One is someone who has what another party may want (so he or she is a haver). The taker is someone who wants what you or someone else has. This is the fundamental basis of all exchanges. Havers and takers make up a major part of the exchange world. It is very easy to get caught up in this tax savings element of exchanges, but as you will discover in this book, exchanging is a universal form of exchange, tax or no tax.

A conversation among several real estate exchangers could easily go like this:

> *First Exchanger:* "I'm a taker for any fairly priced ag [agricultural or farm land] located near Orlando. Do you know any havers?"
>
> *Second Exchanger:* "No, but I noticed on Brad's want list that he indicates he is also a taker for that kind of property. Why not ask him if he has come across any havers that he has turned down?"
>
> *Brad:* "I overhead that. I ran across one guy in Tampa who is up to his ears in farmland alligators [property that is financially eating him alive], but he only wants to cash out [get as much cash as he can out of the property]."
>
> *First Exchanger:* "I can give him a combination of exchange and cash. Let's talk to that guy."

How Tax Laws Are Interpreted

Tax codes tend to make for difficult reading at times, and it is even more difficult to understand exactly what the authors of the text mean. This creates a situation where the codes themselves are in flux regarding the correct way to follow the code. Resolution of this dilemma often requires one to look at how the tax courts have interpreted the codes. The process of letting the courts assign a true definition to a code is slow, tedious, and not always helpful. Why? The courts view every case as a different situation from the next one, and it is rare for every situation to be exactly the same. When it comes to Section 1031 we are dealing with intent of the parties, which may be difficult to prove unless there is past history that supports a contention that the exchange was indeed intended to qualify for 1031 treatment. Top that off with the fact that every real estate asset is different, too. The form of ownership and use of the same asset by a different party could qualify for 1031 treatment for one taxpayer and fail for another. Remember, to qualify the real estate must be held for use in business, trade, or investment, and not primarily as inventory or product for sale.

To speed things up the IRS gives the practitioner rulings or procedures that illustrate what the IRS calls safe-harbor steps. These procedures, although not written into the codes, outline acceptable behavior that if followed gives taxpayers a level of comfort that the steps they have taken are correct and they are less likely to be challenged by the IRS.

In the final analysis, all laws enacted eventually have to meet the test of the courts. Every time there is a decision it tends to set the bar of standards for another similar event. The problem is that the only court that puts the burden on *you* to prove yourself innocent is the Tax Court. Double ouch.

How You Can Become an Insider to Real Estate Exchanging

A year or so after I first went into the real estate brokerage business, I was introduced into the magic of this fantastic technique. That introduction came when I joined a local real estate exchangers club that was made up entirely of real estate brokers and salespeople. There the members arranged seminars and informative talks by local certified public accountants (CPAs), title insurance experts, and real estate and tax lawyers to give us what knowledge they had on the subject.

As we were all new to this thing called exchanging, we learned by using every aspect of the tool right in the field and by using the procedures in the practical application of the trade. It was hands-on learning that covered a wide range of situations and circumstances. As I mentioned earlier, we were all in the brokerage profession, and as such our main goal was to use this technique as a tool to help our clients and to obtain listings.

Real estate exchanging, then, is simply a tool that has the ability to do a variety of things for the real estate investor, buyer, or seller. After all, most investors who purchase a property may eventually want, or need, to dispose of it. Exchanging is also a good extension of the obligation of a broker or salesperson to offer clients, either the buyer or the seller, a different approach to help those clients reach their desired goals. If I, as a broker, could improve a seller's chance to dispose of a tough to sell property in a buyer's market, then I would be doing that client a service and helping him or her solve a problem. In the same way, helping a buyer decrease the amount of cash that might be needed for a transaction by showing the buyer how to include one or more dormant assets as a part of the offer to buy benefits everyone.

Many times the broker ends up with some of this exchange property as a commission. While there is nothing wrong with this, I have seen and heard managers of real estate companies rant and rave at the suggestion that a deal will be closed only if the firm takes the offered real estate as its fee.

No two exchange transactions are the same. As the people differ, so do their goals and approaches to solving problems. For this reason, the best way for you to continually improve your working relationship with real estate exchanging is to associate with other real estate investors. For those of you who are not directly in the real estate profession the task of making such an association might seem to be difficult, but that is not the case, as I will show you.

Where the Insiders Hang Out

The best way to find where real estate insiders hang out is to first make a list of the most important things a true insider does. You can emulate these things that real estate insiders do.

- **Insiders stay on top of current events within their comfort zone.** This means read the local newspapers and continually tour the community. Real estate investing requires constant visual input of the facts and the physical changes or opportunities that exist.

- **They attend city meetings (development review, planning and zoning, commission meetings).** This is important when subjects (new projects for example) that are important to them and their investments are scheduled.

- **They meet all the important decision makers within the local government.** There are not so many people. The most important are these: mayor and commissioners; city manager; head of the building department; head of the planning and zoning department; heads of the city, county, and state departments of transportation; state government representatives; and congressional representation for your area. These people are all public officials or work for them, and they are easy to find and easy to meet. The key that a true insider knows, though, is that meeting them is just half the goal; getting them to associate with you as a real estate insider is the rest of the goal.

- **They give something of themselves to the community.** Leaders of a community know this is important, both for themselves and for the community. It is so easy to do, too. Join one or more community help organizations. There are many to choose from and they all welcome new members with open arms. Be a ready and willing helper and you will rise to the top of that organization quicker than cream on milk.

Start your process by attending city meetings. The most interesting for a real estate investor are the planning and zoning board meetings. This is the place where real estate projects are introduced to the public. Later on you will discover that there are even more preliminary meetings that you can attend that precede the P&Z meetings, called the development review committee meetings. But at the P&Z meetings you will see all the local real estate players show up when important (to them) projects are presented. This is a great way for a newcomer to real estate to see all the stars of the profession in one place. Keep in mind, however, that your goal is not just to see them, but also to meet them and make sure they know who you are.

Rediscover the Oldest Game in Town— Barter and Exchange

One of the best and most effective techniques for a new real estate investor is called sweat equity. This is where an investor exchanges a talent that he or she possesses as all or part of the cost to acquire a property. Someone who has carpentry skills might agree to fix up a property for the seller of, say, a small apartment complex to the point where the property has increased in value enough that the buyer (the carpenter) can finance 100 percent of the purchase price. Or it might be a CPA, an architect, or a civil engineer offering a credit for their time in their profession to a developer as payment for one of the new condominium units to be constructed. All these situations are a form of barter, and barter is the oldest exchange of value that exists.

When it comes to real estate, the methods of using non–real estate assets to acquire real estate should never be overlooked. Most of us have some asset, either talent or physical assets, that we could use as all or part of an acquisition of real estate. I have acquired real estate giving jewelry as the down payment for a rental condominium. I have given up holiday time in time-shares I own (and not the actual time-share) as a down payment for a vacant lot. I have used property I own as security on a note I gave as a full payment on a fixer-upper and traded land for an office building. In my brokerage business I have been involved in countless real estate exchanges where part or all of the transaction was non–real estate.

In your community you are likely to find at least one club or organization that specializes in barter. Become a member, and you will be instantly thrown into a pond of more insider exchangers. Learn from them.

CHAPTER 4

The Nitty Gritty
of IRS Tax Loopholes

The goal of this chapter is:

To Expand Your Knowledge of Tax Loopholes

Let's review each in detail.

Parties to the Exchange

Many thousands of real estate transactions close each year without the taxpayers taking full, if any, advantage of the Internal Revenue Code tax breaks and end up paying more tax than necessary. There are many reasons that this occurs. Generally, though, the reason for this is the taxpayer (either the buyer or seller in the transaction) does not understand how these codes work and can easily be intimidated by their complexity when attempting to use them. A vast majority of bookkeepers and even some certified public accountants are not comfortable enough with these codes to advise their clients on the full extent of the tax savings possible.

There are sufficient reasons why a 1031 exchange may fail to close in its tax-saving mode, but there is no reason for a buyer or seller not to know that there is light at the end of the tax tunnel—that it is possible to sell your investment property and avoid the tax, and to reinvest your full equity into a new investment.

About now you might be wondering why I have used the words *buyer or seller* in connection with a tax code that centers around the *exchange* of a piece of real estate. All real estate exchanges originate with one party who is actually a buyer *and* a seller. Some exchanges evolve with a second party who is also a buyer and seller, and still another type can have a third party who comes to the exchange solely as a buyer. Let's look at how the parties relate to each other.

The First Player

Jennifer, whose investment goal was to ultimately own one or more large office buildings, started out by buying a well-located, but old, complex of retail shops consisting of almost one and a half acres of land (63,162 square feet) on which there was approximately 20,000 square feet of rental space. At the time she purchased it, using inheritance money left to her by a wealthy parent along with financing, she believed that eventually the value of the land under the complex would far exceed what she paid for the property. This turned out to be the case sooner rather than later, and developers were suddenly clamoring to buy the property. The offering prices hovered around $60 per square foot, meaning that there was a good chance she would end up with a price close to $3,800,000.

Jennifer had heard me talk about the tax-free opportunities provided by using IRC Section 1031 in classes at the local board of Realtors where she once worked. It was something that seemed too good to be real, but she decided that if she was going to have a windfall in the sale of her retail complex, she would want to reinvest those funds without having to pay the capital gains tax that would be due.

She and I discussed her goal of wanting to own one or more large office buildings. I played devil's advocate in the discussion to see how strong were her convictions about that type of property. In the end, I was convinced that she had done her homework and I agreed with her that the area where she wanted to own such buildings was ripe pickings for a category of real estate that was going to have a very strong appreciation in the next few years. It was a very good time for her to make that kind of a move, and her good fortune to have started with a small investment (the old retail shopping complex) that was about to pay off with a multifold return. Here is how the numbers looked in her situation.

Jennifer had purchased the shops for $960,000 using $300,000 of her inheritance as the down payment and financing the balance of $660,000 with a local savings and loan institution. At the time of that acquisition, she had paid just about the top price for a retail complex of that size. The shops were more than 50 years old and not in tip-top condition. But they were well located nearly in the center of town and surrounded by a high-paying employment base that included hospitals and banks; law offices galore; city, county, and federal office buildings and courthouses; high-end retail shops; and chic restaurants. One of the upper-priced residential areas was just a few blocks away to round out the advantages to the area.

By the time she and I were discussing the now pending turn of events, she had owned the property for nearly seven years. As mentioned, in that span of time the property had appreciated to around $3,800,000. Even after deducting the amount of the mortgage (she still owed around

$600,000) she would have a reinvestment potential of $3,200,000 in cash. With this sum, and using a very conservative ratio of 30 percent down and 70 percent financing, that $3,200,000 would allow her to purchase an office building in the $10,670,000 price range—that is, if she did not have to pay any capital gains taxes in the deal. I calculated with her what her capital gains tax would be.

Jennifer's Tax Situation in a Sale

Purchase price of property	$ 960,000
Less depreciation over seven years	25,000
Tax basis at time of sale	$ 935,000
Net profit	$3,800,000
Less tax basis	935,000
Capital gain	$2,865,000

Keep in mind that she had paid off $60,000 of her mortgage over the seven years. As the original mortgage was $660,000, the amount owed at closing would be $600,000; so at closing she would get:

The buyer pays	$3,800,000
The closing agent deducts the mortgage owed	600,000
Cash in Jennifer's pocket before tax	$3,200,000

(I have not taken into account any expenses that might change the gain we calculated.) Even at the tax rate of 2004, she would have to pay $429,750 in tax and end up with $2,770,250.

I know that no one needs to feel sorry for Jennifer at this point, but as you know by now, she does not have to pay that tax. But if she did, and still reinvested the cash left over at a 30 percent down payment, she would be able to purchase a building worth $9,233,416.60 ($2,770,025 ÷ 30% = $9,233,416.60). By paying her tax, Jennifer loses the reinvestment potential (based on a 30 percent down payment) of $1,436,584 ($10,670,000 – $9,233,416). You can see that it is not just paying the tax that hurts, but the loss of reinvestment potential.

The Second Player

In this transaction, the second player is the owner of a 100,000-square-foot office building that is for sale. It is a modern building in a very nice location, except that it has suffered from the 9/11 terrorist attack (despite being nearly 1,400 miles away from New York City), and has only 70 percent occupancy. The asking price of $11,500,000 was just a tad bit high, and it sat on the market for some years.

The owner then reduced the price of the building while at the same time the management company was negotiating several leases that would jump the occupancy up to nearly 90 percent. Other positive events were going on, and Jennifer had been eyeing the building for some time.

However, the first player wanted to sell the building outright, not exchange it, as he had other investment plans elsewhere in the United States.

The Third Player

In this transaction, the third player is a ready, willing, and very able buyer for Jennifer's property at a price she will accept. Sometimes this player could be the one that starts this whole transaction. He or she comes along, sees a property he or she would like to own, and makes an offer. "Not so fast," Jennifer says. "I've got to get this set up right so that I can do a tax-free exchange." Other times everything goes on hold while Jennifer or her real estate agent seeks this third player out. In any event, if the owner of the property Jennifer wants to end up with won't wait until she finds a buyer for her property, or someone else buys the office building before she can get to it, then the deal just doesn't move forward.

The Fourth Player

Usually this facilitator handles the money and acts as an intermediary in the transaction. The terms *facilitator* and *intermediary* identify this player. You might say that the intermediary is a neutral party that functions to keep the seller, in this case Jennifer, from controlling or having access to the funds.

When the transaction draws near to a transfer of titles on either or both properties (Jennifer's shops and the second party's office building), the second party is likely to initiate a new 1031 setup where he (or she) becomes a buyer of a replacement property. The tax-free benefit of the exchange can be had by both parties who give up and receive replacement property. Or perhaps only one party qualifies for 1031 treatment, or even needs it at all.

Special Caution to the First Player

Jennifer is the one who is giving up the exchange property. In this example, it is her commercial shops. She is also the person who will end up with the replacement property. No matter what route the exchange takes, the party giving up a property must take title to the replacement property in the same name as he or she held the original property. This is something that the parties often overlook, especially if one spouse owned the exchange property, later got married, and now takes the replacement property in both names (husband and wife). If this might present a problem, it is best to straighten out the names on the title of the exchange property well before entering into the Section 1031 transaction.

Starker Exchange

The Starker exchange is also called a *deferred* or *delayed exchange*. It is a technique that allows a taxpayer to actually sell his or her property and use the proceeds to acquire a replacement property. This technique has become very popular and has created an entirely new form of real estate transfer. It originated when a taxpayer named Starker took the IRS all the way to the United States Ninth Circuit Court and won (*Starker vs. Commissioner*, 602 F.2d 1341, 44 AFTR2d 79-5525 [CA-9, 1979]). The case centered around a very complicated exchange of timber rights, which in some situations and circumstances, are considered a property right. Following the favorable decision for Starker, in 1981 Congress enacted a new provision to the already existing Section 1031, adding (a)(3), which created the procedure allowing a taxpayer to transfer the exchange property (also called relinquished property) to a party different from the one delivering the replacement property. This provision also established the 1031 45/180 timetable clock, which has already been discussed.

Because of the *Starker* ruling, the whole IRC Section 1031 has gone through a development and evolution that allows a wide range of sales and exchanges to take place. This evolution is likely to continue, which, if the trend continues along its present path, is good news for the real estate investor. Although some of the current rules are cumbersome and difficult to understand and follow, there is hope that elements such as the 45/180 timetable clock will be one of the next factors to soften. The chapters to follow show some of the new techniques that are available to real estate investors who choose to use the benefits of Section 1031.

Reverse Exchange

Prior to getting into the details of a reverse exchange, please be careful not to confuse this with a reverse mortgage, which was discussed in an earlier chapter. To remind you at this point, a reverse mortgage is one where the lender gives you money over a period of time, often monthly, until the amount given to you plus the growing interest due reaches the amount of the mortgage agreed on. All the while, your property (usually your home) is the security for that loan. At the end of the period, once the amount promised is reached, you would start to pay off the loan.

A reverse exchange, by contrast, is an event where a taxpayer interested in exchanging his or her property for another property engages an exchange accommodation titleholder (EAT) to acquire and hold title to a replacement property before the taxpayer has disposed of the exchange property.

Frank's Reverse Exchange

Frank owns a shopping center, but he wants to get rid of it and acquire the marina where he keeps his yacht. He has negotiated with the marina owner and has put it under contract. He then hires a 1031 facilitator to act as the EAT in this transaction and arranges for the EAT to take title of the marina. The owner of the marina, in essence, sells the marina to the EAT.

Frank eventually finds a buyer for his shopping center. There are special rules that he and the EAT must follow, and I will get to them in a moment. But at this point, things proceed, and when Frank has a buyer the center is sold, the facilitator who is also acting as the EAT completes the transaction, and Frank ends up owning the marina.

The rules governing reverse exchanges came about when the IRS issued its safe-harbor procedure on September 15, 2000. It is called Revenue Procedure 2000-37 and it officially sanctions reverse exchanges made after that date. This procedure provides a safe harbor for a parking style exchange so that the title to either the relinquished property (owned by the exchanger) or the replacement property can be held by the EAT for up to 180 days while the taxpayer attempts to sell the relinquished property.

In short, this safe harbor procedure says that the IRS will not challenge: (1) the qualification of the property as either replacement property or relinquished property in the exchange, or (2) the treatment of the EAT as the beneficial owner of such property if the property is held under a qualified exchange accommodation arrangement.

Although the IRS has issued Revenue Procedure 2000-37, which has opened the door on more of this kind of exchange, this type of exchange should not be used if a more direct form of exchange can be accomplished. Consider Frank's example a few paragraphs ago. If he could negotiate a purchase of the marina that would not close until he could sell his shopping center, he could arrange a simultaneous exchange and avoid the potential problems of the reverse exchange. In addition to the fact that the reverse exchange can be costly due to double closing costs and added legal and facilitator fees, there is always the possibility that the IRS will challenge the exchange anyway.

Intent to Exchange

I have noticed that in reading tax court cases that involve Section 1031, there are instances where the court rules in favor of the taxpayer even when all the rules have not been met, because the taxpayer was able to prove that he or she fully and completely intended to exchange and to do so in a correct and an acceptable way. With this in mind you should make an effort to leave a very clear document trail of your intent to exchange throughout the exchange process. This process, by the way, should begin very early in the buy-sell-exchange transaction. Follow along with such a transaction.

Kevin's Exchange

Kevin had been purchasing small condominiums in northern Florida for several years. He looked for buildings that would allow the units to be easily rented out, and then purchased them, fixed them up with the best used furniture he could find, and rented them out. (This kind of property will qualify as an investment when the owner can document that he or she did not purchase the property for the purpose of living in the units.) Kevin now owned 10 such condominium apartments in the Daytona Beach community, all within an easy walk to each other and to the famous Daytona Beach. Kevin decided that his package of 10 rental units, even though spread over four different condo complexes, would be a good investment for someone else. He figured this because condominium prices were climbing, and the units would be easy to hold for a few years for more appreciation. He put a price on the entire package, and was not surprised when an investor who also thought condominium prices would not stop rising for the next dozen years at least made an offer.

Kevin had a good lawyer who drafted the agreement and suggested a facilitator who would handle the detail side of the Section 1031 exchange. The contract for the sale of the condominium package spelled out that the sale was predicated on Kevin's successfully obtaining a binding agreement to purchase a replacement property that passed his due diligence inspections and could be closed. A number of letters passed between Kevin and the other parties in the transaction (lawyer, accountant, buyer of his units, and seller of a replacement property Kevin located). All this correspondence mentioned conversations between those parties about the 1031 exchange, and confirmed that the exchange was in progress.

This documentation trail would also include mention of Kevin's intent to exchange and meet the procedural requirements of Section 1031 in the contract with the seller of the replacement property. It seems that Kevin was doing everything right anyway, so why did he have to be so careful?

No matter how well things seem to be going, when it comes to real estate closings, especially when there are two sets of transactions that are greatly dependent on each other, something can easily go wrong. What kind of things? Here are just a few.

Eight Things That Can Hold Up a Closing

1. Title problems exist that have to be cleared up before the closing of that property can take place.

2. One of the parties' lawyers cannot be contacted and he or she has vital data needed to close.

3. One of the parties is stricken ill or dies.

4. A disaster (storm, fire, flood, whatever) strikes and property is damaged or wiped out, or the disaster makes it physically impossible to close.

5. A lender holds up the deal because the appraisal (that the lender wanted) is late for reasons that they say they have no control over. (After all, they generally don't care whether you meet your deadlines.)

6. One of the parties is trying to sandbag the deal because of a change of mind.

7. You discover the real reason you got such a "great price" on the replacement property and need more time to evaluate the situation.

8. An unavoidable event makes the property or the buying entity temporarily uninsurable, which in turn causes the lender to hold up releasing the funds until its interest is properly insured.

The list can go on and on, but you get the point. Any one of these events might not eventually affect the potential sale of a property in a normal buy-sell situation. The parties might have to renegotiate, the lender might have to find another appraiser, the insurance companies might settle on the cost to rebuild, or whatever. But does this deal have the time to suffer through all that? Likely not. So, by having documented everything leading up to one of the possible delays that can strike a deal, Kevin has built a good case to present to the IRS that even if he runs over the 180 days, he should still be allowed to use the 1031 treatment. Remember, a safe harbor is just that: a safe way to go. The IRS has, and will again, allow circumstances that create obstacles to that route to be detoured when the intent to exchange can be documented and the substance of the transaction has, in good faith, been properly carried out.

Safe Harbors

Safe harbors are specific rules that come from revenue procedures that are issued by the IRS from time to time to give taxpayers (and those who help them deal with IRC Section 1031 exchanges) some guidance on steps to follow to ensure that the IRS will look favorably at the transaction. Keep in mind that this does not mean that these procedures *must* be followed for the exchange to be allowed. It is possible that other circumstances are present in a specific situation that would cause the IRS or a court to decide in a taxpayer's interest even if the safe-harbor rules were not followed. This book aims to discuss all of the important such safe-harbor procedures. However, remember that every IRS ruling is subject to change in future codes. It is not uncommon for the IRS to issue new rulings that replace old ones or further clarify the IRS's position on any aspect of the tax code.

Why Not All Tax-Free Exchanges Are Free of Tax

Many exchanges that can qualify under Section 1031 as a tax-free event are never attempted by the taxpayer. This generates substantial revenue for the government and is a good motive for a complicated procedure. There are several reasons why people do not use Section 1031 even though it would save them taxes.

Election Is Made Not to Use Section 1031 Rules

There is no rule that forces a taxpayer to use the benefits of Section 1031. Unfortunately, many exchanges that would qualify are not processed under those rules not because the taxpayer chose not to, but because the taxpayer did not know he or she had a choice. If the property qualifies as a property held in business or trade or for investment, then every taxpayer who will otherwise pay a capital gains tax should make an educated decision prior to entering into any sale or exchange, if it is to be accomplished under Section 1031 rules and benefits. This decision must come early and be documented every step of the way in close harmony with the IRC Section 1031 rules.

However, in the event of relatively insignificant tax savings and/or the proceeds from the sale are needed for some use other than reinvestment, the taxpayer could simply elect to have normal capital gains treatment apply and pay the tax.

Or perhaps there is a loss carryover in the property to be sold. In an exchange a loss cannot be used, whereas in a sale it can reduce the taxpayer's adjusted gross income, thereby having a beneficial impact on income tax owed for the year of the sale. The only time a loss can have a benefit in an exchange is if the loss is a deferred passive loss that is related to the relinquished property. In this instance, the taxpayer may offset taxable boot received in the exchange.

There Is Net Mortgage Relief

In the event of an exchange where the taxpayer has more mortgage relief from the relinquished property than new debt assumed on the replacement property, the excess will be treated as receipt of cash boot and be taxable. However, some credits can offset some of the excess mortgage relief. Here is an example where the first party (Ken) has a taxable net mortgage relief, and the second (Rod) has net mortgage relief that is not taxable.

Ken exchanges his office building valued at $500,000 with a $200,000 mortgage against it and his $300,000 equity for a smaller office building owned by Rod that is worth $400,000 with a $100,000 mortgage. Ken has a net mortgage relief of $100,000, all of which will be taxable to the extent of the gain. Assuming that Ken's adjusted basis in his property was $350,000, this would give him a gain of $150,000 (price of his building was $500,000 less the tax basis results in the $150,000 gain). If Rod's adjusted basis were $300,000, he would have a gain of $100,000.

Recap of Ken and Rod's Office Building Exchange

	Ken	Rod
1. Value of property exchanged	$500,000	$400,000
2. Less mortgage relief of	200,000	100,000
3. Equity exchanged	$300,000	$300,000
4. Value of property received	$400,000	$500,000
5. Less new mortgage assumed	100,000	200,000
6. Equity in property received	$300,000	$300,000
7. Adjusted basis in old property	$350,000	$300,000
8. Gain realized from exchange— value of property exchanged (line 1) less old basis (line 7)	$150,000	$100,000
9. Adjusted basis in new property— value of new property (line 4) less deferred gain (line 8)	$250,000	$400,000
10. Result of adjusted basis—compare old basis in line 7 to new basis in line 9	–$100,000	+$100,000

Ken goes from $500,000 in value down to $400,000, yet his equity remains the same. His adjusted basis also drops from $350,000 to $250,000, leaving him with less assets to depreciate. Ken will have $100,000 of his gain taxed.

Rod goes up in value from $400,000 to $500,000, yet his equity remains the same. His new tax basis is also up from $300,000 to $400,000, giving him added future depreciation. Only Rod has a fully tax-free exchange. See the following explanation of the rules.

Three Rules for Net Mortgage Relief Calculations

1. To have a fully tax-free exchange, the exchanger must trade up or equal in both value and equity when going from the relinquished property to the replacement property. This means that in the example just shown, to be fully tax-free Ken would have to exchange into a building worth $500,000 or more, with $300,000 or more in final equity.

Naturally, if Ken's property were free and clear of any debt his equity would have to be $500,000 in the new property.

2. If the taxpayer trades down in either value or equity, the difference is taxed, but not more than the extent of the realized gain in the transaction. Ken traded down in the value of the two office buildings, and although his equity was the same, he would be taxed on the reduced value. As equity is the result of deducting the mortgage from the value, the two numbers are closely related to each other. If Ken's adjusted basis in his old property had been $450,000 (and not $350,000), his actual gain would have only been $50,000 and his taxable portion of the transaction would be limited to the $50,000.

3. The new tax basis in the replacement property is equal to the fair market value of the replacement property less the amount of the gain that is deferred in this transaction. The results of the new tax basis are shown in the chart for both Ken and Rod.

Clearly, this exchange had little benefit for Ken, except that it might have been exactly what he wanted to do. Consider this: What if Rod had come along and offered the exchange to Ken, and after review of the data presented to him, Ken realized that the office building Rod was offering was better for Ken. It might have allowed him to downsize his business into a freestanding building that was, perhaps, only five minutes away from where he lives.

A Portion of the Exchange Is Cash or Nonqualifying Real or Personal Property

When a part of the exchange is a nonqualifying real or personal property, the value that is assigned to that real estate will be taxable (but only to the extent of the gain realized). Here is an example of such an exchange.

Non-qualifying Real Estate and Personal Property

James exchanges his $500,000 F&C commercial lot to Scott for $300,000 in cash, plus a condominium worth $150,000 that James plans to live in and a diamond necklace that is worth $50,000. The cash is used to purchase a replacement property under the rules of Section 1031, but neither the condominium nor the diamond necklace is like kind. If James has a gain in the commercial lot, he could be taxed on that gain up to the combined value of the condominium and the necklace, which would be $200,000.

Look at these following rules that deal with balancing boot given and/or received in exchanges.

Four Rules to Balance Boot

1. When balancing boot, liability assumed will offset liability relief. So, if you assume a $200,000 mortgage that is on the replacement property and are relieved of a $150,000 mortgage in the relinquished property, you have no net relief as you have increased your total liabilities by $50,000. But if the mortgage on the replacement property was $90,000 and you were relieved of $150,000 you would have a net mortgage relief of $60,000 ($150,000 – $90,000 = $60,000).

2. If you add cash to the escrowed funds (from the sale of the exchange property) to acquire the replacement property, the new cash can offset a net mortgage relief. For example, you want to acquire a vacant tract valued at $500,000, so your exchange property worth $500,000 with an existing mortgage of $200,000 is sold and the $300,000 cash from the sale goes into your facilitator's escrow account. You plan to acquire a tract of land as an investment that is worth $500,000 and has a first mortgage on it of $150,000. Because you are relieved of your $200,000 mortgage and are assuming only $150,000, you have a net mortgage relief of $50,000. However, because you are having to add another $50,000 in cash to acquire the tract of land, the cash you add to your escrow of $300,000 will offset the net mortgage relief of $50,000. In essence, it is as though you had paid down the existing mortgage you had on your property in the first place.

3. Revenue ruling 72-456 (1972-2 CB 468) states that in some circumstances cash that is paid by you when you acquire a replacement property can be used to offset cash that you received in the sale of your relinquished property. However, this applies only if you have followed the rules and have not had constructive receipt of those funds. For example, you sold your exchange property and $300,000 in cash went to the facilitator to handle the transaction to acquire a replacement property worth $700,000 that had a $400,000 mortgage on it at the closing. However, the seller underestimated the amount

of the mortgage and you realized the week before the closing that the real amount of the mortgage was going to be $450,000. This means that it will take only $250,000 of the escrowed funds to close and you will get back $50,000. That would be considered cash boot and taxable. The solution in this situation would be to provide funds *in advance of the closing* to pay down the mortgage by $50,000 so that there would be no cash boot at the closing.

4. If you received cash at the closing of the replacement property that cannot be offset by the assumption of additional debt there is, in essence, a slight twist to the previous example in the third rule. Assume you went to close with the $300,000 of escrowed funds from the sale of your relinquished property. The new property is worth $700,000 and has $400,000 of existing debt. The seller of that property agrees to increase that debt at the closing table by adding a seller-held second mortgage. In this scenario, there would be a surplus of $50,000, which comes from the escrowed funds. The IRS will treat this as unused cash that would be boot to you and taxable up to $50,000 of any gain.

Application of State Law That Conflicts with IRC Section 1031

Some states' laws may conflict with the rules in IRC Section 1031. Generally, rules that come into conflict deal with withholding of taxes due the state and definition of like-kind property. While it is not within the scope of this book to get into these differences, it is important that your facilitator and legal advisers become aware if there is any such conflict. Residents of states that have state income tax for individuals or corporations and other entities are likely to have such conflicts, but even states that do not have income tax can have conflicting laws.

Absolute Dread and Fear of IRS

This is a very good reason why some people avoid seeking Section 1031 treatment. There is no solution to this except to state that thousands of 1031 transactions occur every year, it is legal and proper, and the avoidance of paying a capital gains tax is not an act to fear.

CHAPTER 5

How a 1031 Exchange Will Put Money into Your Pocket

The goal of this chapter is:

To Expand Your Knowledge of Creative Real Estate Techniques

Terms and Concepts You Need to Know

The Exchange Web
Slide Debt to Other Property
Legs
The Exchange Presentation
Offers to Exchange
Balance Exchange Equities

Let's review each in detail.

The Exchange Web

There are exchange groups scattered around the United States and beyond. If you are into surfing the Web, you can spend hours viewing many sites that generally look far more promising initially than they turn out to be. The problem is many of the sites are poorly maintained, and I have found that much of the information they contain is out-of-date. There is little that provides less value for your time than to be looking at properties offered for sale and/or exchange that have been disposed of by those owners several years ago. Despite that, there is some value to these sites, no matter how out-of-date they might be. This value comes in the form of a contact. Within an hour or so, you can find a real estate professional or firm in or near just about any city in the United States proficient in real estate exchanges. If you need to find out something about a property offered to you or you want to find a property in another area, this is a good way to start. It sure beats hopping a jet and flying several thousand miles to get firsthand data.

You will discover exchange clubs and associations of real estate brokers and investors who use real estate exchanges as a part of their business and their investment practices. They meet on some regular schedule, once a week or less often, and may have regional and national get-togethers from time to time. I participate in a number of such organizations either as a speaker on exchange topics or as a broker/investor interested in seeing what kind of deals I might generate there. I encourage you to seek out such organizations because you will learn from the members.

Slide Debt to Other Property

This is a real insider technique that can work wonders in many kinds of real estate transactions, and is especially useful in exchanges. It is based on the concept that a loan, such as a mortgage, is often tied to real estate that is pledged by the borrower as security for that loan. In essence, the borrower says to the lender, "If I don't meet my obligations under the loan agreement, then you have the right to foreclose on my real estate that I have pledged as security to the loan." So far this is a normal situation. Let's take it one step up the creative ladder.

At the time the loan is made, or at some future date, the borrower may want to sell or exchange the pledged property without paying off the loan, or for that matter without letting the new owner assume the loan. One way to do this would be to change the security for that loan to some other asset. This substitute security can be anything that the lender will agree to accept—a bag of diamonds, a sack of gold coins, other real estate, whatever works for the lender. Often the lender in this kind of situation is the former owner of the property, who was motivated enough in the first place to take back seller-held financing. In this circumstance it is a good idea for the buyer, or exchange new owner, to negotiate this potential substitution of security during the initial steps of the original acquisition. Here is an example of how that would work.

Charlie's Sliding Mortgage

Charlie owns a duplex in Atlanta that is worth $400,000. There is a privately held first mortgage on the property with $200,000 remaining. Jim, the former owner who sold the duplex to Charlie three years earlier for $300,000, holds this mortgage. At the time Charlie purchased the property from the seller, Charlie had inserted into the purchase agreement the following provision:

> The seller will hold a purchase money first mortgage in the amount of $200,000 payable with monthly installments of interest only, at an annual contract rate of 6 percent, over a 20-year period of time. At the end of that 20-year period, the principal outstanding will come due and be payable. This mortgage will be secured by the property that is the subject of this sale. The mortgage will allow either the buyer or the owner (in the event of a subsequent new owner) to substitute another property as security to the loan, provided that the substitute property have an equity equal to twice the amount of the outstanding balance of the mortgage. This equity must be appraised by two independent bank-approved appraisers who are local to the area of the substitute property to an equity amount equal to no less than twice the amount outstanding of principal plus any unpaid interest. The substitute property must be located within the State of Texas, and the owner of the subject property will maintain the same level of liability insurance and casualty insurance as provided for in this mortgage for the initial property pledged as security.

As the seller was anxious to sell the subject property and liked the idea of 20 years of income with the balloon payment at the end of that time, he agreed to allow Charlie the future option to slide the mortgage to another property provided there was an obvious equity in the other property worth more than the remaining amount owed.

A few years later, Judy offers Charlie her office building in Hilton Head, South Carolina, for his duplex, which she values at $400,000. The value of her office building is $1,000,000 and the building is F&C.

She tells Charlie that she will take his duplex as long as it is F&C plus $600,000. So far this is a good deal for Charlie, only he doesn't have any extra cash to close the gap. Charlie knows he can obtain $600,000 in the way of a new mortgage and he still has the ability to slide the mortgage on the duplex to another property.

Charlie tells Jim, the holder of his $200,000 mortgage (on the duplex), that he is going to slide it over to a second position in the office building. Even after Charlie puts a new $600,000 mortgage on the office building, there will be a clear $400,000 equity in the office building. This meets the terms of the substitution of security and makes the duplex F&C of any debt.

Charlie now has $400,000 in equity in his duplex, so to match the equity in that part of the deal he has to add $600,000 in cash to give to Judy. This cash he can raise from the new mortgage on the office building.

At the end of the day, Charlie ends up with the office building without having to reach into his pocket for additional capital. There are two bonus factors here, too: Charlie will have no capital gains tax to pay (on the gain on the duplex of $100,000), and as he has no net debt relief he actually increases his depreciable assets by the amount of the new mortgage ($600,000). Here is a recap of this deal.

Charlie and Judy Exchange Properties

What Happened	Charlie	Judy
Value of properties at start	$ 400,000	$1,000,000
Debt in beginning	200,000	0
Owner's equity	$ 200,000	$1,000,000

Charlie slides Jim's mortgage:

Add equity from Jim's mortgage	200,000	
Revised equity	$ 400,000	$1,000,000

Judy gets:

Revised equity	$ 400,000
Plus cash given up by Charlie	600,000
Balanced transaction	$1,000,000

Charlie's situation:

Gives Judy cash from new mortgage	$ 600,000	
Gives Judy equity in duplex	400,000	
Balance of equities	$1,000,000	$1,000,000

The cash that Charlie obtained from the added financing would not be taxable as it is borrowed funds, so not only would he have no tax to pay on his $100,000 capital gains ($400,000 value of the duplex for which he paid only $300,000), but also because he was able to slide the mortgage to the office building, he increased his equity in the duplex by that amount. This enabled him to keep the attractive interest-only loan until he would ultimately pay it off or slide it to another property.

Legs

In a real estate exchange a *leg* is where you generate different options and are able to expand the opportunities to broaden the exchange. Here is how it works. Say you have a duplex in Atlanta, Georgia, and you want to sell or exchange it so that you can eventually end up with an investment in South Florida. It is fairly priced at $200,000 and is free and clear. This presents an attractive exchange property because the owner (you or a new owner) can crank cash out of the property by obtaining new financing. You show up at an exchange group meeting in Sarasota, Florida, which is one of the areas where you would like to own property. You make a presentation to the members and distribute brochures you have printed up with photographs and pertinent data about the duplex. Within a very short time you are likely to get several offers from members where they will take your duplex in exchange (full or partial equity) for property they either own or represent as a broker.

Here are three such offers.

1. A vacant residential lot in Citrus Springs, Florida. This is a nice retirement area north of Tampa. The lot is priced at $50,000 and is free and clear of debt. The offer is the vacant lot and you hold the balance of $150,000 in the form of a first mortgage on your duplex.

2. A 20-unit apartment complex in Naples, Florida. The complex is a blue-collar tenant type building, and caters to couples with children. Priced at $1,200,000, it has a first and second mortgage that total $900,000. The offer is for you to give up the duplex and assume the $900,000 in debt and you pay the offering party $100,000 in cash.

3. A small condo near the beach in Fort Lauderdale worth $200,000 with a first mortgage of $50,000. You are asked to exchange your duplex and hold a $50,000 first mortgage on it.

Let's assume that none of these properties are interesting to you at the first review of the material. What you do have is added elements that might allow you to do a deal with a different party by incorporating what you have generated with one or more of these three offers.

For example, perhaps you have discovered that one of the parties at the exchange group meeting has a property that you would want to own. It is a five-unit apartment building in a nice area of Sarasota. It seems fairly priced at $450,000 and has a $300,000 first mortgage that can be assumed. But the owner is not interested in your duplex in any way; he just does not want to own property in Atlanta. However, if you can come up with some cash he would be happy to deal with you.

Here are some of your options using one or more legs from the three offers made to you. You take the first offer of the Citrus Springs lot and the $150,000 first mortgage. You then offer the Sarasota owner one or all of the following options:

1. The lot and $100,000 cash.

2. A $150,000 soft mortgage on your duplex (i.e., a mortgage with terms that are less stringent than market rate terms).

3. The $150,000 equity in the condo in Fort Lauderdale.

There are other combinations of course. I have avoided even attempting anything using the 20 units in Naples as the apartment complex seems to be overly leveraged with debt already.

Oh, by the way, where did you get the cash in the first offer you made? When the owner of the lot wanted you to hold a $150,000 mortgage, what he really said was, "If I can use my lot and no out-of-pocket cash I will take your duplex." That deal should be easy to close (if he likes the duplex after seeing it, and the value on the lot should be relatively easy to check out), then you could crank out cash by arranging a first mortgage on the duplex from a local Atlanta lender, and let the lot owner assume that mortgage. That would put $150,000 cash in your pocket of which you can spend some and keep some. Alternatively, you might decide to keep the duplex, borrow the money, and buy the Sarasota property.

Exchange groups help these deals by providing moderators who assist in the presentation and discussion of the properties presented. They are aware of what other deals and combinations can be made and push and pull the members to bring these potential situations to light. It will surprise you, as it frequently does other members there, that potential combinations are not so obvious until the moderator brings them to light.

The Exchange Presentation

Everything you do, when it comes to the pursuit of being a professional, should demonstrate that fact. This will be seen most importantly in the way you approach making an offer to exchange (or for that matter to buy or sell) your property. You begin the process with the presentation of what you have to offer. Presentations come in many different forms. Some real estate professionals grossly overdo this process by supplying far more information than is needed to attract a taker or buyer. Give that prospective taker or buyer only the most important data on the property so they will want more information because what they see interests them. What you *do not* want to do is to give the taker or buyer (or his or her broker or lawyer) a book of data that will take more than 10 minutes to read; if it contains data that is not important (at this stage, if ever), that will do more to turn off the taker or buyer than anything else you could possibly do.

The actual presentation of a property that is for sale and/or exchange should contain the following data and nothing more:

Owner's Value of Property

If you have an appraisal, that would be helpful. Otherwise, a comparable property analysis that can be made by you or a local real estate broker showing how your property compares to others in the neighborhood. Do not include the entire appraisal, but provide the summary page only. On that page will be a statement such as this:

Owner's value	$5,500,000
Tax appraised value	$4,500,000
Appraisals (available for interested parties):	
Replacement	$7,250,000
Economic	$5,700,000

Indicate that the full and complete appraisal is available to interested parties.

Recent comparables of sales would be good, too, provided they can be confined to one page and relate closely to the area and the category of real estate in question. There is nothing worse than a comp of another property that is 50 miles away and is an apartment building whereas the property in question is a shopping center.

Total Debt on Property

If you have a mortgage on the property, then show it along with the payment schedule, interest rate, and term. It is a good idea to say if the holder of this debt would slide it to another property as security. This might be done in a simple statement such as this:

There is a first mortgage in the amount of $2,500,000 principal remaining, payable over the next 22 years at 7 percent interest only in monthly installments with a balloon at the end of the 22nd year. The holder is the former owner of the property, who has indicated he would consider accepting other security for this debt (will slide it to something else).

Owner's Equity in Property

Your value less your total debt would be your initial equity. If any debt could move to other properties you own, that could increase your equity. A buyer or new owner in an exchange could also increase their equity in this property by sliding your original mortgage to another of their properties. This could be shown as:

Existing Debt

1st Mortgage	$3,500,000
8%—20 year amortization	
2nd Mortgage	$1,000,000
12%—10 year amortization*	

* Can be moved to other security by new owner

Motivation to Sell or Exchange

Why do you want to sell or exchange? If it is to take a profit, that is fine. Often the motivation is to take advantage of tax-free cash and to move up to property that has a greater tax shelter through more depreciation. This motivation can be shown like this:

Owner is retiring from real estate management and wishes to obtain passive holdings. As he is moving to North Carolina, he is motivated for holdings within 100 miles of Blowing Rock, North Carolina.

Area and Category of Properties Desired

As this is an exchange offering, one will presume that there are some areas of the world that are more attractive to you than others. Try to be specific as to your needs and desires. If you want Florida but will consider Spain, then say so. If you like Atlanta but hate Macon, then say that, too.

Positives and Negatives of Property

The key here is what the positives and negatives are from *your* perspective. If you are sick and tired of managing a property, that is a very strong negative for you, but might be a positive for someone else who loves property management. Sometimes it is difficult for the owner to realistically come up with positives. It is a good idea to ask a real estate agent who deals in the kind of property in question how they would best market the property. It is possible that as an owner (sick and tired of the property) you will overlook something not so obvious.

Financial Data (If an Income-Producing Property)

The key with giving financial data on the income and expenses of a property is to be as accurate as you can be. No one is going to acquire your property based on its reported income without making a thorough investigation of the facts. Save time by having the right data from the very start. This is one of the areas where people (and big real estate companies) go astray. The key here is to be as brief, and yet as accurate, as possible. Remember, stick with net operating income (NOI). Do not show debt, because the new owner may have an entirely different debt structure than you do.

Gross income
Less expenses:
Payroll
Cost of sales
Bad debts
Repairs and maintenance
Insurance

Real estate taxes

Utilities

Other expenses

Net Operating Income

Photos of Property

Four photos are enough to start with. You can provide more for the interested party if you have a digital camera, or if not you can easily have a CD made containing several film rolls' worth of photos. These can be viewed on a laptop computer and are a great way to provide many different angles and views of the property and its neighboring properties. Some professionals have web sites where interested parties can view as many photos as the owner wants to provide.

General Demographic Information

Not everyone is as familiar with the area where your property is as you are. Get data from the local chamber of commerce and other organizations that supply this kind of data, and combine the material into a comprehensive presentation of the community where your property is located. Be sure that information such as population growth, employment base, demographics of the community, and third-party opinions of the future of the area is provided. This data can be shown in a single paragraph. If you have a 20-page demographic report in your file, keep it there unless someone interested wants to see it. The problem with these reports is they can vary greatly and are quickly out-of-date.

Maps and Other Data

A series of maps that will take an interested party from where he or she lives to where the property is located is essential. There are several great web sites that give you free access to just about anyplace in the world.

Mapquest.com is a good one, and there are other great sites as well. Search the Web for maps and you will find them.

Once you have all the material together, compile it into a nice-looking presentation. If it can be viewed and comprehended in five minutes, do not try to add more. Keep it simple and accurate.

Offers to Exchange

Offers to exchange can vary greatly depending on whom you are dealing with. When you are working through a broker or dealing within an exchange group, one of the best ways is what is called a mini-form or mini-offer. It contains only the most basic of information and is used to see if there is any interest from the other party. This form should be used only in the exchange group setting as it is too basic to present to an owner not familiar with this informal contact. Like a letter of intent (which generally contains far more information), these initial contacts are not binding agreements. They do, however, serve the purpose of allowing the parties to relate the data and form an opinion if they should move forward to a binding agreement. The form of an offer will vary depending on its author and designer. Figure 5.1 is one mini-offer that makes it easy to get the ball rolling. These forms work best if they are filled out with a copy (either carbon paper or direct transfer).

Figure 5.2 is the same form that has been filled out. As the mini-offer is usually filled out and presented during an exchange group meeting, the information is almost always handwritten.

Dan's Mini-Offer

Here is the setting. Dan is attending a monthly meeting of an exchange group he belongs to in Miami, Florida. A property is being presented and it sounds like something that would interest him. The presentation is made by the property owner's broker, who has stated that the owner, Albert, will join the group during the lunch break to review any offers that might be made on the property.

The property is an 80-room hotel located on the beach in Delray

DATE:

FROM: TO:
Phone: Phone:
Fax: Fax:
E-Mail: E-Mail:

FIRST PARTY   SECOND PARTY

HAS   HAS

VALUE   VALUE

DEBT   _____   DEBT   _____
EQUITY   EQUITY

BALANCE   BALANCE
Cash   Cash
Mortgage   Mortgage
Note   Note
Other Property   Other Property
Personal Property   Personal Property
Other Value   _____   Other Value   _____
Balance   Balance

DETAILS   Note: Numbers in parentheses are deductions from value.

Signed by: Signed by:

Figure 5.1   Mini-Offer to Exchange (Blank Form)

Beach, Florida. Dan knows the hotel and has actually attended several social functions that have been held there. Dan also anticipates one of the reasons the property is on the market, and suspects that the owner is motivated to do a deal. It turns out that there was a fire in the hotel's kitchen a month ago and although the fire damage was confined to the kitchen and dining room there was substantial smoke damage to the entire building. The value of the property as presented is $4,400,000. The

DATE: *March 3, 2006*

FROM: *Jack Cummings*
Cummings Realty, Inc.
3015 North Ocean Blvd.
Fort Lauderdale, Florida
Phone: 954-415-6896
Fax: 954-561-0687
E-Mail: CummingsRealty@aol.com

TO: *Sally Rhimes*
Rhimes Realty

Phone:
Fax:
E-Mail:

FIRST PARTY
Dan Vega

SECOND PARTY
Delray Beach Hotel Group, LLC

HAS *4-acre commercial tract*
  On Seralago Blvd., Orlando, FL

HAS *80-unit hotel on the sand*
  in Delray Beach, FL

VALUE	$1,250,000	VALUE	$4,400,000
DEBT	(250,000)	DEBT	(2,700,000)
EQUITY	$1,000,000	EQUITY	$1,700,000

BALANCE
Cash	$250,000	Cash	
Mortgage	450,000	Mortgage	
Note		Note	
Other Property		Other Property	
Personal Property		Personal Property	
Other Value		Other Value	
Balance	$1,700,000	Balance	$1,700,000

DETAILS   Note: Amounts in parentheses are deductions from value.
Debt on four acres is interest only for seven years at 7.5%—monthly payments.
$450,000 represents a second position Dan gives to Delray Beach Group, secured by
the hotel.
Deal is subject to Dan refinancing a conversion of the hotel into time-share units.
Dan to have reasonable time to accomplish this.

Signed by:

Signed by:

Jack Cummings

Sally Rhimes

Figure 5.2   Mini-offer to Exchange, Filled Out

presentation touches on all the highlights of the deal. The existing debt is $2,500,000 and repair estimates to correct the fire and smoke damage of $650,000 are covered by insurance, less the policy's $200,000 deductible. This puts the owner's equity at $1,900,000 less the insurance deductible amount of $200,000, or $1,700,000. The hotel is closed pending the outcome of an offering to sell or exchange.

Dan reviews what the owner has indicated are the kind of properties he would consider taking in exchange. He would look at vacant commercial land or any improved residential property in the south Florida area. He does, however, need to cash out at least $500,000 at the closing.

Dan has a good idea of what to do with the property, and the fact that there is fire and smoke damage could be turned into an advantage for him. He fills out a mini-offer and presents it to the owner's broker.

Look at Figure 5.2 to review what Dan offers. First of all, Dan keeps the value as presented. This mini-offer is to see if the idea of the exchange or transaction will be accepted by the other party. There is a lot of time between mini-offer and final binding contract. Besides, each party will expect to have a period of due diligence where they can inspect the property they are asked to take in the exchange. Even though Dan's property is F&C, he shows it with a mortgage of $250,000 against it.

This serves two purposes. If Delray Beach Group accepts the deal with it, Dan knows that before the closing he can put a new mortgage of that amount and terms against the property. This frees up $250,000 in cash that he can now give to the owners of the hotel. The $450,000 mortgage is the amount he wants to put against the hotel after he refinances it. Again, in the mini-offer little is said about that mortgage. In the final analysis it would have release provisions that would allow Dan to obtain releases from the mortgage as he sold time-share units in the property.

There are many different ways Dan or another party could make such offers. In the next part of this chapter where we get into the balancing of equities we will see how different exchanges can be structured. This aspect of exchanges is very important because the idea is to stress the method of balancing the equities more than the actual amounts used to arrive at the value it will take to do the deal.

Balance Exchange Equities

Here are the different elements that can be used to balance equities in an exchange. Keep in mind that values that show in the balance section of the form (and not in the equity calculation) will be placed under the party's name when those values are added by that party to the transaction. In the details section of the form there should always be some comments as to these aspects of the exchange which explain how the amounts are treated.

Cash

Cash can come from any source. It might be refinancing the property you are going to receive, as Dan anticipated doing in his Delray Beach deal. It might be a new loan on another property, or even right out of your pocket. Usually the cash part of the deal is kept at a minimum during early negotiations, and often is just enough to entice the owner of the property you want to sit down with you to hammer out the final deal.

Mortgages

Mortgages can be generated on the properties that are being exchanged or tied to other properties. To balance his deal Dan asks the Delray Hotel Group to hold a second mortgage with the hotel as the security for the deal. He has not gone into the details of that or what the new first mortgage might be when he refinances the hotel to convert it to a time-share. Mortgages that show up in parentheses (e.g., $250,000 and $2,700,000 in Figure 5.2) are existing mortgages. If they are in the balance section of the form they are placed there to show that they will become a positive value to the relinquishing party and an obligation by the party that receives that property. Such an increase to the value of the exchange property (e.g., $450,000 in Figure 5.2) is not in parentheses.

Note

A note differs from a mortgage, as it usually does not have real estate as a security. A personal note would have only the person's name backing it up. Other notes may have other kinds of security, such as equipment, cars, boats, gems, gold bars, and so on, backing the value of the note. In many parts of the world personal notes are commonly used in all kinds of transactions, and are often purchased in bulk by banks, depending on the discount they can negotiate and the value of the person behind them. Notes are obligations against a person or entity; if they show up as a deduction from value they are existing obligations that reflect on the equity of the owning entity. In that instance they will be in parentheses. Notes that are in the balance section of the form are added value to the property owner of the column where indicated and will not be shown in parentheses. See Figure 5.3 for such an example (Robert's zero interest note).

Other Property

If Dan wanted to add other real estate instead of cash to his offer, he might have put a block of time-share units into the deal. Those could be from another building, or the Delray Hotel Group might have a selection of choice units in the building prior to their offer to the public. That kind of other property is often the case when a developer acquires a property for condominiums (office or residential use) to be built. Dan might have brought in a partner who had some real estate to add to the deal.

Personal Property

The sky is the limit here. Anything that is tangible and not real estate falls into the category of personal property. You name it, from cases of apples to cases of wine, to bags of zircons and other gemstones to everything between. I have participated in exchanges where the parties traded cars, boats, airplanes, jewelry, unset gemstones, cases of wine, cases of apples and other produce, store credit for merchandise, restaurant food and beverage credit, and so on. Any transaction can absorb some personal property in the deal. The key to that is to leave personal property out of the negotiations until the last stage, except where it is a major value in the transaction.

Other Values

This is the rest of what can go into an exchange. What is left? Here is just a partial list: personal services, prepaid rent, use of time (say a vacation in my mountain lodge), advertising credits, endorsements, discounts, and the like.

Two Examples of Equity Balances

Robert's Deal: Robert has eight acres in the mountains of North Carolina valued at $80,000. He owns the land free and clear and can add up to $43,000 in cash, equity of $300,000 in a large home in Tampa, and discounted travel (use of time-shares owned).

Robert wants a 45,000-square-foot warehouse owned by Jones that Robert can use in a new business he is about to launch, valued at $2,000,000 F&C. (See Figure 5.3.)

Robert adds $20,000 cash to his equity, plus a first mortgage in the amount of $1,750,000 secured by the warehouse he receives, plus a $25,000 zero interest note due in 36 months and $100,000 in vacation time anywhere in the world (time-share availability) up to $25,000 per year.

Bill's Deal: Bill owns a 30-unit apartment complex valued at $2,500,000 located in Fort Lauderdale, Florida. There is a first mortgage against that property with $1,000,000 remaining. Bill can add $100,000 in cash, plus up to $500,000 in appraised gemstones, $50,000 in time-share weeks, and a vacant commercial tract worth $125,000 that is F&C of any debt.

He wants to acquire a 400-acre tract of land in the eastern mountains of Tennessee where he hopes to develop a golf course, mountain lodge, and inn, together with a complex of retirement condos and townhouses. The property, owned F&C by Mountains Inc., is on the market at $4,000,000. However, there is one partner in the deal who wants to cash

FIRST PARTY		SECOND PARTY	
Robert		Jones	
HAS 8 acres + some cash		HAS 45,000 sq. ft. warehouse	
+ equity in home and travel			
VALUE	$ 80,000	VALUE	$2,000,000
DEBT	0	DEBT	0
EQUITY	$80,000	EQUITY	$2,000,000
BALANCE		BALANCE	
Cash	$ 20,000	Cash	
Mortgage	1,750,000	Mortgage	
Note	25,000	Note	
Other Property		Other Property	
Personal Property		Personal Property	
Other Value	$ 100,000	Other Value	
Balance	$2,000,000	Balance	$2,000,000
DETAILS Note: Numbers in parentheses are deductions from value.			

Figure 5.3   Robert's Deal

out. The partner's percentage in the land is 20 percent, so his equity in the deal is $800,000. (See Figure 5.4.)

In this case Bill uses several other balancing techniques. His introduction of $1,000,000 cash into the deal gives the partners a way to solve the problem with the one dissenting party to the deal, which is likely one of the reasons the property is on the market in the first place. How the partners make this dissenting party go away is up to them, and Bill does not want to negotiate directly with that party. His idea (the right one, too) is that if the remaining partners need to take a cut in what they get to get out of their relationship that is up to them.

One might think that Bill has left himself a lot of room to negotiate in this deal. That will depend, of course, on the relative values of the real estate. Once any deal gets past the initial balance of equities and the parties can agree, at least in principle, to the merits of the deal, more detailed proposals leading up to a formal agreement to exchange, and then the inspections and approvals of those inspections must take place.

FIRST PARTY		SECOND PARTY	
Bill		*Mountains Inc.*	
HAS *30 units in Fort Lauderdale*		HAS *400 mountain acres in Tennessee*	
VALUE	*$2,500,000*	VALUE	*$4,000,000*
DEBT	*1,000,000*	DEBT	*0[1]*
EQUITY	*$1,500,000*	EQUITY	*$4,000,000*
BALANCE		BALANCE	
Cash	*$1,000,000[2]*	Cash	
Mortgage	*$1,000,000[3]*	Mortgage	
Note		Note	
Other Property	*$ 125,000*	Other Property	
Personal Property		Personal Property	
Other Value	*$ 350,000[4]*	Other Value	
Balance	*$4,000,000*	Balance	*$4,000,000*

DETAILS   Note: Numbers in parentheses are deductions from value.

---

[1]There is an $800,000 obligation that must be satisfied at closing (takeout of 20% partner).

[2]Cash payment to the second parties to divide however they want. This cash will come from a new development loan (first mortgage) in the amount of $3,000,000 to cover acquisition balances and initial phase of the project.

[3]Second mortgage Bill will give to Mountains Inc. This mortgage will be subordinated to the new development loan. Each (both first and second mortgages) will have release provisions to allow development rights. This second mortgage will be at 7% interest only, monthly installments, due in full by the end of the seventh year.

[4]Credit given to Mountains Inc., which can be used against a purchase of any condos or townhouses in the first or second phases of the development at a preconstruction price with a 10% discount off that price.

Figure 5.4   Bill's Deal

Use an Exchange as a Buyer's Tool

Any real estate investor who is anticipating making an investment should already know if there is anything in his or her existing portfolio of assets that can be disposed of in the upcoming transaction. This only makes sense. Yet most investors do not take that approach and sit around with assets that are taking them nowhere and do nothing for them. Let's look at the benefits to George, who is an investor interested in buying a $5,000,000 office building that is owned by Offices LLC, a development company that builds commercial structures, then sells them. Assume there is a $1,000,000 mortgage on the office building. George wants to use the office building for his own expanding offices. Let's now look at a short list of assets that George has at his disposal.

George's Assets

George has $1,000,000 in cash he can spend, but believes he will need much of that to remodel the building to suit his needs. He is a certified civil engineer, and his fee for such work is $150 per hour. He owns two vacant commercial tracts of land whose total worth is $1,200,000. He has $800,000 in advertising credit with a major media company, which he got as payment for work he did for them. Moreover, his borrowong credit is excellent.

Here are steps that George can consider in making any offers.

Ten Steps Available to George

Houseclean the Portfolio: A quick review of George's assets suggests that the two vacant tracts may be doing nothing for him at this moment, nor is the $800,000 in advertising credit. After all, the seller might be able to use either of these two assets, either all or part of them.

Sweeten the Offer: Sweeteners to any offer come after the initial rejection by the other party. It is a good idea not to offer them up front, so George might want to hold back some of the advertising credit as a sweetener. If the seller takes some, the seller might also take some more. Other sweeteners from his asset pool can be additional cash, engineering work, added mortgages that the seller holds, or something that George can obtain for the seller by using any of his assets that the seller rejects. This last element is the one that most people overlook. A quick review of what the seller, Offices LLC, is at present spending cash to get would reveal a long list of items and services it pays for each month. As George is in a related business to Offices LLC's development enterprises, he might be in a good position to barter with other development services to pass on value in things like building supplies that require civil engineering testing, architectural work from clients that hire George for his time, and so on. In large development projects these fees can climb up into the hundreds of thousands of dollars.

Maximize Use of Investment Capital: Whenever George or any investor can get an immediate capital return on a stagnant asset that is not increasing in value (or hardly so) there is an instant benefit in the deal. This relates to current assets, as well as the presale of sweat equity, which almost any investor has the potential to supply.

Increase Return on After-Tax Investment: If the assets that are included in the transaction qualify for 1031 treatment, there will be no capital gains tax on them. Clearly in most transactions this would be limited to like-kind real estate, but one should not overlook that IRC Section 1031 also qualifies certain other assets for similar treatment. If, as an example, George has equipment of the same category as equipment that is included in the sale property, that could also become a tax-free transaction for one side of the deal. How would George get that kind of equipment? Again, this could be by separate barter that George can make between the wholesale supplier of such equipment and George's services or advertising credit. Remember, anytime you can get an increased cash value for an asset you paid for years ago or have not yet purchased or delivered, you will increase the bottom line on the cash you actually pay out in the deal.

Offer Seller Benefits: Sometimes this item comes from knowing more about the seller. What benefits does the seller seek? What benefits could the seller use? Those two alternatives may not be the same. Do your homework in this respect. Seller's benefits may be the cheapest way to go. For example, I brokered a transaction of the sale of a shopping center that had many coconut trees as part of the landscaping. The buyer discovered that the seller's son had a restaurant and bar that had a special drink that used half a green coconut as the container for the drink. The buyer told the seller that he would welcome the son coming anytime to pick the green coconuts, as long as it was during off hours when the shops were closed and there would not be cars in the parking lot.

Help to Solve a Seller's Problem: Anytime you can help the other party solve their problem you are moving closer to a deal. Like knowing what benefits they seek or can use, finding out their problem can take time and homework. In the final analysis you may never discover the real problem or reason the seller has put the property on the market. Say, however, you believe, from what you have found out, that they want to acquire another tract of land to build an office park. After all, that is their business, so it is logical. What about that side of the deal? If George can give the seller assets that can be used toward that acquisition, then George benefits, and so do they. Don't you just love win-win transactions?

Become a Proactive Investor: Getting active in using all your asset talents to make your investments come together is the proactive way to approach investing. Making offers is a major part of this concept, and neither George nor you should worry about sellers who respond with something like, "Are you nuts? I am insulted at your offer." Oh, sure, some may say this, but my reply as a broker to such sellers is this: "If you are insulted because a person who is genuinely interested in acquiring your property (which you want to dispose of) makes you an offer, how do you feel about the millions of people who are not even the slightest bit interested in your property to the extent of making you an offer?"

Create New Financing for New Deals: By using some of the exchange techniques I have shown you thus far, you can see how easy it is to create additional investment potential. Remember Bill's future credit he offered

Mountains Inc.? That was a value that did not yet exist. George's offer of engineering services and the potential for his bartering some of his other assets for what Offices LLC could use are examples of new financing to the deal. As all of these assets come with a discount built in (George's profit or your capital gain), this generates greater leverage of the capital actually spent.

Make a Move Closer to Your Goal: Any exchange that moves you and/or George closer to a desired goal is a good exchange. Try to keep that concept in focus as you maximize both Section 1031 exchanges and exchanges in general. If, as I have already shown, you can advance closer to your goals while at the same time moving the other party to the transaction closer to his or her goal, then the deal can indeed be a win-win situation.

Compare What Is Offered, Not What Is Hoped For: One of the hardest things to overcome, despite its simplicity, is a seller who compares offers with what they believe should happen. Let me explain. An owner of a $4,000,000 office building has a reason to offer it for sale. The seller's idea of how to meet or satisfy that reason might be based on facts that are unrealistic, yet a broker agrees to market the property to meet those ends, and actually has some initial investor response; however, nothing seems to move in the direction of a sale. Along comes a potential user for the building. This is what I call a very strong motivation for a buyer. No matter what that person offers, every effort should be made by all parties to close whatever gaps exist.

I have been in countless situations like this where a seller has an unrealistic set of demands for a buyer, yet the seller is motivated to sell and in some situations is getting close to losing the property in foreclosure. Often, the best approach in this situation is to say, "I will pay your price, if you accept my terms."

Price can be a function of terms. The very idea that I can actually meet your price, if you are flexible in accepting my terms, will work wonders. But it requires sellers who can get off the pedestal of price and terms that they have indicated they want. Sometimes the stumbling block in the deal is a broker who doesn't understand how exchanges work, or who is simply intimidated by the seller.

When you encounter this kind of situation it is often helpful to have a face-to-face meeting with the seller. I have had such meetings that have resulted in deals coming together, once the seller understood what the deal was really about and the brokers saw that they were actually going to get a cash commission, even though a major part of the value of their listing was in exchanged, noncash assets. I will touch on this concept in the next section of this chapter, and in other chapters of this book.

Use an Exchange as a Seller's Tool

Be a Proactive Seller

Picking up right where I just left off, let's take a look at the benefit to a seller whenever a prospective investor comes along. Let's not think exchange yet; let's just look at a prospective investor who expresses the willingness to purchase your property. What have you already learned about this investor? For sure you have discovered that they like what they see, see a need they have being filled by that property, and have made the decision that they will purchase it if the deal makes sense.

Moving from there to a closed transaction is far easier than stopping someone on the street and trying to convince that individual to purchase your property. So be proactive and make sure your broker (if you are using one) is proactive. The idea here is, do not let them get away until all avenues are exhausted.

The problem is some brokers and salespeople in the real estate business are proactive only to the extent that they will answer your phone call, they will take your check as a down payment or deposit, and best of all, they will thank you for your business after the closing.

Many transactions that start out including an exchange, end up quite different by the time the investor has really gotten into the property and now wants it no matter what. Likewise, many sellers who have indicated they would never take an exchange end up doing so. Why? They do so because they come to the realization that:

■ They were unrealistic as to what they wanted to get out of the deal.

■ Their problem still exists, and perhaps is getting worse.

- They realize that the offer on the table, includes taking something they would not go out and purchase (even if they had the money to do so). Why? Because they don't have the cash burning a hole in their pocket, so they take the exchange.

- Getting rid of the property moves them closer to their goals.

Expand Your Available Inventory

Every time a buyer offers you something as a part of the deal, that additional asset becomes an extension of what you might have to work with. Take George's deal with Offices LLC as an example. If he offers $500,000 in advertising credit, and all the other terms of the deal are acceptable, this deal should close if Offices LLC:

- Has a use for the advertising credit.

- Can sell the credit at a satisfactory discount and convert it to cash.

- Can barter or exchange that credit or most of it for what Offices LLC wants to buy.

- Can give the broker(s) all or most of what would be the commission in the form of this credit.

- Makes a counteroffer that incorporates the credit into the deal somehow.

You may have to think about these aspects every time something is offered to you that you do not want. How you reject such offers should also be carefully considered. It is very easy to burn a potential investor's bridge by using that classic "Are you nuts?" response.

Entice a Buyer to Consider Your Property

Just by offering your property on the market where you would consider an exchange, you begin to entice buyers who might not otherwise ever know about your property. Remember that the number one rule of advertising (of any product or service) is to attract a buyer of that product or service who may not have ever considered that service or product. Once buyers are attracted and want to learn more about it, the rest of the transaction is in the hands of a savvy investor and/or a good broker/salesperson.

Replace a Big Problem with a Small One

One of the advantages of offering a property for exchange is that you may attract a far smaller problem that would be acceptable to you so you could get rid of a much larger one. In some situations you might actually discover that the small problem can be fixed and turned into a profit. As an example, I took two lots in Port Saint Lucie, a development south of Vero Beach, Florida, as a part of the sale of a retail shop I had fixed up and put on the market. I didn't exactly want the lots, but as I was making a large profit on the retail shops I was satisfied to make the deal. The lots were F&C and the taxes were low, so I didn't mind sitting on them for a while. As it turned out, I sort of forgot about the lots as they were out of sight and out of mind for four years. Suddenly they came back to my attention when I received a letter from a developer who wanted to make an offer. Two days later the deal was cut and I had sold the lots for three times their value when I took them in exchange four years earlier. I never say no to any exchange offered to me now without taking a very hard look at the possible benefits from the deal.

Move Closer to the Desired Goal

This is what a good real estate exchange can do. Buying, selling, exchanging, leasing, giving options, taking options, these are all investing tools. Some of them may have, as do Section 1031 tax-free exchanges, some positive cash-saving benefits. Others simply allow you to take advantage of a ready and willing buyer so that you can enter into a Starker type exchange and park the money for up to 180 days while you set up a reinvestment purchase.

The key factors to the concept that any good deal moves you closer to your goals are:

- Do you have a good grasp as to what your goals really are?
- Have you made an effort to maximize your benefits in the offer before you?
- Is there a more promising option potentially ready to come to you?
- Do you have the time to wait for that other deal?
- Should you take advantage of the deal on the table because of other deals you can make with other investment opportunities?

Many people have a hard time making a decision, especially one that can shape one's entire future, or put an investment portfolio at great risk. However, the worst way to make a decision is to make it by indecision. Indecision comes in many forms. Some people sit back and worry about making a decision so long that the deal passes them by. Others dive into their due diligence process to such an extent that they crunch the numbers to death and another buyer who recognizes the opportunity snatches the property right out from under them.

The best approach to making sound decisions is to develop a strong understanding of what is going on in your comfort zone. That zone is the geographic area about which you will learn everything that is meaningful. You will become a wizard at understanding zoning rules and regulations, and observant in what is being planned in the community and how that can affect the future values of the area.

All it takes is a little time and patience. Everything you need to know and learn is right in front of you. The teachers are the city planners, elected officials, and developers in the community. The classrooms are the city council meeting hall, the planning and zoning meetings, and quiet chats from time to time with a multitude of staff members who just love to show off how much they know.

Only then will making a decision about what you should do come easily. Let this book be your tour guide to financial success.

CHAPTER 6

Advanced Elements of the Tax-Free Exchange

The goal of this chapter is:

To Provide a Final Touch to Understanding IRC Section 1031

Although this is not the last chapter to deal with Section 1031, this one is designed to fine-tune the remaining steps that will put you ahead of the game. The explanations and examples that have preceded this chapter should have given you a good understanding of what IRC Section 1031 is about. You have seen the actual Section 1031 as it appears in the Internal Revenue Code and learned what all that government talk means.

You have discovered, if you already did not know it, that IRS codes have a life of their own. The interpretation of a code more often than not will depend on the situation, the circumstances of that situation, and the people's intent—what they really wanted to do. Intent plays a big role with the IRS, as does "substance over form." Substance over form means that what it appears to the IRS to be is more important than what you say it is. This is extraordinarily important when it comes to what the IRS says is a violation of one of its codes. The IRS takes a position as to how it sees the substance of the possible violation, and it is up to you to prove that you did not violate that code.

As an investor's tool, you now know that IRC Section 1031 offers you the opportunity to own and invest in real estate and to build wealth without paying capital gains tax. With proper timing, your reinvestment of capital following the sale of your investment property can continue to grow without any gains tax ever being paid.

Both buyers and sellers can use the technique of exchanges as a way to bring deals to the closing table. Exchanges can become a way of life, and many investors *never* would think of paying any of their otherwise due to be paid capital gains tax because they understand Section 1031, have good legal counsel, and know a competent facilitator to take care of the details of this government kickback program.

However, you should never be so tied to the *tax-free* aspects of real estate exchanges that you overlook any exchange that moves you toward whatever your goal is, even if it does not give you any tax-free benefits. Exchanges have benefits all on their own, and investors, brokers, and salespeople who grasp those benefits will discover many ways to improve their own portfolios, as well as help their clients get closer to their desired goals.

Terms and Concepts You Need to Know

Date the 1031 Clock Should Start
Constructive Receipt
FIRPTA
State Laws versus Federal Laws
Foreign Property

Let's review each in detail.

Date the 1031 Clock Should Start

I have shown you that the 1031 clock encompasses a 180-day period that begins the day following the closing of title on the relinquished property. However, this timetable is becoming increasingly difficult to meet, especially the initial identification period, which is the first 45 days of that clock time. Because of this challenge, all investors should be continually looking for ways to improve their investment portfolios. This "always observant" strategy is important for any kind of investor in whatever the commodity, but is even more critical when it comes to using Section 1031 benefits in the rollover of your real estate investments. In essence, all real estate investors should be on the lookout for a property to become a replacement to their investment portfolios. This may require you to work harder than just focusing on the investments you have, but the effort will prove to be very beneficial in the end. How so? Consider the following key elements to an always observant strategy.

Five Key Factors to Always Observant Strategy

1. **Better market awareness.** By making an effort to seek better investment options, you will be more aware of the marketplace. By being more aware of what is going on in your comfort zone, you will be expanding your knowledge of that area to the point where more opportunities for reinvestment will be available to you. In essence, you will see more opportunities because you are looking for them.

2. **Stronger focus on your portfolio's value.** By constantly looking for a potential replacement for one of your properties, you can better judge the worth of your existing portfolio. There should be no question about this. The more you know what is going on in your marketplace, the better and easier it will be for you to weigh how your investments compare to other similar properties or other categories of properties. Because you will be reviewing information on these other properties, you will quickly ascertain where your rent structure is with respect to the competition. By knowing this, you can take early steps to correct imbalances you may have overlooked in this respect.

3. **Early detection of problems.** Early detection of imbalances between your properties and others in the area may point to an ideal
time to sell a property. For every investment plan and every investor's unique goal, there is an optimum time to sell and move on
to another property. This can be considered an absolute statement,
except that no one knows what will happen the day following that
sale or reinvestment. To improve your edge in developing a more
reliable opinion on what these future events might turn out to be,
the greater your involvement in the market, the quicker you will
learn from what happens there.

4. **Constant review of the portfolio.** The best time to move an asset
from your portfolio is when you find another that has greater
promise. Remember the same real estate asset can provide a wide
and diverse package of benefits to different investors. Therefore
each investor should carefully and in a timely fashion review one's
investment plan and how well those desired goals are being attained. This periodic review, coupled with the greater knowledge
of what is going on in that investor's comfort zone, may indicate
that what really needs to be changed is not the asset, but the plan
and the goals.

5. **Help in formulating goals.** Holding the wrong asset at the wrong
time for the wrong reason (goal) is a fast way to lose money. But
worse is having the right asset at the right time but disposing of it
because you did not recognize that your goals and investment plan
were wrong.

Therefore, the writing on the wall should be clear. You need to
watch the market. Have a plan that is directed toward specific goals. Continually review the plan and the goals and make adjustments accordingly
to ensure your portfolio's benefits are taking you toward your goal.

If you can do this, then you won't have to worry much about when
the 1031 clock should start. You are ahead of the game so that if that
"golden wallet" investor who is dying to buy your property comes along
with an offer you just cannot refuse, you will not only recognize the value
of the offer, you will already have your eye on one or more investments
to acquire.

Constructive Receipt

Did you receive something? Or perhaps you did not. When it comes to the IRS, anyone using Section 1031 must take great care with respect to the proceeds of a sale/exchange. Remember, when you sell your real estate investment with the plan to use the proceeds of the sale to purchase a replacement property, you *must not* be able to exert control over the funds once they come out of the closing of your old property. If there is the slightest hint that you can still direct the funds, then the IRS will likely take the position that you have constructive receipt of those funds.

All Section 1031 exchanges that evolve from the sale of the taxpayer's property and the holding of those funds by an intermediary or EAT prohibit the taxpayer whose property has been sold to have any control over the funds from the sale. This means that if your property is sold and you anticipate acquiring another property with the proceeds from that sale, you cannot touch, or even direct, the funds once the money has been paid by the buyer and deposited with the intermediary. Not until you have closed on the replacement property will you have benefit from the sale. It is not uncommon for the IRS to challenge the qualification of a 1031-treated exchange when the evidence suggests that the taxpayer has had constructive receipt of these funds. This "receipt" of the funds does not mean that the money actually has to pass to the taxpayer. All that has to happen is for the taxpayer to have the unilateral right to change the escrow instructions and/or to withdraw the proceeds.

In a deferred exchange, the taxpayer must not receive any monetary benefits such as rent from the property while the intermediary or EAT holds it. In the event of a deferred exchange where there is construction or improvements to be made to the replacement property, the use of any proceeds of a deferred exchange sale at the direction of the taxpayer (either directly or indirectly) can cause the loss of qualification for 1031 treatment.

FIRPTA

The Foreign Investment in Real Property Tax Act (FIRPTA), passed by Congress in 1980, provides a set of rules that must be considered if a foreign person or entity is a party to the exchange-seeking Section 1031 treatment. A foreign person would be any nonresident alien individual, whereas a foreign entity would be a foreign corporation, partnership, trust, or estate.

Any transaction with a foreign person or entity that results in the transfer of real property from that foreign person or entity to a taxpayer in the United States requires the withholding of 10 percent of the total price from the proceeds from the foreign seller, no matter how much cash actually changes hands.

The foreign person or entity may enter into an exchange where they end up with a replacement property and successfully benefit from the tax-deferred portions of Section 1031. However, the real estate must be United States real property that would be subject to United States taxation immediately following the exchange on its subsequent disposition or future sale or exchange. Any taxable boot received by the foreign person in a Section 1031 exchange would be subject to the withholding.

The withholding is an obligation of the closing agent, intermediary, or facilitator of the exchange transaction, and it is that agent's responsibility to properly execute the necessary documentation. Failure to do this correctly and in a timely fashion can cause the agent to be held liable for the payment of the tax and any applicable penalties and interest.

The withholding may be reduced or eliminated if either the transferor or the transferee obtains a withholding certificate. The complexity of FIRPTA need not unnecessarily discourage a taxpayer from entering into an exchange with a foreign person or entity provided that the closing agent or intermediary has experience and knowledge in properly handling the paperwork involved.

State Laws versus Federal Laws

It is easy to assume that the laws of the state in which you live and do business are mirror images of the laws of all the other states in the nation. While they may be similar in general, there can be vast differences between such laws. To complicate things further, federal laws, particularly when it comes to tax codes, do not always mirror state laws. While it is not within the scope of this book to point out all the diversity between different states and how the federal laws and codes may conflict with state regulations, it is important that the professionals who are closing your real estate transaction and acting as intermediaries in the deal be current in this subject.

If a state has personal and/or corporate income tax, it is also likely that local state law may also have a capital gains tax as well as further define some of the rules of the IRS. For example, the states of Georgia and Mississippi tighten the knot on which kind of property can qualify for Section 1031 treatment by limiting the replacement property to another property located within state boundaries. Oregon has adopted a similar but more lenient law by allowing an out-of-state property to qualify as like kind, but still expects to collect any gains tax payable in the state of Oregon when the property is sold.

Other states, of which California is one, have laws that mirror the FIRPTA and require withholding of any tax that might be due to the state as a result of a sale or exchange transaction when a nonresident taxpayer exchanges out of a property located in the state. California has a withholding procedure for its own residents as well, and any closing agent in California will be held responsible for meeting the rules of this withholding requirement. Because some state laws may define like-kind property differently than the IRS has intended, you should be cautioned that there can be other important conflicts that may also impact your treatment under 1031, depending on the state where either your property or the one you intend to exchange into is located.

Foreign Property

Subsection (h)(1) of IRC Section 1031 states, "Real property located in the United States and real property located outside the United States are not property of a like kind." Here the term *United States* includes only the 50 states and not areas outside of the states themselves. This would mean that property within the Virgin Islands, Guam, and Puerto Rico is not given favorable tax treatment under Section 1031. One exception to this rule, however, is that the IRS will allow a 1031 exchange involving U.S. Virgin Islands property if the taxpayer is a citizen or resident of the United States and either receives income from sources within the Virgin Islands, is closely connected with a trade or business there, or files a joint tax return (say, with a spouse) who meets the requirements.

Effect of a 1031 Exchange on Your Tax Shelter

One of the benefits that comes with owning already improved investment real estate is the tax shelter that the owner gets. This tax shelter is the depreciation that is taken over a period of time after having made the initial investment at the time of purchase. Say you purchase a $1,000,000 office complex. There are two main components to this, and any other improved investment property. These are the land and the improvements. The land is not a part of this tax shelter equation because it simply is there, and only the improvements will, in theory, be diminished in value over time.

The amount of depreciation that you (or your accountant) take each year will depend on the method of depreciation that you select at the start of the process. The comprehensive IRS Publication 946 (2003), along with just about everything you ever wanted to know about the IRS, is available on the IRS web site at www.irs.gov. On the home page you are shown two search windows. Forms and publications are found using the lower of the two windows; for everything else use the upper window. Type in "946," click on Go, and you will be transported to a long list of publications that will begin at Publication 946. You can then click on that publication (or any of the others in the list), and that document will appear before you. It is printable with Adobe (you can download an Adobe reader for free if you do not have it). Adobe allows you to print selected pages so you can view the document on your screen and then print out what you want to have in hard copy form. I suggest you do not simply print out entire forms as there will not be enough paper in your machine, nor ink or toner to do it justice.

The essence of depreciation is that the amount of this expense deduction reduces the taxable income from the investment. If you have gross income of $100,000 and operating expenses of $60,000 and no other deductions, you would have taxable income from that investment of $40,000. However, if you could take $30,000 in depreciation that year your taxable income would drop to only $10,000. The beauty of this is you did not really pay out expenses that year of $30,000; that $30,000 is really a part of the original purchase price of the property when you bought it. And because most real estate is purchased in a highly leveraged state—in essence, a small down payment and a big mortgage—you did not actually pay that price in cash when you purchased the property. Moreover, if you understand the magic of other people's money (OPM), you do not even make the payments on the mortgage—your tenants do.

Example of Depreciation

Bob purchases a shopping center worth $3,000,000 on January 1 of the year. He put $600,000 down and financed the balance of $2,400,000. The land under the center is worth $250,000, so he has a total investment of $2,750,000 of improvements and $250,000 in the land. Remember, only the improvements can be depreciated.

Because of other income he has coming in that year, he wants to maximize his tax shelter on this property, so he selects the most attractive straight-line method he can to get the most shelter out of the property. Looking at tables A-7 and A-7a provided for nonresidential property (page 74 of Publication 946 from www.irs.gov), Bob sees that he can choose either a 31.5-year schedule of depreciation or one for 39 years. Selecting the 31.5-year straight-line method, his depreciation would be approximately $87,300 a year. That means that Bob can put $87,300 in his pocket at the end of the year from that investment and not have any tax to pay on that sum.

Over a 10-year period of such annual deductions of depreciation, Bob will have accumulated $873,000 of tax-free earnings from the investment. At the same time his book value or tax basis of the property is going down by exactly the same amount as the depreciation he is taking.

At the end of 10 years, then, Bob would have a tax basis situation that would look like this:

Calculating Tax Basis

Original purchase price	$3,000,000
Total depreciation taken over 10 years	873,000
New tax basis (with no other calculations made)	$2,127,000

The IRS does get a chance to tax that money provided Bob sells the property and now recovers the depreciation in the form of capital gains. Suppose there is an outright sale by Bob for $5,000,000 10 years after his acquisition.

Sale 10 Years Later

Sale price	$5,000,000
Present tax basis	2,127,000
Capital gain	$2,873,000

This capital gain is the $2,000,000 profit over what Bob had paid for the property 10 years earlier, plus the amount of depreciation he had taken all these years. If Bob had added any capital improvements to the center, such as new buildings or additional parking, for example, those costs less their depreciation would be added to the original cost.

Price when Bob sells the center	$5,000,000
Price Bob originally paid for the center	3,000,000
Gain	$2,000,000
Depreciation taken over 10 years	873,000
Total taxable gain	$2,873,000

Value of the Shelter

The value of a real estate tax shelter will depend on the tax bracket for the periods in question for both earned income and for capital gains taxes.

For the sake of this example, assume that Bob's earned income would be such that had he taken in the extra $87,300 in income each year on top of all else that he has earned, he would have paid 33 percent tax on that sum each year. That is an annual tax of $28,809 or a grand total of $288,090 over the 10-year term.

However, he did have the advantage of this deduction, so he did not have that tax to pay. Now, even if Bob sells the property and must now pay tax on this sheltered income of $873,000, he is (at the writing of this at least) looking at a 15 percent gains tax, or a total of $130,950, which is less than half what he would have paid over the 10-year period in regular income tax. Therefore, even paying the capital gains tax Bob had the use of $87,300 each year plus what it would earn with compounding interest.

It should be clear that what depreciation ultimately does is allow the investor to convert all of the now tax-free money in the form of depreciation into income that may be taxed at the lowest rate. So Bob goes from the highest rate he would pay each year into the much lower and deferred capital gains rate. If Bob elected to enter into a transaction that is qualified for 1031 treatment, he would completely escape any tax on the resulting gain from a sale.

Compare a 1031 Exchange to a Sale

Setting the Ground Rules

The Investor's Goals: People purchase real property to serve a purpose. A house is purchased by one person to serve as a place to live and raise a family and then to live out retirement. That same house owned by an investor may be an income-producing property that at some future date becomes a vacation home, and even later, a place to retire to. A motel might be a place for a whole family to live and work together, or simply an investment by an absentee owner who has managers who operate his or her chain of such properties. A young family just starting out might plow every dime that comes in from renting out a small duplex into fixing up the property with the goal to sell it at a profit and to reinvest in another fixer-upper to repeat the process again and again. They are looking for appreciation, and not earnings. Other people may need every dime from their income properties to pay for their children's university educations or their own retirement medical bills. How the property is purchased and operated can be a major part of the results, so the planning of any investment should be directed toward that desired goal.

The Investor's Investment Position: Investors in the United States have the best of all worlds with respect to real estate investing. Chapter 2 discussed the unique form of financing available to investors here, as well as modest tax rates, discounts off those taxes for capital gains, and the ease by which to seek and find opportunities in the real estate market. All these are elements that are taken for granted here but do not come easily to investors in most of the rest of the world. Despite the many options that are available to finance an investment, not all are open to all investors. Credit ratings, financial statements, earnings history, and experience in the type of property being purchased all have a bearing on what a lender will lend that investor, if anything at all. Some investors must rely on the opportunities granted them by their service to the country via Veterans Administration (VA) loans, others look to special minority-based loans, while some have to struggle through their early investments by the sweat equity they build with their own hands and talents.

The limitations that some investors have by not being born with silver spoons in their mouths does not, interestingly enough, limit the advances that a person can make in the real estate investment arena. Many multimillionaires have made their way up from sweat equity, while at the same time many silver spoon guys (and girls) have lost the family fortunes like spitting out chewing gum (so to speak). I like to think that the difference between those two circumstances has more to do with the quality of the goal and the drive to reach it than it has to do with the metal of the spoon.

The Investor's Negotiating Options: The ability to negotiate your way out of a wet paper bag or into a skyscraper is not something that anyone is born with. The ability to learn how to do it, and the environment one is brought up in does. The more tools that are at your disposal, the greater your flexibility for you to present an offer that you hope will not be refused. We have already seen that there are many different ways to approach a transaction. What people want, or say they will give, is a bit like that wet paper bag. Your offer to acquire or counteroffer to their proposal may bring reality to the negotiation table.

The key to negotiations is to let the other party see that he or she won something if not everything. Is this possible? It should be possible because both a motivated buyer and a motivated seller have the same goals in mind. One wants the other's property, as in cash for land or vice versa. The enemies of a real estate deal need not be the two parties who seem to be at odds; it is all the other elements that stand in the way. These are factors like the IRS, taxes, late appraisals, title problems, lawyers who want to renegotiate deals, real estate brokers who can't negotiate deals, mothers-in-law who want the master bedroom instead of the guest room, and so on.

What an investor has to offer and how the offer is made are critical. It is a law of inverse values that goes like this: The less I have to offer you, the more I have to make you trust me. In the final analysis, I have seen deals come together not because the parties ranted and raved about how "honest" and how "respectable" they were, but because they conveyed how genuinely they loved the seller's property and how much they wanted to own it.

The Investor's Chosen Reinvestment: When going from one investment to another, the whole story is to choose wisely. This means going all the way back to what was the original goal that motivated the acquisition of the property that is now being disposed of. Did the property help that investor attain the desired goal? Did it, at least, take the investor closer to the goal? Has the goal now changed? If so, what kind of new investment will best serve the new goal? These are all worthy factors to consider and to incorporate into the ultimate decision.

The Situation to Be Compared: The balance of this chapter shows a comparison of two investment techniques. Multiple examples could actually result in each of these techniques, and I leave it up to you to revisit each example to see if you might have done it differently than do Jacob and Eva, who are looking to expand their portfolio of real estate investments. Let's look at Jacob and Eva's situation.

Examining Jacob and Eva's Transaction

Jacob and his wife, Eva, own a condominium apartment in Miami in which they have lived for three years. It is a nice two-bedroom apartment worth $300,000 against which they have a first mortgage of $100,000. They also have a 10-unit apartment building nearby, worth around $850,000, which they purchased for only $400,000 six years ago. At present they have a first mortgage on the 10 units in the amount of $200,000.

Over the six years, they have used $52,000 of depreciation in the apartment building, which has dropped their tax basis to $348,000. If they sold the units at $850,000, they would have a capital gain of $502,000. At a 15 percent capital gains tax, they would pay $75,300 in tax.

View the following calculation:

Value		$850,000
Less adjusted basis:		
Original purchase	$400,000	
Depreciation taken	52,000	
Adjusted basis		$348,000
Taxable capital gain		$502,000
Tax rate		× 15%
Tax to be paid		$ 75,300

During their ownership of these 10 units, they have plowed most of the cash flow from the building into fixing it up. They have total savings of $75,000 and their parents have indicated that if they found another investment that made sense, they would contribute a total of $100,000 as a loan to help with the investment. Both Jacob and Eva are ready to give up their apartment if the hotel they acquire has decent living quarters for an owner/manager. As some hotels do have such quarters, this decision will free up the equity in that apartment to add to their investment potential.

Jacob has been working in the hospitality field for nearly seven years, and has taken every night course possible in the field from local colleges. Eva has also been involved with hotel work, specializing in the management area and in hotel accounting. They dream of owning a hotel.

Jacob and Eva's Assets and Liabilities
and Investment Capital Available

Condo worth $300,000 with a mortgage of $100,000	Net value $200,000
Ten units worth $850,000 with a mortgage of $200,000	Net value 650,000
Cash	75,000
Parents' loan	100,000
Total value they have to work with	$1,025,000

In the hotel market, values vary greatly, as do the terms that a seller will accept or that are available through conventional financing. However, to purchase a property that will at least break even from day one, a down payment of 30 percent of the total purchase price would be a conservative approach. To stay on that conservative side, Jacob and Eva should not blow their entire bankroll of value on the down payment. My recommendation would be to hold back the safety net of the parents' $100,000 for use only if it is needed. This means, then, that they have a total value, if they choose to use it, of $925,000 that they can commit. If this is the 30 percent down, their total investment could be found by the following two-step formula:

Backing into the Down Payment Amount

1. If $925,000 equals 30 percent of the total price,
2. Then the total price would equal $925,000 divided by 30 percent, which is $3,083,333.

If Jacob and Eva were to look at hotels (and/or motels) in a price range of $3,000,000 to $3,500,000, they might end up with their dream.

A decent interstate highway motel can be found in a good area at a price of $40,000 to $55,000 per room. This gives Jacob and Eva a potential motel of between 65 to 90 rooms, anticipating some variance in all these numbers at negotiation time. Full-service hotels can cost more than this per room, because of the added public facilities, meeting rooms, and higher standards than in motels that generally cater to one-night in-transit traffic. First-class hotels and resorts in major tourist areas can cost more than $100,000 per room.

Because under the current IRS tax code investors are each exempt for $250,000 of gain in a personal residence in which they have lived for two out of the past five years, Jacob and Eva can cash out of their apartment and pocket all the proceeds from the sale, less the amount to pay off the mortgage. So they will have no problem moving that cash into a new investment. Their savings is also no problem, because they have already paid the tax on that in past years. What they have to deal with now is their 10-unit apartment building. They have a $502,000 gain on the apartment building should they sell it. Take note that in these examples I will not introduce any expenses of the transaction; let's look just at the basic deals as they happen.

Conventional Sale and Reinvestment: Here is what Jacob and Eva's reinvestment in a hotel or motel would look like if they sold the 10-unit apartment building and paid the tax on their gain.

Value	$ 850,000
Less mortgage that is assumed	200,000
Gross proceeds from sale	$ 650,000
Less gains tax	$ 75,300
Reinvestment capital from 10 units	$ 574,700
Other capital	
Cash from sale of condo	$ 200,000
Savings	75,000
Total reinvestment capital	$ 849,700
Divided by	30%
Maximum value Jacob and Eva can afford	$2,832,333

If $849,700 equals 30 percent of the total price, you ascertain the total price by dividing the $849,700 by .30 which is $2,832,333.

Section 1031 Exchange to Reinvestment Property: As we already know that if Jacob and Eva structure a deal using Section 1031 to remove any capital gains tax liability on their part, they will get a full reinvestment potential of the capital available for them, a sum of $3,083,333. This is, of course, saving the $100,000 loan promised by their parents as capital to fall back on if needed.

They find a hotel property they like that is relatively near to where they live, and for which the seller is asking $3,500,000. It is basically in good shape, and needs just a little TLC to spruce it up. Best of all, the beginning of the tourist season is still several months away so they can close on the deal and then be able to count on the best earning months right off the bat.

They have $925,000 to work with for a down payment, so if they are forced to pay the full 30 percent down this property would be just beyond their economic reach. However, if the seller will help them with the financing they might be able to put less cash down and still keep the condo so they wouldn't have to occupy revenue-producing facilities at the hotel.

The seller agrees to reduce the price to $3,350,000. Nevertheless, that still does not quite put the property in their hands. The seller's broker suggests that the seller hold a land lease under the hotel. If the land is worth $400,000 and the seller would accept an annual lease payment of $20,000 per year with a 60-year lease, with options by Jacob and Eva to purchase the land anytime within the first 20 years of the lease, that would change the entire financing structure.

As long as the seller agrees to subordinate the lease to the new first mortgage, then here is how the lender would view the situation.

Outright sale price	$3,350,000
Less land value	400,000
Total to be paid at closing	$2,950,000
Less loan available (70% of $3,350,000)	2,345,000
Cash to close	$605,000

Revisit what Jacob and Eva had to deal with. I would like you to seriously think what they might do to improve their situation with this turn of events.

Here are some suggestions based on what we know. Let's assume that they can borrow $280,000 against their condominium. To reach that loan amount the lender may, however, require the borrower to live in the apartment. Keep in mind that residential loans are often at the lowest rate, whereas a hotel loan is considered commercial and would be at a higher interest rate. If they borrowed $280,000 and paid off the existing mortgage of $100,000, how would that benefit them?

It would contribute $180,000 to their cause. This leaves $425,000 remaining to meet the $605,000 cash at closing on the hotel. This puts them in a great position. They can now choose between keeping the 10-unit apartment building and simply refinancing it or going ahead and selling it and focusing their full attention on making the hotel a success.

The great thing about this situation is they can choose which way benefits them the most, in several ways. Cash flow should be a major consideration, because if they refinance the 10 units they will generate tax-free cash, which is good, but they will also have debt service to consider. While the extra income coming in will look good on their financial statement, they may rather cash out, use the proceeds in a Starker type exchange (and pay no capital gains tax), and have a greater cash pillow for improving the hotel.

A cash sale of the 10 units would net them $650,000 and also mean they would not have to refinance or sell the condo. They still have their savings, and they keep their equity in the condo. Perhaps best of all, they do not owe their parents a thin dime, so that $100,000 can go to the next investment (or perhaps the first grandchild's education).

How This Deal Affects Tax Basis: Let's look at their new tax basis situation if they go ahead and do a Starker type exchange on the 10 units and purchase the hotel with the land lease in place. Keep in mind that this is solely a financing tool. They have all the benefits of ownership of the improvements and the land, and it is as though the seller has held a second mortgage at interest only (only 5 percent) for the period until they later refinance the hotel again (if they still own it 10 to 20 years down the road). The seller gets a potential benefit from this kind of deal, too. If the majority of the appreciation of the hotel since he purchased it is in the land, by not selling the land right now he has no capital gain on that part of the deal and therefore no tax to pay.

Here is the recap of the deal:

1. Jacob and Eva kept the condominium, and sold the 10 units.
2. They entered into a long-term lease of the land.
3. The seller subordinated the land to a new first mortgage.
4. The lease was $20,000 per year with a fixed option price to purchase it later.
5. They paid $2,950,000 for the improvements on the property.
6. They borrowed $2,345,000 from a local lender.
7. They added $605,000 in cash to the deal.

This cash came from the sale of the 10 units, which actually netted them $650,000. Their option here is to reduce the amount borrowed by that overage of $45,000 to fully shelter the proceeds from the sale of the 10 units, or to pay the gains tax on that amount ($6,750) and have the extra cash in their pockets. They still have not touched their savings of $75,000. Let's assume they want to maximize their tax savings so they reduce the amount they borrow only $2,300,000 and add their full $650,000 in proceeds from the sale of the 10 units to close on the hotel.

New Tax Basis Calculation

Sale price of 10 units		$ 850,000
Less adjusted basis of 10 units:		
Original purchase	$400,000	
Depreciation taken	52,000	
Adjusted basis		$ 348,000
Deferred gain by virtue of deferred exchange		$ 502,000
Price of hotel only (not land)		$2,950,000
Less deferred gain		502,000
New tax basis in hotel		$2,448,000

How did all this happen? First of all, the deferred gain of $502,000 is what Jacob and Eva would have had to pay tax on had they not completed a Section 1031 exchange. Even though they did not buy the land, they entered into a long-term leasehold arrangement that also qualifies under 1031 treatment.

Because Jacob and Eva did not have to pay tax on the gain, the IRS says that they now must reduce the tax basis of the new property by the amount of that deferred gain. Therefore, as they paid $2,950,000 for the hotel, that basis has to be reduced by the amount that has been deferred. They will now have a full $2,448,000 of value to depreciate as they have not purchased the land at this time. Land, by the way, is not a depreciable item, so by separating the land from the improvements they have achieved an added benefit.

CHAPTER 7

How to Make a
One-on-One Exchange

The goal of this chapter is:

To Show You the Steps in Creating an Exchange

The method of introducing the idea of a one-on-one exchange to the owner of a property you want to acquire is a bit more complex than to make an offer to buy that same property. While the idea of an exchange may interest you for tax savings reasons, the other party may have no tax problem to deal with. In fact, the owner may not have thought of even selling the property, let alone exchanging it. This chapter takes you into the real-life aspect of how to get a reluctant seller to enter into an exchange of the property for equity in something you own.

Terms and Concepts You Need to Know

Value versus Marketability
Dual Values
Justifying Value
Tax Appraisal Value
Lender's Appraisal
Common Area Maintenance (CAM)

Let's review each in detail.

Value versus Marketability

There are times when some real estate is offered for sale without a prospective buyer ever walking in the door for years. Then there are times when five offers are waiting at the broker's office when he returns from putting up a For Sale sign on the property. This is an interesting phenomenon about real estate and its marketability. There is no doubt that real estate is not as liquid as stocks and bonds, or for that matter not even as liquid as a three-year-old car. Those are items that have an instant value. A stockbroker can dump all your stock in a few minutes, and your three-year-old car will disappear on the car lot in seconds, provided you are willing to take the price offered.

The speed with which things like stocks and bonds and used cars sell says something about how quickly they also can go down in value. For example, take that brand-new car across the street from the dealer where you just purchased it and see how close you can get to the price you just paid. Stocks have a life of their own that many people in the business of buying and selling them do not fully understand. But we all understand and expect, in general at least, that over time all real estate will go up in value. And while this is a nice and comforting thought, it does not always happen on the timetable that the owners would like to see.

A number of factors cause property to go up and down in value, and they are discussed in detail in several of my other books, especially *Commercial Real Estate Investing: 12 Easy Steps to Getting Started* (John Wiley & Sons, 2004). In that book I show how the same factor, such as change in infrastructure, can first have an adverse effect on value, then a positive boost to the value. Other factors, such as supply and demand, can swing property values in big arcs as the supply of any category of property is exhausted. Any continued interest in that type of property will tend to push up the value of the remaining supply, as well as draw a new supply as prior owners now take profit in selling the higher-valued real estate.

No matter what is the underlying cause that starts the rise or decline in value, the ultimate value of property in any area generally has to do with a change of the highest and best use of the real estate. With respect to investment real estate, where the bottom line of the income less expenses equals profit, real estate tends to change in value in respect to the use it can be put to. The change that is the cause of a declining neighborhood might have been a new superhighway that sliced through a part of town and split off one section that can now no longer economically support the kinds of businesses that existed there. The former uses may degrade, slowly going from a modestly upscale clientele, to a blue-collar crowd, to a part of town on its way to becoming a slum. In each step the use that was economically viable was a continuing downgrading of the property, because as the condition of the real estate deteriorated the potential rent possible also declined. In contrast, the other side of this superhighway may benefit greatly because all the upscale shops have migrated there. Any single infrastructure change in a community can have similar effects. Fortunately, land planners are aware of this kind of impact and generally make an effort to either eliminate this kind of result or at least limit the negative side effects.

But any use is still likely to be temporary compared to the long-range thinking of a community. A use that will produce an economic return that is in excess of a prior return can raise the value of that property. One such improvement may catch on, and over a period of time the entire neighborhood moves up in economic stature. Then another use comes along that improves another neighborhood, and so on. Neighborhoods that become trendy see this effect and continue to prosper. The fact that a property has not sold because of what it is does not diminish the value of what it can become. The beauty of real estate is that change is not only inevitable, it is always present.

The underlying causes of change may be slowly developing, often out of your perspective. Events that create massive bridges or new highway systems require years of planning, months of political debate, and eventual public referendums just to get approval to go ahead with the project. Then, and usually only then, does the average member of the public become aware of the magnitude of the project, and its impact. I am sure you have experienced this, as when you suddenly are aware of a new building and remark, "When did they build that?"

The name of the game is to be aware of what is going on, and to understand what a change in use can do to the neighborhood, and to the values of the property located there. Your ability to grasp this aspect of use will help you to use exchanges as a special tool to acquire property and enable you to convert a losing proposition into a win-win transaction.

The effect of all of this is that one person's problem can be your ticket to wealth. The owner who has a problem on his or her hands can be a very motivated seller to be sure, and in the absence of a ready, willing, and able buyer, that owner may be ready for a property exchange you will offer him or her. The cash, mortgage money, *and* property you offer may not be the dream the owner has been waiting for, but your offer can take the owner closer to his or her goals.

The exchange you offer should never be compared by the other party to what they have expected they would get; it should be compared with what else has actually been offered. Remember about the "bird in the hand?" Well-rephrased it would be, "an exchange that can help solve your problem, is much better than a sale that will never happen." Having just said that, I can tell you that many property owners who have a genuine problem on their hands can become narrowly focused on how they see the solution to that problem. Usually the only solution that comes to mind is a direct sale, tomorrow would be nice, and yes, cash at the closing table.

Astute real estate investors learn that this kind of seller can be highly motivated, but will also need to be carefully walked through the alternative transaction. I have found a three-step approach to this kind of situation that can work wonders.

Three Steps to Get a Motivated Seller to Focus on an Exchange

1. **Praise.** A good way to start moving the seller in a direction you need is to praise the seller and the property. After all, you do want to own it, so there must be something about it that you can praise. If you can praise the property, then there must be something about the property owner you can also praise. A statement like this will give you an idea of what I am talking about. "Mr. and Mrs. Seller, I admire you for developing such a successful motel (restaurant, office building, apartment complex, etc.) and understand that you want to retire from active management of such properties. My wife and I have some great ideas on how we can continue in your footsteps, and we would love the opportunity to make improvements to the property and to expand its potential. We hope we can come to terms. We have been looking for an opportunity like this for several months now, and we have narrowed our investment choices down to three properties. Yours is our number one choice."

2. **Respect the seller's goals.** It does not matter if the seller has told you the real goals or just something that sounds good. The key is to respect what they say. "Mr. and Mrs. Seller, both my wife and I respect the fact that you would like to cash out on the sale of this property. We also respect that you value the property so highly; we know you have worked hard to make it what it is. Your price of $2,000,000 is a grand amount, and we hope that we can come to terms with you. We are anxious to put together a deal that works for you, as well as for us."

3. **Offer regret.** Explain that you regret not being able to meet the seller's terms. "Mr. and Mrs. Seller, we regret that, no matter how hard we have tried, we don't see how we can meet the terms you have presented to us. We love this property, and would like to own it. We would like you to consider a proposal that we feel is a fair offer to you, and is one that will enable us to close on the title as soon as possible. It is not an all-cash deal, but it can enable you to move on with your lives."

Dual Values

Within the real estate exchange world it is not uncommon for property owners to set two separate values for their offered property. "Okay, if you want to buy my property, then pay me $500,000 cash. Want to exchange something with me (that I will be willing to take)? Then my price is $700,000." Even old-timers in the real estate profession will do this. The problem here is they have missed the whole point by setting two prices and having the exchange price higher than the all-cash price. Why? Because by using Section 1031 in a qualified exchange, the very act of making an exchange can save the seller money that otherwise would be paid to the IRS in the form of capital gains tax.

However, because you are likely to run across a situation where two prices are actively quoted, my suggestion is to ignore the issue of which price to negotiate on, and simply make your offer. Remember, "I will pay your price, if you accept my terms."

Justifying Value

One of the most difficult things you will do is to accurately estimate the value of a property you want to acquire. As difficult as this process is, when sellers withhold information or provide inaccurate data about the subject property, the task can be nearly impossible. However, there are ways in which you can ascertain what the property would be worth to you. This process will depend on the nature of the real estate market in the time and place you find yourself, as well as your motivation to own, and the owner's motivation to sell. All these factors will come together once negotiations begin.

The process of justifying the value of any real estate starts with your own homework about the property and the owner of that property. This process can be very elaborate and entail the review of virtually every aspect of the physical nature of the real estate, as well as the financial details of the investment. Many investors seek to discover every minutia of a property before making an offer to acquire it. These investors frequently lose out because other investors seek first to tie up the real estate before spending time, effort, and money in doing a complete study of the property.

My own thoughts on this subject are to take a quick look at the basics of the property, which would include a personal visit to the property and neighborhood where it is located. If the property is a rental (apartments, offices, retail shops, etc.), then four types of statistics would be required at this stage.

Initial Data Needed Before Making an Offer

1. **Monthly rent per square foot.** This should be base rent only, and not include any common area maintenance (CAM) amounts. CAM costs are generally accepted in most commercial rentals such as retail, office, and shopping center rents. There is more about CAM later in this chapter, so for the moment stay focused on base rent. The base rent is critical because it gives you a benchmark to use in comparison to other rents in the area. If, for example, the rent for a one-bedroom apartment is $700 per month and the average size of the one-bedroom apartment is 700 square feet in the building you are considering acquiring, then that base rent is $1 per square foot per month. Calculate forward to one full year and you would have a $12 per square foot rent on an annualized basis. If you invest in apartment rentals you would already know what the rental market is for the category of building and location you are now reviewing. If that $1 per square foot per month is below the market then there likely is room to increase the rents.

2. **Review of the rent roll.** The rent roll is a chart of the status of all the tenants. It should have data about the tenants and their lease terms. Important information would include: start date, term of the initial lease, options to renew, rent increases built into the lease, deposits held, and on-time payment history. If you find that the rent is below market, and that the leases are for a long term with options to renew at the same rent, it may not be immediately possible to improve the income by increasing rents.

3. **Personal inspection of the property.** It is obviously important to view the property because a poorly managed property is likely to be in need of cosmetics. A badly managed property may have a

combination of deferred maintenance, defects in need of correction, and a bad mix of tenants as well as under-market rents. You will want to have a professional opinion of the condition of the property much the same as you will have your lawyer review the leases. However, in the initial stages of deciding if you want to own this property in the first place, do not take the time for the more detailed inspections.

4. **Review of ownership history of the property.** The ownership history is generally quick and simple to obtain. A tax assessor's report of the property will show when it was built, the tax appraisal, past sales history, and the ad valorem tax against the property.

With even minor seller cooperation, all four of these factors can be obtained and reviewed by you in a few hours. Your ability to make sense out of the data will depend on how well you understand the current market conditions. That process is an ongoing one, which you would be updating on a regular basis by continual study of what is available for rent, and the terms landlords demand and get.

One of the first steps you should make is to let the other party "teach you" the value of their own property. In essence, you might ask the seller to show you how they have come up with the value of $2,000,000 for their property. A well-versed seller who understands what you need to know will be anxious to explain the value of his or her real estate. Unfortunately, most sellers are first-time sellers and may not know how to justify value. Here are three explanations you might get from first-time sellers, and how to deal with them.

First-Time Seller's Defense of Property Value

1. **"It's worth $2,000,000 because that is how much I need to get from the sale."** This is a common answer to the question, and yet it offers no justification to the real value at all. If the seller has a broker or salesperson handling the sale, then, in the presence of both the seller and the agent, ask the agent what comparable sales of similar properties would show the value to be. It is helpful for

you to first know the answer to that question, and critical that the seller be present. It is likely that the seller is well aware that the property is priced above the real market value, and both he and the agent are fishing for someone to come along and buy at that high price.

2. **"The market is hot right now, and there are several buyers discussing this deal with me right now."** This, too, is a common answer, and might even be true. Still, there is no justification of the value offered. Mind you, you will have done your homework and would know what the owner paid for the property. This information is more critical if the time period of ownership has been short, and the price paid substantially under the asking price. A logical follow-up question would be for you to ask what improvements have been made to the property since it was purchased for only $1,000,000 two years ago. It could be the owner did a lot of work, even added more square footage and so on. This kind of question gives the seller an opportunity to give justification to the price. If he or she did nothing, then another follow-up question would be to ask if the revenue has been increased substantially to warrant the increase in value.

3. **"We don't need to sell, so if we don't get $2,000,000 cash in our pocket, we'll just hold on to the property until we do."** I wish I had $10 for every time I have heard this one. This kind of response defines one of two kinds of property owners. The first is a person who doesn't know exactly what the property is worth, and is hoping that someone will make an offer considerably higher than its real value. The second is a person who does know exactly what the property is worth, but is nevertheless trying to entice a higher offer out of a prospective buyer. The best approach here is to make an offer that is not quite as much as you would pay for the property. If the seller or the seller's agent comes back with something like, "The seller is insulted at such a low offer," then remind both the seller and his or her agent that you really like the property and think enough of it to make an offer; if that is insulting, how do they feel about all the thousands of people who do not even care to make an offer on the property?

Tax Appraisal Value

The local property tax appraiser keeps track of what is going on in the local real estate market. They see the sales data from the recording of deeds, and are quick to respond to the rising values of property in the community. This response is generally in the form of higher tax appraisals, which is reflected in increased ad valorem tax bills at the next billing period.

This is important information to know because an excessively high tax appraisal can occur. If you acquire the property and are successful in getting the tax reduced, you can add the savings directly to the bottom line of your net operating income. How does an excessive tax appraisal occur? A lot has to do with the price the previous owner paid for the property, what has happened to the neighborhood in the meantime, and how much of a bargain you got when you put it under contract. It is not all that uncommon for a shopping center that the present owner paid $20,000,000 for 10 years ago to slip out of fashion and decline in value to the point that it needs major rehab, new tenants, new uses, and an overall new point of view. If the property has been milked by the past owners, they might have still made money selling it for $10,000,000.

There is an interesting factor about the tax appraisal value. It is rarely a value that an owner would take in a sale, yet it is always too high a value on which the property owner has to pay taxes.

Lender's Appraisal

Virtually every lender will want to review a recent appraisal of the subject property. Some lenders may have their own in-house or preferred appraisers whom they use on an exclusive basis, while others accept outside appraisers who meet certain criteria and have been preapproved by that lender. These appraisals are designed to justify to the lender that the value shown by the appraisal is sufficient to warrant the loan. As each lender may have a different loan-to-value formula, depending on the type of real estate in question, different lenders may end up offering a greater loan amount at better terms than other lenders reviewing the same appraisal.

A comprehensive appraisal on a major investment property can be expensive and can take a considerable time to prepare. The time aspect of this factor can become a major part of the negotiations to acquire that property. Sellers do not like giving a buyer a long period of time on a contract where the buyer can back out of the deal. Buyers, in turn, do not like to be fully committed to the deal where financing is essential to close the transaction, and until the lender has committed to the deal, buyers generally will not do so, either.

Common Area Maintenance (CAM)

I mentioned CAM earlier. This is another one of those nonhomogeneous terms that tend to confuse people when they attempt to make comparisons of properties. Originally, common area maintenance referred to the cost to maintain the common area that all the tenants in a specific property, say a retail strip store or a shopping mall, used or had access to. The total cost for such maintenance would be divided between all the tenants, usually on a per-square-foot basis. However, in more modern use, CAM can mean all the cost to maintain, manage, and otherwise operate the subject property. This might even include institutional advertising for the mall or shopping center.

These costs could include everything from the management fee charged by the operators of the facility to insurance, taxes, reserve for replacements, and so forth. If it is a potential cost of the facility, it could be found in most CAM calculations. The importance in this issue is that you can never assume that CAM for one building is going to include the same elements and costs as CAM for another building. It is important to know exactly what is included, how it is calculated, the annual or other periodic adjustments to it, and how it is paid. If the CAM is totally inclusive of all costs and reserves, then the base rent would be much the same as a triple-net lease. However, the advantage that a CAM lease has over a triple-net lease is substantial. First, consider that a triple-net lease is one where the tenant, often a single tenant, agrees to maintain the property, pay the taxes and insurance, and cover other costs attributed to the property. The tenant may or may not, however, maintain the property in the same condition as would the management under a CAM situation. In addition, CAM, in its most liberal use, includes management and a reserve for certain replacements, such as a new roof and/or new air control systems.

The Five Steps to Making an Exchange

1. Establish Your Goals

Goals are important in everything you do. Yet most people either do not establish goals or become frustrated because they set unrealistic goals that cannot be attained. Frustration sets in quickly in those instances, and the whole process of establishing goals is abandoned.

I want to stress the fact that an improperly established goal is not worse than no goal. The key is to be able to recognize that the goal is unrealistic or without merit and that you need to step back, take a long and hard look at your goals, and reset them. Proper goals are made up of interim goals that lead you to target goals that in turn lead you to new goals. Here is how this works.

2. Understand Interim Goals

An interim goal is like the baby steps that are important to ultimately be able to run a marathon. Far too many people skip over the interim goal and head directly for the target goal. Let's say that you set a target goal to become a jet pilot. At your starting point the most sophisticated mechanical apparatus you know how to operate is your car. A jump from car to jet pilot is a rather large hurdle to overcome. What about some of the other important, if not critical, elements like finding the source of funds to pay for pilot training, ascertaining if you have the right qualifications to learn to fly, finding a flying school, taking a sample flying lesson, committing to the time it takes to learn to fly, and so on? Each of these requires some effort, and as easy as some of them might be, each element is another step up the ladder toward your target goal.

3. Form Target Goals

Target goals are what you want to reach; then once you reach them, new target goals can be established. In essence, a target goal is a form of interim goal, only it occupies a greater position in the scheme of things. To graduate from a university with a master's degree is a target goal, as there are many interim goals that must be reached one after the other to attain that degree. To rise to the head of a department in your work, or to reach an annual sales quota that you have established for yourself, is also a target goal. Like the goal to earn a master's degree, each goal, once attained, must now be replaced with some other target, and a new set of interim goals developed to take you there.

To be truly effective, both the target goal and the initial interim goals need to be written down. This serves several purposes. First of all, you get to reinforce your mind every day by looking at them, reading them, and confirming that you can and will achieve those goals. Secondly, the written word binds you to what you have established as your goal. There is no equivocation about, "What was it I said I was going to do?"

However, just because a goal is written down, it is not something etched in stone. You are likely new at this task. Goals are something you have tended to think about—sort of wishful thinking, I would bet. Nevertheless, this is serious stuff now. You are likely to bite off more than you can attain. You may even select a target goal that is impossible for you to reach because you fail to back up that target with a plan of action and the interim goals that go with that plan.

Because of this, you need to pay close attention to those interim goals. If you are meeting all your deadlines and achieving all your interim goals, you likely have been too easy on yourself. Ratchet up the levels you can attain and shorten your timetable. But if you have set goals that are too high and have no plan to get you there, then rethink the goals and reset them; apply a stricter set of interim goals that are smaller steps and more realistic for your ability; and then move forward.

In the business of investing in real estate, a great target goal for you to have would be: "Within 10 months I will become an expert in the real estate that is within my defined comfort zone." This target goal is attainable based on the success you have in meeting and attaining your interim goals. Here is what your interim goals might look like for the first 16 weeks of your progress toward your target goal.

4. First 16 Weeks of Your Goal Formation Process

1. **Within the Next Few Months.** Read a couple more real estate books, such as my *Investing in Real Estate with Other People's Money* (McGraw-Hill, 2003) and *The Real Estate Investor's Answer Book* (McGraw-Hill, 1994).

2. **Within four weeks.** Obtain the essential local zoning maps and codes, drive around the neighborhood and define your initial comfort zone area, and order business cards that show you to be a "real estate investor."

3. **Within eight weeks.** Attend two planning and zoning (P&Z) meetings and one city council meeting, pass out your new business cards to each board and city council member, and follow up with a thank-you card to each member.

4. **Within 14 weeks.** Attend two more P&Z board meetings and one more city council meeting. Learn how to access data from the property appraiser's web site by computer. (If you do not have a computer, most public libraries have them available free of charge and offer low-cost or free lessons on how to use them.)

5. **Within 14 weeks.** Have tax appraiser reports on at least half of the properties in your comfort zone. Inspect 15 properties that are for sale and make note of similar properties that have sold in the past year (as found on the tax appraiser reports).

6. **Within 16 weeks.** Begin to follow the rental market in your comfort zone. Inspect at least 15 properties that are for rent, and make note of rents charged, CAM requirements and details, and amount of space that is vacant.

These goals have several factors in common.

5. Understand the Common Elements of All Goals

- There is a timetable to the goal.

- The goal has an element that can be measured. This is important as it enables you to gauge how well you are doing. If you cannot achieve the goal in the time period, you may need to readjust that goal or make better use of your time.

- The goal is clearly attainable as all it requires you to do is be proactive. It is impossible for you to fail to attain the goal, even if you need to adjust the timetable.

- The goal is clearly focused to an end result, your target goal.

- The interim goal is a building block that not only takes you on a path to the target goal, but it also builds your confidence, puts you into a learning situation, and helps you establish yourself as you move toward that target goal.

Remember that any exchange that takes you closer to your goal can be a good exchange.

Where to Find Potential Exchanges

I caution sellers who focus only on a sale as the best way for them to dispose of their property. Likewise, let me caution the exchanger who spends all his or her time at exchange meetings, dealing with people who live and breathe exchanges. It is easy to forget that if a buyer comes along, that, too, can produce a tax-free situation by using a Starker type deferred exchange. With the birth of the Starker type exchange, it doesn't matter whether you sell or exchange; as long as you follow the rules of IRC 1031 you can accomplish the goal to avoid having to pay capital gains tax on your qualified investments.

Therefore, the key is not to look for exchangers to the exclusion of finding a real live buyer of your property. Indeed, a good marketing program will take into account either situation. The first party to come along, either buyer or exchange party, can have the property. In reality, if you are motivated to sell and will consider an exchange, then it is to your advantage to let your agent know this. If the agent does not have a clue how to find an exchange party, then you may need to shop around for a more versatile real estate company to represent you.

Here are some sources of takers for your real estate or other properties you would like to dispose of.

Nine Sources of Takers for Your Property

1. Motivated sellers.
2. Owners of free and clear properties.
3. Owners of problem properties.
4. Owners with problem partners.
5. Sellers with difficult-to-sell real estate.
6. High-profit sellers.
7. Exchange clubs.
8. Local Realtors.
9. Buyers without sufficient cash to buy your property.

Let's look at each of these in some detail.

Motivated Sellers

I have discussed motivated sellers in earlier chapters, and they do exist. A motivated seller generally is one with an agenda that is pressing for a solution—a divorce, a move to a new job, triplets born so a larger home is needed, management difficulties, a need for capital for other personal circumstances, and so on. Each reason for the motivation will have a clear and obvious solution, which generally is a cash sale. Equally, each situation can be solved in other ways, if the motivated party will open his or her eyes and consider what is offered, and not what the seller has prayed for, but which is not on the table. Any motivated seller who can sit still and give a genuine offer some careful consideration may be an ultimate taker for a full or partial exchange.

Owners of Free and Clear Properties

When the property that is for sale is free and clear of debt, there is always a chance that an exchange can be possible. The reason for this statement is that an exchanger can offer a property plus cash in this kind of situation. Why? Because an F&C property will generally enable the taker for that property to crank cash out of the deal. If it is an income-producing property and represents good loan potential, then cash can be had by all. Here is an example of one such situation.

Julie's F&C Property Exchange: Julie owns an office building that she inherited several years ago. She has been told that now is a good time to sell, so it has been put on the market by her real estate agent. The offered price is $7,000,000, which is just $1,000,000 above its value when she received it in the inheritance. In a sale she would have to pay a capital gains tax on that excess value of $1,000,000.

Joe had always invested in vacant land because he knew that big profits were possible in land deals. Now he wanted to cash out some of his land holdings and move into some income-producing real estate. He saw the offering data on Julie's office building and after looking at the property and the data he made her this offer:

He offered her $6,750,000 with $5,000,000 cash and a 200-acre tract of land near Vero Beach, Florida. The land was, in fact, a producing orange grove that was managed by a local Florida juice company. The income paid the annual taxes, and there was a small cash flow of $100,000 on top of that.

Julie's immediate reaction was a loud "No" to the deal. However, Joe persisted and gave her a DVD made up of video images that he had taken of the property and the operation of the orange grove, along with chamber of commerce type data of Vero Beach and the growth potential for that area, as well as central Florida in general. What he did was sell Julie on the idea of the property. Of course, he was also a buyer of her property, so it did not take Joe long to close on the deal.

Because Julie's property was an F&C income-producing office building, Joe was able to finance the $5,000,000 to balance the exchange. As Joe was trading up, he benefited by getting a fair value for his 200-acre grove, added a substantial asset to his portfolio, gained tax shelter from the value of the improvements of the office building, and did not have to reach into his pocket for anything. Julie likewise qualified under the conditions of Section 1031 and was able both to take the grove as like-kind property for part of the transaction and to complete a Starker exchange with the $5,000,000 portion of the deal.

Owners of Problem Properties

Problem properties offer great potential for patient investors. Remember, one person's problem is another person's piece of cake. If you have a talent and can turn a problem property into a moneymaking venture, then cultivate that talent. Generally the key is finding a use that fits the property rather than attempting to nurse a use that is outdated or inappropriate for the area and/or the property.

There are several types of problem properties that you need to be careful of. If the problem is financial—that is, there is more debt on the property than it is worth—the battle to turn it around can be dangerous. However, even in this kind of situation there may be a silver lining tied to the debt: a lender who is anxious not to foreclose on the property.

A little due diligence about the lender may reveal information that opens new avenues to approach. Just because the existing owner is up to his or her ears in debt does not mean that the lender would be unwilling to cut a sweet deal with a new buyer (you) who has a sound plan to turn the property around. Some lenders will even go deeper into their pockets and lend that new owner the funds to make the turnaround.

Owners with Problem Partners

When you come across a situation where the motivation is to break up a failing partnership or joint venture, you may have just met Santa Claus. The partner in control of the situation is the only one you can deal with, but his or her problem might not be the property but rather a conference room full of partners who, for one reason or another, are driving the controlling partner crazy. I know from personal experience how easy it is for a joint venture or syndication to end up with one or two sour faces that want to take over and run the show. Only they do not have a controlling vote, so what do they do? They drive everyone up the wall until the partners would rather sell at any close to reasonable price to end the relationship.

These sellers are ideal for exchanges, and my company has closed some rather interesting partial exchange transactions to help the controlling partner save face, while ending the pain for everyone except that one sour face who had become the thorn in everyone's side.

Sellers with Difficult-to-Sell Real Estate

Just because it is difficult to sell does not mean it is worthless. Some real estate is not hot when you want to sell it the most for many different reasons. Perhaps the 200-acre orange grove that Joe traded to Julie is just a few years away from development, but what is hot is ready-to-go development property. That happens, so orange groves may sit without a ready buyer, for the moment, at least. Sometimes there is a political situation that renders a property unusable for the time being. Building moratoriums can be placed on whole towns while a three-year traffic study is made or new water sources are found and built.

If you are looking to solve a problem and can entice someone who has a difficult-to-sell property to let you have the property along with solving your problem, you might be a taker for that real estate. Remember, people will do whatever it takes to solve a problem or reach a goal. To accomplish that they will reach out to what is available. Take my offer, I would say; it is real, it is on the table now, and I can close tomorrow.

High-Profit Sellers

People who have real windfalls in value appreciation are prime takers for an exchange. Tie that to a difficult-to-sell property or a problem situation, and almost any reasonable partial exchange is possible. The tax assessor's reports can give light to this kind of situation. When a property is put on the market and it is F&C or has low loan-to-value debt, that is a sign that the owners have held the property for a long time. A quick look at the tax report might show that the present owners purchased the property 30 years ago and paid $100,000 for the property then, and it is on the market for $25,000,000 now.

While this seller can use a buyer with that kind of cash, then park the cash with a facilitator and complete a Starker type exchange thereby saving the rather large capital gains tax that would become due, it is not so easy to find a replacement property for a $25,000,000 deal within the 180-day Section 1031 time period.

Because of this, these sellers are ripe and sometimes anxious to close within that time period and are open for any creative solution.

Exchange Clubs

I have already mentioned exchange clubs as a viable source for takers of your real estate. However, here the key is to be proactive. Do not sit back and wait for someone to offer you something; go out and use your real estate as a partial deal to a much larger investment.

Exchange clubs exist around the country and can be found by surfing the Web. The Internet is full of self-described experts, however, so be careful whom you deal with. Be sure to have real names, phone numbers, and addresses that you can check out. Get references, and anyone who is worth their pinch of salt will be glad to supply you with references who are not related to them, and are still alive.

Local Realtors

A large percentage of members of exchange clubs are local Realtors or real estate brokers. They frequently deal with their own properties, and they understand the finer points of making exchanges. Seek out one or two of these people in your own neighborhood. You will be glad you did, and they can generally help you with any real estate exchange.

Buyers without Sufficient Cash to Buy Your Property

You are a seller with a property that no one wants to own—that is, until you let it be known that you will take some vacant land as a part of the down payment. What you are doing is making it easy for someone to buy your real estate. Just the offer to take someone's vacant land (or time-share, or diamond ring, or 1950 Ford coupe) may bring you a buyer who falls in love with what you have. I have seen such deals turn into all-cash sales when the property owner turned down the trade property offered.

CHAPTER 8

How Real Estate Exchanges Work

The goal of this chapter is:

**To Demonstrate Different Motivations
of How and Why Exchanges Work**

Terms and Concepts You Need to Know

Importance of Timely and Effective Due Diligence
Outside the Comfort Box
Greener Grass Syndrome
Expanding Your Horizons and Options with Exchanges
Eight Motivations of Exchanges

Let's review each in detail.

Importance of Timely and Effective Due Diligence

I have mentioned due diligence in several past chapters, and would like to wrap this subject up with emphasis on the element of time as it relates to due diligence. Let's first review some of the other elements of due diligence.

Cold Turkey Due Diligence

This is the worst kind of due diligence you can make. By "cold turkey" I mean you enter the picture knowing absolutely nothing about the property, where it is located, the owner's motivations, and the financial nature of the real estate. This does not mean that you cannot be successful doing cold turkey due diligence, only that it puts an added burden on you and your inspection team, and can be more costly than a more deliberate approach to due diligence.

What Comes First, the Chicken or the Egg?

What do you do first—tie up the property or expend time and effort with detailed due diligence? If you have developed a comfort zone and have established an ongoing learning process of properties in that area, this question will never come up. The comfort zone will give you advance information about the market so that you will be able to recognize opportunities before they become apparent to the rest of the real estate investors in your area. Before? Yes, most property owners begin to give subtle signs that their property may be available for sale long before it actually goes on the market. Evidence of sustained vacancy of space or apartments, a decline in the level of maintenance to the property, or signs of poor or bad management (which may indicate absentee ownership or illness) can be such preludes to putting the property on the market.

An investor who is observant in his or her comfort zone will be proactive to ferret out such property owners. This would include phone conversations with the manager or owner of property that is beginning to show some or all of the signs I just mentioned. Take care to distinguish between the manager and the owner. Managers can be very defensive of their position, and questions such as "Do you think the owner will sell?" can fall on deaf ears, or the answer you get will generally be a resounding "No." If you forget this warning and ask that question, remember this paragraph when you get that "No" answer.

Regardless of the length of time you are aware of a property being on the market, your efforts to become the expert in your comfort zone will prepare you to move forward on this newly recognized opportunity without having to do any preliminary due diligence other than, perhaps, a quick walk through or around the subject property.

Importance of Timing

Due diligence should be accomplished in as comprehensive a way as possible. This process will take time, and as I have mentioned earlier, time is usually a critical part of negotiations. This reinforces the need to have some initial knowledge of what is going on. Therefore, if the property rings your "opportunity" bell, then spend a day going over the initial elements of due diligence pointed out in the previous chapter; then do what it takes to tie up the property. Not all the due diligence in the world will help you get the property if someone else jumps in ahead of you and locks up the deal. Mind you, your competition did that with a provision in the agreement that allowed them a due diligence period, and if they were not totally satisfied with the property at the end of that period they could walk away from the deal.

When Do You Go Hard?

Going hard means your deposit (all or part of it, according to the terms of the agreement) is at risk. This is the put-up-or-shut-up time where the investor has to make a decision either to go forward, to back off from the deal, to try to renegotiate for more time, or to renegotiate the entire terms of the deal. Many savvy investors do not pull the plug on a deal at the last minute, but rather have their lawyer or agent send a letter to the seller that says something like this:

> Based on the buyer's current due diligence investigations, they have found several elements that will take longer to conclude than they first anticipated. As it is, the buyer's due diligence period ends in 7 business days from today, and I have been informed by my client that unless they receive a 20-business-day extension of the existing due diligence period, they will be forced to withdraw from the agreement.

Did they pull the plug? Not exactly; by using their lawyer or agent as an intermediary, all they did was suggest that they would do that unless granted an extension, and they did so in time to renegotiate the deal if the seller does not respond positively prior to the end of the period. By then, the bridge might already be on fire and there might be no more time left to save the deal. However, by providing a buffer between the suggestion they will bail out and the actual deadline, they demonstrate an example of good negotiation where the decision maker stays remote and uses intermediaries to deliver the messages.

By using the time allotted, this method is generally successful. Nothing is more frustrating and potentially deal-ending than investors who wait until the last moment to say they need an extension or to threaten some legal action if they don't get it (like suggest that the seller gave them incorrect data).

Outside the Comfort Box

Your comfort box is your comfort zone. Anytime you step out of that box you run the risk of needing more time to do proper due diligence, which you may not get. My advice to you is to never stray outside your comfort zone. It is that baby blanket that will keep you as safe as you possibly can be when it comes to real estate investing. If you feel tempted to move into new territory, then do so with an expansion of your comfort zone. Start the learning process of that new area over again and build your sphere of reference and contacts for that area just as you continue to do in your existing comfort zone.

Greener Grass Syndrome

I tend to talk about the Greener Grass Syndrome a lot these days. It has always been an important issue in real estate investing, but as it becomes more difficult to find good investments, it is more prevalent than ever. The Greener Grass Syndrome is that feeling you get when you see something that is out of the comfort box that looks so good to you that you feel you have just died and gone to investor heaven. I tell the story of my first trip to Bermuda, where I could not believe what a beautiful paradise I had found (as if no one else had made that same observation). I was about to plump down a sizable down payment on a property when my subconscious told me to hold off. Do your due diligence, it shouted to me.

It turned out I would have made a horrible mistake. Once I began to learn of the nightmares of ownership of the type of property I was about to purchase, I realized that I had strayed too far away from my comfort zone.

The Greener Grass Syndrome can strike any investor at any time. The exchanger who agrees to take a property that is outside the comfort box needs extra time to be able to accomplish an effective due diligence on the property. A drive past will not do.

Expanding Your Horizons and Options with Exchanges

You can benefit from exchanges as an additional investment tool whether you are a buyer or a seller. Anytime you have an asset that is not moving you closer to a goal, you should consider including that asset in your offers to acquire other property. Not only can you improve your chances of getting a fair value for the property, but you may save paying the capital gains tax on that asset if it qualifies as a 1031 exchange property.

I have illustrated this concept several times now, and want to make sure you have grasped the point that exchanges are simply a tool. Like all tools in the investment field, the exchange has its benefits and its drawbacks. Generally, however, the drawbacks occur when investors push exchanges where they will never work, or become so focused on making an exchange that they lose track of where they are going. After all, many great deals have been lost for investors pushing exchanges when if they had only abandoned the idea of an exchange and paid cash the deal was theirs to take. This works for sellers, too, so remain flexible and consider any reasonable offer.

Eight Things You Have That You Can Exchange

Let's look at some of the different kinds of properties you can use in exchanges. Keep in mind that you are not tied to an all-or-nothing exchange. Sometimes the exchange element is the kicker that brings together a deal that has avoided you.

Section 1031 Property: Section 1031 property includes any real estate that qualifies as like kind. The benefits with this kind of property are that it will qualify for tax-free treatment for at least one of the parties. If both parties qualify, then so much the better. Remember, like kind is not necessarily a farm for a farm, or an office building for an office building. When it comes to real estate, it is generally the intent of ownership that will govern the status of like kind. If you have purchased a tract of land or a vacant lot and have held it for investment purposes, you will likely qualify for almost any other real estate. The key is to be able to prove to the IRS (if you need to) that you are not going to live there (for the moment anyway) and it is not inventory that you are going to put back on the market for sale.

Nonqualifying Real Estate: Real estate that does not qualify under the 1031 rules could be property that is outside the United States and would not qualify for the U.S. Virgin Islands, either. Or a home that you plan to move into immediately. Or inventory that you plan to add to other similar inventory and sell. Say you are in the mobile home business and I offer to exchange 100 mobile home pads in a mobile home park I own for a tract of land you are holding as an investment, perhaps for a future mobile home park. The fact that you would not qualify for Section 1031 treatment by taking the lots has nothing to do with the viability of the transaction in other respects. Even property abroad may be an ideal exchange if it fits your needs, serves a purpose, and takes you closer to your goal. In fact, it might be nice just to have that condo in Paris.

Personal Property: Personal property is any tangible object that is not real estate. I have attended exchange closings where everything from old cars, boats, trucks, and recreational vehicles have been traded for homes, apartments, office buildings, vacant lots, and so on. Generally, there is also cash on the table, and often the personal property was added to the negotiation near the end of the transaction as a kicker. Many times the kicker part is that final sweetener that clinches the deal.

Here is an example of personal property as a kicker to close a deal. I was negotiating to acquire a lot on which I wanted to build a retail center. I had gotten closer to the seller's asking price of $150,000 but we were still around $30,000 apart. In the midst of a conversation with the owner, he appeared anxious and kept looking at his watch. I asked him if he was late for something. He told me that it was his wife's birthday and that he had already hinted that he was going to get her something really nice. As we were in my office at the time, I went over to a safe, opened it, and took out a small strongbox. I removed two black velvet ring-size boxes and let him open them. Inside each was a different style ring set with a very high-quality ruby over one carat, circled with 10 5-point diamonds. I suggested he take whichever ring he thought she would like, or both for that matter and let her choose. I told him I would add either of the rings to my offer. He was free, I said, to take the rings to any jeweler and have them appraised and if he did not feel he got a good deal, then we would forget about my buying his lot.

Now, my cost in the rings consisted of taking the stones as commission in another deal, plus the cost to buy the setting, and the diamonds set with the rubies, which came to around $15,000 for each ring. I knew that either of the rings would be appraised at close to $30,000 in a retail environment. I also knew that if he gave his wife a choice of the two rings that he would have a very difficult time getting her chosen ring away from her later on.

We closed the deal a few days later. Since that transaction, I have done several other deals with this same person. Mostly they were transactions where I was representing him in deals where he was offering small exchanges as part of larger deals.

Certain Leasehold Interests: A leasehold interest comes in many different categories. If you have a three-year lease on an apartment in New York City, and your rent is well below the current market rate, then your leasehold may have value. If the terms permit, someone would buy your leasehold interest and pay you to take over your lease. What would they pay? That will depend on two things: how much below the market rate your current lease is, and how desirable your apartment is for that person. If, for example, the market rate for a small studio is $1,500 per month (plus utilities) and your lease is $850 per month, there is a spread of $650 per month. I might offer you a sublease where I pay you $1,500 per month and you keep the $650 each month, but I might rather pay you $5,000 in a lump sum to take over your lease altogether.

Okay, that was a simple example, but what if you were a major developer who had just negotiated a deal to lease a tract of land for 99 years? Your plan is to build a parking garage on the site to serve an office building you want to build next door on land you already own. The deal is signed and you start your lease while you go through the planning stages of the office building. A year goes by and a real estate investment trust (REIT) comes along and makes you an offer to buy the office building you have not yet constructed. In your deal with the REIT, you enter into a sublease with the REIT for the parking lot property. Your lease with the former owner is $50,000 a year fixed rent for the first 50 years and then tied to a cost of living index starting on the 51st year of the lease. However, the REIT will pay you $150,000 a year in rent.

Your leasehold interest in this parking lot is now worth some serious money. Likely, you could sell the leasehold for $1,000,000 or more. Best of all, the sublease would also likely qualify for Section 1031 treatment and be viable as either a sale and then Starker type exchange or a direct exchange.

Mortgages: Existing mortgages are great exchange items. They will not qualify for 1031 treatment but it is not difficult to get a motivated seller to take one as a part of a transaction. Many real estate investors become bankers of property they sell. They hold first or second mortgages on property they have sold or exchanged to facilitate the transaction. The interest rate will vary, sometimes higher than the market (especially if the price of the property sold was lower than the market), and other times below the market because the seller-held financing was a secondary reason to the transaction (the goal was to get rid of the property and not to create an income stream in the form of a mortgage).

For example, Philip took back a first mortgage on the sale of his mountain lodge in Boone, North Carolina. The sale price was $210,000 and Philip held a first mortgage in the amount of $150,000. The terms were interest only at 6 percent interest per annum (at a time when bank financing was closer to 7.5 percent) for a period of four years. At the end of the fourth year the buyer had the option of paying the mortgage down by $50,000 and continuing for another four years at interest only with a balloon at the end of that term, or simply paying off the mortgage in full at the end of the fourth year.

After three years, Philip made an offer to buy a new home in the Boca Raton area of Florida valued at $650,000. As a part of the offer, he included the $150,000 first mortgage on the mountain lodge, which was the amount still owed. Philip's plan was to use that $150,000 equity as the down payment and to finance the balance of $500,000 with a local savings and loan. The seller of the home reviewed the document, had a quick appraisal made of the mountain lodge, looked over the financial statement of its owner, and countered to Philip that he would do the deal but wanted Philip to discount the mortgage to $135,000. Philip took him up on it and the deal closed.

As it turned out the seller of the home anticipated that the new owner of the lodge would refinance it when the fourth year was up. If that happened, he would get a full payoff of $150,000 plus one year's interest (6 percent of $150,000 = $9,000). As he was guaranteed $15,000 in discount ($150,000 less the $135,000 he allowed for the mortgage) plus the $9,000, he would have a profit of $24,000 on his $135,000 investment. Not a bad deal for him. Philip was satisfied, too, as he had sold the lodge for at least $15,000 more than he had anticipated he would get (at the time).

Options: An option in the stock market can be a valuable commodity, as most stockbrokers will agree. So, too, are options on real estate. For example: You have a lease on the condo apartment you are renting.

You arranged for an option to purchase that same apartment anytime within the first six years of the lease at a fixed price, say $300,000. Suddenly the real estate market goes nuts, and values of condos like the one you are leasing go through the roof. Current sales comparisons indicate that the same model apartment as you have are selling for more than $500,000.

You wake up that morning when those statistics appear in the local newspaper and realize you are in for a potential windfall profit. Realistically, if you want to, you could go ahead and exercise your option and buy that apartment. With the spread between the current market value and your option price you could easily finance the deal, and even put cash in your pocket at the same time. But assume that you want to move on to other areas of the city, county, state, or country. You have a distinct and very salable value. You can use that value by offering it for sale to someone, or you can offer to give that value in an exchange.

Option values are, however, only as good as the terms of those options. Generally there is a time limit to the option, and often that is a specific date, say, the fifth anniversary of the lease or nonlease option to buy.

Nonetheless, options can become valuable. This is something that most people who lease real estate fail to anticipate. The whole idea is this: Often an option to buy that is tied to a lease does not cost you anything—perhaps you got it as an incentive to lease the property in the first place. With this in mind, never lease any real estate without either asking for an option extend the lease for umpteen years at the same rent (which you may have to negotiate for) or asking for an option to purchase the property anytime during the term of the lease (or extensions thereof) at a fixed or negotiated price.

It costs you nothing to ask for an option, and who knows, it might pay off with a big dividend to you in the future. And in the long run, it might give you something of extreme value to sell or exchange.

Use of Your Property: The use of your property has a value, so if you own something that you do not use all the time, you can package the use of it as a value to sell or exchange. What am I talking about? A boat, an airplane, a vacation cottage by the sea or in the mountains, your own home while you are away on a vacation, your new sedan with a driver, an empty office where you work, and so on. I have found that a vacation-type perk is a good way to close a transaction, and as I own several time-share weeks I use them that way. The nice thing about time-shares is there is a nearly endless list of places where they are found. The ones I own are in Orlando, and as Disney World is one of the most sought-after places, the units I own have a high ranking in the exchange pool. This means that when I bank a week with RCI I have an advantage over owners who have banked their weeks from less desirable areas of the world. (Resort Condominiums International is the largest time-share exchange organization in the world. To find out more about the organization and what it offers to time-share owners, check the RCI Community web site at www.rci.com.) Because I rarely have time to use all my weeks we constantly are either giving them away to family, friends, and business contacts to use or including them as perks in exchange offers. What do I exchange for? No one said that you have to exchange for real estate, so I have exchanged the use of one or more weeks of holiday for landscape material, mechanical work, dental work, house painting, handyman help, holiday time in places where there are no time-shares, a boat, charter time on deep-sea fishing boats, charter time in aircraft, cases of wine, scrip at restaurants, jeweler's work, and so on.

People who own fishing boats generally have no problem getting a friend or two to come along for a free afternoon of relaxation and fishing, but no matter how much you use your boat, it generally sits at the dock or on its trailer most of the time. The same can be said for airplanes, mountain lodges, and so on. Put a value on that time and offer it for something you would like to use or do.

If you join an exchange or barter club in your hometown area, you will find that there are many people willing to give you things, or time, or items of value in exchange for time with your assets. Later in this chapter I get into barter and trade organizations in greater depth.

Services: I just mentioned several services that I have exchanged things for: dental work and house painting, just to name two. What do you do? Are you a lawyer, accountant, decorator, mechanic, plumber, landscaper, or electrician? No matter what you do or know how to do, it is likely that your spare time (if you have any) could be put to work as services for exchange. Keep in mind that you do not have to take 100 percent of the value of your service in trade—you can ask for some cash, too.

Eight Motivations of Exchanges

1. Tax-free benefits.

2. Added revenue from lost time.

3. Preforeclosure exchange.

4. Down and then out exchange.

5. Opening closed doors.

6. Face-saving steps.

7. "Why not" exchange.

8. "Spring cleaning" exchange.

Let's review each of these in detail.

Tax-Free Benefits

Tax-free benefits come from exchanges that can qualify for Section 1031 treatment. This is one of the primary motivations to do exchanges, and once the process has begun, real estate investors can plan the rollover of their assets in such a way that they never have to pay the capital gains tax. Not ever.

Using Section 1031 should become a major strategy in your arsenal of investment tools. It should not be a last-minute thing that you do. If you know you are going to sell a property where there will be taxable gain, then before putting the property on the market you must review your situation. If your goal is to move the equity from your present property and reinvest in another investment, then start looking for the new investment right away. Be very careful about accepting an offer if you have not located a suitable replacement property, or if you do, be sure to give yourself substantial time to look around prior to your closing of title. Remember, your 1031 clock begins the day after you close.

Added Revenue from Lost Time

In the list of items to exchange, getting value out of the time that is lost with your investments can increase your bottom line. Many property owners let their personal assets sit around unused. If we are talking about mechanical elements, such as cars, boats, airplanes, and so on, periodic use is good for them. Keep in mind that I do not mean that you have to be a charter boat captain or an airline pilot (unless you already are, of course) to get value out of the time in your boat or airplane. You can generate contacts with those professionals who would be paid for their part of the services while using your boat or airplane.

Lost time is like the airline seat or cruise ship cabin that is empty when the vehicle has departed. There is no way to fill it once it is under way. The same goes for restaurants that do not fill every seat, and end up with leftover food, or cooks that had lots of time to cook more than they did. The point here is that most businesses and services have lost time in one way or another. As a big part of the cost of any service is the combination of rent, overhead, and employees, there has got to be lost time in the operation of any business that is not operating at 100 percent full blast. If you own or operate a business of that nature, then consider what you can exchange your lost time for.

Preforeclosure Exchange

The sharks and wolves are out tonight. That seems to be what happens when the word gets out that you are in deep economic trouble and are headed for foreclosure. Mind you, that is not the end of the world if the property has gained in value and you can recover all of your equity through a sale of the property. But if a buyer does not come along and offer a decent price, you should consider offering your property for exchange.

Many people are ashamed to admit that they are in financial difficulty. They let the situation develop into a nightmare where there just is not enough time to accomplish a well-planned exit from the financial problems. I have been called into situations like this many times when the foreclosure sale was just a few days or weeks away and attempted to salvage something for the owner. One example was a motel that the owner listed with my company for sale. There was absolutely no hint at any financial problems, and the reason the owner gave for wanting to sell was that he was tired of managing the motel. This is a logical reason to sell, but as it turned out he was up to his ears in debt and had run the business into the ground.

Not knowing anything was going badly in the financial department, we launched a marketing program targeting the top price we felt we could get. Four offers came in almost immediately. Two of them included property exchanges for a small part of the equity, but all four of them were off the asking price by 10 to 14 percent. I urged the seller to make counteroffers, but he said he would rather keep the motel than take an exchange, and he was insulted at the low offers.

The end result was that one morning I saw an article in the newspaper that the motel had been closed down and was in receivership. The owner had lost all his equity and was being sued personally for nonpayment of a third mortgage.

If you are approaching a financial difficulty, plan your exit early. Keep an open mind for any potential solution to your problem. Become proactive as a buyer using your property and its equity as a down payment in some other kind of real estate—ideally one that will not have the same financial difficulties.

Down and Then Out Exchange

One of the best ways out of a difficult situation is to go down, then out of the real estate or exchange property. For example, had the owner of the motel mentioned in the prior subsection been honest about his financial difficulties, we might have been able to finesse one of the offers that had been made into one that would have worked. Here is what the deal was. The motel was listed for $2,450,000, and the owner had said the debt was $1,650,000. That would have left him with $800,000 in equity. However, there was another $400,000 (plus or minus) in the form of second and third mortgages and other supplier debts, which brought the total debt to $2,050,000. This dropped his viable equity down to $400,000, which he ultimately lost. One of the offers was for $2,250,000 and included a single-family F&C home that was worth around $375,000. If we could have gotten that party up just a little bit, even another $75,000, the motel owner could have walked out of the motel with a home at least. Even if he had to go into his pocket he could have borrowed against the home, say $100,000 from the present owners of the house, and they could have taken the house at $275,000 equity and dropped the price of the motel to $2,325,000.

Recap of the Motel Solution

Home worth	$ 375,000
Less new mortgage	100,000
Equity in home goes to new motel owners	$ 275,000
New motel owners take over motel and debt	2,050,000
Total paid by new owners of motel	$2,325,000

Opening Closed Doors

Because many highly motivated sellers understand that they are forced to consider any option, they openly look for them. As exchanges are a good way to entice a buyer who may not have considered their property before, they will respond to offers of exchange. Knowing this, savvy exchangers will advertise items for exchange, and will constantly make offers of exchange to any such party when the real estate in question is of even the slightest interest to them.

If you want to test this theory, run an ad in the local newspaper, and make up 20 or so flyers that also advertise that you are a real estate investor who wants to exchange (whatever it is) for real estate and you will also consider other items, which you include in a short list. Here is the information the flyer might contain:

Local Real Estate Investor Wants to Exchange

A beautiful seven-acre single-family tract of land
On Beech Mountain, in western ski territory of North Carolina
Free and clear of debt—zoned for up to six homes
Off main highway, five minutes to Banner Elk, NC
Valued at $150,000
Owner will hold financing, and will exchange equity
into single-family homes, condos, or apartment buildings
in Broward County up to $300,000.
Will also consider vacant farm or grove land
in other areas of Florida up to $400,000.
Contact Jack Cummings—Fax: 954-563-4354

Send the flyer to anyone who calls, and as an additional measure send some to local real estate companies and other sellers of property that is advertised "for sale by owner." Note that one of the keys to an ad like this is that the property you offer, whatever it is, be F&C. You can include jewelry, boats, cars, improved real estate, whatever. If you try this you should price your property fairly and keep an open mind, and you will get some response.

Face-Saving Steps

An exchange of any kind, whether it takes you closer to your goal or not, can be a way of saving face for a motivated seller. You have seen it happen on television when a people will exchange a handful of cash that Monty Hall had just given them for something, they know not what, that is in the big box on the stage. Well, to some degree this is a motivation for some people in real estate exchanges.

Soften this just a little, and you will find that some people will commit to an exchange for something they have not yet seen, but are willing to spend a thousand dollars to fly to Hawaii to inspect. I have entered into exchanges for property thousands of miles away from where I was at the time based on photographs and a description of the property. Fortunately, I did take the time to inspect the property, and have turned down most of such offers after doing my due diligence.

I did this, not because I was trying to save face, but because I recognized that the other party was anxious to make an exchange, no matter what.

"Why Not" Exchange

This kind of exchange motivation is akin to the saving face situation, except that the party who ultimately says, "Why not?" is willing to take the offered property usually for one of two reasons. First, perhaps the exchange item is an insignificant value compared to the overall deal at hand, or second, he or she is convinced that the deal will fall apart unless he or she agrees to take the exchange offered.

Sometimes the party that says "why not" is a broker who has put the deal together and ends up taking the item as a commission in the deal. I have brokered many transactions where my fee came out of the pot of items offered up in the exchange. One such example was a gemstone transaction where my client, a jewelry manufacturer and gemstone broker himself, exchanged a substantial value of gemstones for a horse farm in Ocala, Florida. My cut of the deal was that I got a first look at the stones and could choose from them for part of my fee.

Other transactions have involved situations where one of the parties says "why not" because he or she knew that they could pass off what they were taking as a leg on another transaction they were working on. Here is an example of how that works:

Fran offers to give Steve a down payment of $5,000 plus a diamond-studded bracelet worth $15,000 for a condominium in Orlando, Florida. The condo is worth around $100,000 and Steve is going to hold a wraparound mortgage (a mortgage that is made up of an existing mortgage and an extra amount held by Steve) in the total amount of $80,000. Steve takes the diamond bracelet (after he has a jeweler look at it), because he knows he can use it in an exchange he is negotiating with Jim.

Jim and his partner Brad are in the fur business; they buy out inventory of top designers' showrooms in Europe and bring the merchandise to the United States for resale. They offer big discounts on the top designer goods, but are still making a large profit. Jim has agreed in principle to the idea of taking a $15,000 diamond bracelet in part exchange for a $30,000 mink coat.

Keeping your eyes open is a special talent that exchangers have in common.

Spring-Cleaning Exchange

The bargain basement department store has its annual spring sale, and everything is put on the market at 80 percent off. The idea is to get rid of items that are no longer valuable to the owner. In the same way, many people do this and call it a garage sale.

If you have items of substantial value but that are not doing anything for you, then you can spring-clean your portfolio and offer them as a package. I have made up boxes of books, for example, putting one each of 10 or more books I have written, and used them in personal property exchanges at different exchange clubs for other things or property. Each box might have had a value from $300 to $500 depending on which books were included. Naturally, I would personally autograph the books if the taker was so inclined.

A friend of mine who owned a chain of restaurants had several thousand poker chips made up that advertised the restaurants. Each had a denomination of $25 printed on one side, and on the other side the rules of the exchange. The chips could be used, up to $100 worth, at any sitting in any of his restaurants. They expired in 12 months, and a 20 percent tip had to be in cash. He used them in sacks of $1,000 at exchange clubs, and traded them with restaurant suppliers for part of his bills with them. Every so often he would have a special bash at one of his restaurants where people could use up to $500 at a single sitting. Those special bashes were his way of spring-cleaning the supplies at the restaurant.

Enter the World of Barter

The idea of barter goes back to the earliest days of mankind. There was no money, so the only way that people could take advantage of specialization as a way to maximize production was to barter goods they had for goods they needed. This continues today on a growing scale. Not only do individuals barter between themselves, but businesses as well as countries do it as well.

I can remember a time when I was doing business in Czechoslovakia. It was not uncommon to find vast amounts of fine, high-priced goods from China, available in government-owned shops that only accepted Western European cash or U.S. dollars in return. There were items such as silk rugs and tapestries, hand-carved wood and ivory, and other goods that the government of Czechoslovakia had obtained in exchange for goods it had sent to China. What was Czechoslovakia doing with these goods? Simply this: selling them for hard currencies.

Barter and exchange clubs exist all over the world. It is likely that there are several in your hometown or a city near where you live. I just glanced in the yellow pages of my home city, Fort Lauderdale, Florida, and found two ITEX clubs in the area. ITEX Corporation is one of the largest barter companies in the United States, and several years ago it went public, the first one to do that.

In a search on the Internet I found many such organizations. Rather than list them all, I would suggest you search for yourself, or satisfy yourself with those in the local yellow pages.

The Good, the Bad, and the Ugly of Barter Clubs

Let's Start with the Good: There is a lot of that around. Barter clubs come in many different sizes and types. Some are designed more for the businessperson and cater to things like getting rid of excess inventory, taking advantage of that "lost time" item I have been talking about in this chapter, and helping the businessperson maximize the use of facilities that otherwise are getting only partial use.

Other clubs are designed more for the service-oriented person or business. These clubs allow members to "bank" their talents or services, and then use them in exchange for goods or services provided by other members. They may also use their credits to acquire other goods that are obtained by the management of those clubs for the members by using those banked talents or services.

Still other barter and exchange organizations function somewhat like eBay, in that they allow the members to list what they have to exchange—services, goods, or whatever—and then other members can bid against them using barter currency that is issued by the club for those goods or services.

The Formation of Scrip: Scrip, which is a form of barter money, can also be issued by individual members or services. Remember my restaurant friend? His $25 poker chips served as a form of scrip that could be acquired and then spent in his restaurants. By the way, a certain amount of any scrip that is issued almost always falls through the cracks. In my restaurant friend's case, close to 30 percent of the poker chips that he made and distributed or used as exchange scrip never found their way back to the restaurant. Of those that did, as much as 10 percent came back after they had expired. Oh, his instructions to the restaurants were to take them anyway. That made for goodwill, and almost always ensured a bonus on the tip, which the waiters liked a lot.

The nice part of issuing scrip is that the member doing so gets to choose the format and the redemption rules. Almost always there is a blackout period for restaurants, hotels, and entertainment types of services. It might be that Saturdays are excluded, but that is up to the member making the scrip. Generally, the scrip has strict tipping rules, and cash is not returned if more of the scrip is tendered than the amount of the bill. In essence, if the bill is $80 and you put up $100 in poker chips you would not get any change, plus you would be expected to tip in cash. In that instance perhaps it would have been better to use only $75 in poker chips, and add $5 out of your own pocket.

If you look at the many barter and trade organizations on the Internet, you will quickly discover which ones might offer the kinds of goods and services you want. Feel free to contact them and discuss your needs and what you have to offer their members in exchange. If you do not have a service or talent that would be accepted, perhaps you have something you can sell to collect the credits or barter currency you can then use to acquire the goods offered.

What about the Bad? There is some of that, too. Generally the bad part of barter and trade is that you might not find the kinds of goods or services that you would want or need. What happens is that there may be dentists in the club, and you could use one, but try to get an appointment! Somehow you never are able to do that. Mind you, I had a relatively good experience with a dentist in a barter club. He was there when I needed him, I never had appointment problems, and I continued using his services long after both of us stopped being members of that specific exchange organization.

Why did we drop out? In my case it was mostly because I could not spend all the credits I was accumulating. When that happens, then the management of the organization is not doing what it should to bring in goods or services that are needed by its members, or those goods or services just are not available in the area for barter or trade.

Another barter organization I belonged to for several years operated in New York City. I used its services a great deal, mostly hotel accommodations and restaurants when I visited New York City for my several trips a year to talk things over with my literary agent and/or different publishers. That company is no longer in business because the owner moved to Chicago, where I believe he is operating a similar company.

The Ugly: Yes, there can be an ugly side to barter and trade organizations. I have seen several that just could not keep their members happy, and out of desperation they began to print up lots of scrip that would go sour. Here is what was happening. There would be recruitment drives to bring in new members, mostly restaurants, bars, entertainment clubs, and hotels in the community. To get a lot of barter currency out on the street, the management would encourage generous amounts be issued for each service. Generous timetables would be allowed, and large amounts of scrip use at any time. Service-starved members would queue up to acquire the scrip, and overwhelm the participating restaurants with the use of the barter currency. The restaurants either would go out of business for lack of real cash spenders or look like they were doing so much business that they would sell out to someone else. That someone else would post a sign saying, "No barter club currency allowed."

Does this mean you do not join a barter club? For goodness' sake, no. But you should investigate the club and its owners and ask to interview some of the members. Start small in the club and do not build up too large a bank of credits or barter currency. If you cannot spend what you have over a 45-day period, then pull back or drop out.

CHAPTER 9

Thirteen Creative
Techniques Applied
to Exchanges

The goal of this chapter is:

**To Build Your Ability to Mix Different Techniques to Enable
You to Close More Transactions**

Within the art of negotiation, there lies a toolbox filled with techniques and strategies. Experienced real estate investors know how to draw on these tools to help them successfully go to contract to acquire a desired property. When the market is hot, sellers rule the game and investors have to work hard to find good investments. In a hot market there will be other investors seeking the same thing you seek. Spoils of the hunt (the property in question) will go to the investor who acts decisively and is able to tie up the property before another investor beats him or her to it. The later investment steps such as due diligence, financing, and closing will occur once you have completely inspected the property and are satisfied that you have made a proper decision with your initial offer. Alternatively, you will attempt to renegotiate, and if that does not work, you will have to abandon the idea of acquiring that property.

The key to all this is that first element, to lock up the property. With that clearly in focus, think of every element contained in this book as one of the tools available to you. Exchanges and the various techniques of exchanging are simply tools. And they can be highly effective in enabling you to lock up a property.

Terms and Concepts You Need to Know

Creative Financing
Tenant-in-Common Interests

Let's review each in detail.

Creative Financing

Some years ago I submitted one of my "creative financing" lecture programs to the State of California's real estate education board to qualify it for continuing education for real estate salespeople. California, like many other states (Florida included), has annual education requirements that salespeople and brokers licensed within the respective state must take. Failure to meet the requirements will place the license to function as a broker or salesperson in jeopardy, and ultimately cause one to lose that right.

The course in question that I submitted to the appropriate person in California elicited a long, tongue-lashing kind of letter that in essence asked me how I could suggest that brokers, salespersons, and their clients ever consider using some of the highly risky creative financing techniques that were contained in the course. The woman who wrote the letter went on to point out some of the examples of such supposedly highly risky elements in my program. I called her and we had an interesting conversation for about 45 minutes, at the end of which I concluded that this person had not carefully read the program and/or she did not understand the concept of risk.

Everything you do in the way of making an investment has a margin of risk connected to it. The fact that much of my program dealt with either new ideas or old ideas used in new ways had mystified her. She had mistaken the whole point of being creative and, as I had pointed out in the program, the idea was to have a win-win situation where both the buyer and the seller benefit by moving closer to their desired goals.

The lecture program that California ultimately turned down as being about "highly risky techniques" was at that same time being offered in other states that had no such objections, and had been attended by many brokers and salespeople who praised it as an eye-opening way to better serve their clients. This chapter contains all of the creative techniques and strategies that the California person objected to, tied in with using exchanging as an investment tool. To make things very clear, the intent of using anything creative is that it becomes an alternative to having to walk away from a deal that fails to work with conventional real estate investing techniques. I think you will find these techniques no more risky than going to a savings and loan and taking out a loan to buy a property—a loan, by the way, that may be at a higher interest rate and cost you more to close on than some of the so-called highly risky elements contained in this chapter.

Tenant-in-Common Interests

This is a new method of effecting a deferred exchange. What I am referring to is the acquisition of a partial interest in a Section 1031 qualified property that is owned by a group of people with the ownership reflected in tenant-in-common interests. Take for example a family-held office building where five members of the family own the property as tenants-in-common and their interests are all equal. Therefore, each of these five members owns a 20 percent interest in the office building.

Two other members of the family, outside this clique of five, have just sold a real estate investment they have owned for several years as an investment. They have anticipated doing a deferred exchange so have set up the deal in such a way that the funds from the closing on their property will go to an intermediary pending the identification of a replacement property. Once they find a replacement property (within the 1031 clock timetable), they will close. However, they are having problems finding a replacement property, and let the family know that they are in the market and have only a short time to identify a new investment. One of the group of five decides to sell his interest in the family-held office building. The amount of funds, which will be held by the intermediary, is not quite enough, but the investor members decide to add the balance to acquire that tenant-in-common interest.

So far, the only wrinkle in this is the relationship of the parties. All these people are members of the same family, and in the past the IRS frowned on dealings between family members. However, the Section 1031 rules were modified to allow one relative to sell to another, provided that the buying party holds the property for a minimum of two years. This holding period was imposed to keep one family member from selling to another to shelter gain within the family.

This new ruling, together with 12 rather strict management rules established by the tenant-in-common entity, has spawned an entirely new industry in the United States. This is the institutionalization of Section 1031 to the point where anyone who enters into a deferred exchange likely will qualify to invest in a tenant-in-common interest of real estate. Wall Street has jumped on this concept and there are major offerings that are made, so far more or less privately, that give investors the opportunity to place their escrowed 1031 money into large investment properties. These may be $80,000,000 office parks, mammoth shopping malls, and/or hotel chains—investments that heretofore were so large that the only buyers that could afford them were insurance companies, large private and public real estate holding companies who operated such facilities, as well as REITs.

In the circle of real estate exchanging, these kinds of interests are called tenant-in-common (TIC) interests. This chapter concludes with a section about TICs straight from one of the most noted U.S. experts in this subject.

Thirteen Creative Techniques for Exchanges

Each of these techniques has many different uses and formats. Naturally, I cannot give you every example that would exist, but I will try to vary the way the techniques are used so that you will see how you can mix and match them in your presentations. I want you to consider two elements when you read each. First, either side of the transaction could be the one proposing the deal. A party offering to exchange $50,000 of advertising credit at a local radio or TV station as a down payment on a $300,000 developer's home would be one approach. An owner of a $300,000 home (possibly the developer himself) might offer a radio or TV station the home with a $250,000 first mortgage for $50,000 in radio or TV time. All of these techniques, I caution you again, are, according to that California person, highly risky. I would like you to judge for yourself whether they are simply creative or a threat to your family fortune. Here is the list.

1. Accommodation exchange.
2. Paper exchange.
3. Pyramid exchange.
4. Double exchange.
5. Future exchange.
6. Mixed bag exchange.
7. Sweat equity exchange.
8. "No sweat off my brow" exchange.
9. Prepaid rent exchange.
10. Leaseback exchange.
11. Personal property exchange.
12. Commission exchange.
13. Tenant-in-common exchange.

Let's review each of these items in detail.

Accommodation Exchange

An accommodation exchange is one where the party who takes the exchange property doesn't really want it and has no real use for it, but takes it anyway. This exchange occurs when the person attempting to acquire a property has made an offer that includes, as a part of the deal, a property the would-be buyer owns or can deliver. Here is an example.

Curt's Accommodation Exchange: Curt has been negotiating to buy a strip mall of 15 retail shops that is on the market for $4,000,000. The owner, Manolo, built the complex 25 years earlier, and the property is F&C. His tax base in the property is $800,000, which would indicate that his capital gain could be $3,200,000.

Curt has a limited amount of cash to use, and lots of other real estate that is sitting in his portfolio. The negotiations have bogged down with Manolo insisting on a minimum of $3,000,000 in cash, and he will hold either a land lease (with a buyout value of $1,000,000) or secondary financing for the missing $1,000,000.

Curt makes one last stab at successfully concluding the negotiations and offers Manolo $3,200,000 in cash for the buildings and a trade of a commercial tract of land he owns easily worth $800,000 for the land under the center. Curt has divided the retail center into two elements: improvements for which he will pay cash, and land (under the improvements), which he will pay for in the form of an exchange.

This kind of offer has several interesting aspects to it. First, Manolo will be able to qualify for a Section 1031 deferred exchange on the $3,200,000 part of the deal and can accomplish a deferred exchange if he can find a replacement property in time. The land-for-land transaction also will qualify, so that part of the deal works under the rules of Section 1031.

The advantage for Manolo is that it is likely that he will be able to conclude this acquisition without reaching into his pocket for cash. All he has to do is get a lender to put up $3,300,000 (plus costs of the loan) and Manolo can use the $800,000 value of the land-for-land part of the deal as his equity. As Manolo is an experienced operator of strip stores, he may be a reasonable risk to a lender on an 80/20 loan-to-value ratio.

However, Manolo has an ace that he could play if needed. He would agree to lease back the land, with an option to recapture it in a few years if pushed to do that. He had originally acquired the land to build a new center, and could still do that if the seller pushed on the deal. Nevertheless, the seller does not, and the deal goes forward, even though he has no real interest in the land Manolo offers him. What Manolo does do, however, is dispel any doubts about the value of the land being worth the offered $800,000.

Another transaction of a different magnitude would be one where Susan wanted to sell the apartment her mother had left her. It was worth around $250,000 and she had no tax liability at that value. It was F&C, and she wanted to move out of Florida. She understood the essence of exchanges, and had, in fact, contacted several real estate brokers in New York City, where she wanted to move, and had indicated she would consider an exchange into an apartment there.

Several offers came in, and one was three years of prepaid rent in an apartment in Hoboken, New Jersey, that amounted to $45,000 of prepaid rent. Susan knew the area (which was a few blocks from where Frank Sinatra had lived), but she did not want to live in Hoboken, even though it was a quick subway trip under the Hudson River into Manhattan.

However, the offer was for her full price, and the New York broker said that if the offering party would allow Susan to subrent the apartment, he could convert that into a profit over the period of time. Therefore, Susan, not wanting the Hoboken apartment at all, saw the wisdom in making the deal. It was ripe, it had a quick closing, and if she had to, she could actually stay there for a while.

Motivation of the parties (both sides of the deal) and the size of the transaction all affect the outcome of an accommodation deal. Usually each side is making some kind of trade-off. The offering party wants to use some equity other than cash, and the receiving party wants to maximize what cash they do get. In each instance, if the offering party can completely or nearly so finance the cash side of the transaction, there will be more give on the noncash side. In Susan's case, the original offer might have been only 30 months of prepaid rent. Or the New York broker handling the deal for Susan might have contacted some of his clients who owned rental apartments in the New York City area and offered them the opportunity to use prepaid rent instead of cash out of their pockets as the down payment on a beautiful oceanfront condominium in Fort Lauderdale. Now there is a proactive broker in action.

Show Me the Risk: In the accommodation exchange, risk is all a matter of making a sound business decision. If you remove the exchange element from the deal, would you still enter into the transaction? If the answer is yes, then surely there is no risk to you in taking something you do not want or need. However, if the deal is very close and you can get something that has real value—an F&C lot, prepaid rent, or whatever—even if you don't want it, are you so secure that a better deal will come along that you can afford to turn the deal down? Think about that one for a moment. That box behind the curtain may be valuable in the future.

Paper Exchange

The paper exchange is one where a property owner gives up his or her property to a buyer who promises to pay an all or part down payment. This promise to pay is either a mortgage on that or other real estate or a note that is secured by some other asset or is unsecured.

Krandle's Paper Acquisition: Krandle wants to buy your 10-unit apartment building. You are motivated for the profit from the deal, and want to take advantage of the fact that the IRS has reduced the capital gains tax rate to a maximum of 15 percent. You think this is going to go back to a much higher rate, and you do not want to lose the opportunity.

Krandle comes along and offers you your price, but he wants you to hold a first mortgage on his mother's home. That home is worth more than double the amount of the mortgage, so you agree to hold the mortgage. However, you want to limit the term to five years. Krandle agrees, as long as he has to pay interest only and no principal during the five years with a balloon payment at the end of the term.

Everyone agrees, and the deal closes. Krandle likes this transaction because he is able to obtain a construction takeout loan as he is going to convert the units to a condo, and expects to be out of the picture long before the five-year period ends.

Show Me the Risk: Paper may be only as valuable as the person's word, plus the security that backs it up. A bank will charge a borrower based on that person's credit score, past history with that institution (or others they can check on), the loan-to-value ratio (in the event of a mortgage on real property), and what other security the borrower may be able to put up.

What the bank never is interested in, however, is how motivated you are to dispose of the real estate you are selling that person.

Whether you take back secondary paper yourself in a transaction or take existing paper that is secured by other assets, you must first weigh the benefit of the overall deal. Never let the decision on the sale of a $500,000 property that you can no longer afford interfere with a $25,000 second mortgage on the buyer's grandmother's condo in Florida if you can determine that the paper is safe and that you are willing to wait the term of years for full payout. However, do your due diligence, check out the validity of the deal. (Does the grandmother know about this, and has she agreed? What is the real value of the condo? What is the amount of the existing debt on that condo?)

Remember, when you are offered paper of any nature, get personal signatures from as many co-signers as you can, check the title on real estate that is reported to be security on that paper, and run a credit check on the persons co-signing the note or mortgage.

Pyramid Exchange

There is a technique in real estate investing that involves a pyramid. Do not confuse this with pyramid buying schemes that depend on a growing pyramid of friends or other people to buy and sell items on which, it is claimed, everyone will get a commission or bonus of some kind. Most of those ventures are not worth getting into. But this is not that kind of pyramid, and, as you will see, it is rather creative.

A real estate pyramid is a technique where you can end up buying two or more properties leveraging your equity from one property to another. It will require the party who initiates the transaction either to own or control the use of a second property or to have a substantial net worth value to make his or her personal signature worth its weight on a personal note. Here is an example:

Horacio's Dealership Pyramid: Horacio is a car dealer who wants to acquire a tract of land on which he can build a new dealership. He anticipates that it will take him 18 months to build the new dealership and have it up and running once he has the land. But, like many businessmen, he does not want to tie up his cash in the purchase of the land. So, when he finds a tract that is of interest to him, he offers the seller a second mortgage on one of his existing dealerships for 100 percent of the value of the land. In his offer, Horacio spells out the terms of the second mortgage as being 7 percent interest only per year for the first 24 months, and 10 percent per year plus $50,000 principal per year for the next 10 years until paid off. Horacio adds that the loan can be prepaid by him anytime without a penalty. Remember, by the end of 24 months, Horacio expects to be in operation at the new facility (with six months to spare).

At this point Horacio has his site for the new dealership and the initial interest payments on that site have started. He goes to a lender with this F&C land and finances the improvements for the new dealership. A few months later, Horacio finds another site where he would like to build an auto repair complex to serve his several dealerships in the community. He goes to the owner and shows him the plans and photos of the new dealership that he has just started building. He explains what his existing financing is on that dealership, shows bank estimates as to what the value of the completed project will be, and offers that property owner the same kind of deal as was offered the other land owner some few months earlier.

Horacio has, of course, solid equity in this new dealership under construction because he acquired that land F&C of any debt. He now has a second site, which also is F&C for the same reason.

Show Me the Risk: Again we have seen a well-informed investor seek to use the value of an asset as security to acquire a new property or investment. By keeping the new acquisition as free of debt as possible, the investor maximizes his or her ability to finance new development on that project.

Pyramid investment in real estate works best when there is ultimately new construction or remodeling and fix-up of the acquired property. This enables a stepped-up value to occur and new equity to be generated. If Horacio had been building condominiums instead of car dealerships, he would have been able to show the investors his whole pattern of buy, sell, and move on. From the seller's point of view, the risk is the same that any lender would take in making a loan: the magnitude of the value of the property in question. Only, as I have stated, the seller will have other agendas to serve and other goals to meet than just making a loan. As with any loan, the person who holds the mortgage on another property must use prudent judgment and get as much information as possible on the property. Usually, the person asking for this kind of transaction will not be presenting a high loan-to-value ratio. All they are asking for is to leave their cash at work, and as they plan to pay off the loan early once they can refinance the construction, these loans can have a short term.

Double Exchange

The double exchange is a type of pyramid exchange where you can go to contract with two deals at the same time. When using the double exchange you are able to pyramid into two properties you do not own at present, and from them into others. Let's look at an example of the double exchange.

Bill's Nothing Down Exchange: Bill has been looking for fixer-upper properties in his comfort zone for several months, and has found four that have good potential for nearly immediate value enhancement with some tender loving care. Bill knows from past sales in his comfort zone that the majority of fix-up is cosmetic, landscape, new front doors, fresh paint inside and out, and occasionally upgrades to the kitchen and bathrooms of the properties. He targets two of the four properties he knows will fit his criteria.

Property 1: A duplex that is on the market for $175,000. It is on a lot that is zoned to permit four residential units, and has a detached garage that can be converted into a nice apartment. There is an existing first mortgage on this property of $50,000.

Property 2: An older two-story home, also with a detached garage, in the same area of town on a lot that will allow three residential units. It is offered for sale at $150,000 and is free and clear.

Bill does some quick homework on these two properties. His plan would be to convert the duplex with garage into four units. This will re-quire approximately $25,000 of supplies and material plus around 300 hours of his own time in the property. For the older home, he plans to add an exterior stairway and new entrance to the upper level of the home, making it a penthouse apartment, while adding an extra bedroom and bath to the downstairs portion. The roof over the new bedroom and bath will become a screened porch off the living area of the penthouse. The garage will be turned into a large studio apartment.

Bill's estimated cost for the remodeling of the second property is $30,000 in supplies and materials plus another 300 hours of his or other workers' labor. For the labor part, Bill plans to do most of the more com-plicated part himself, such as electrical, plumbing, and finish carpentry, which he believes will be a total of 200 hours total for both properties combined. He values his time at $40 per hour, and for the other work he knows he can hire competent labor for $20 per hour. His total fix-up and improvements for the two properties are outlined here.

Estimated Investment Cost

	Property 1	Property 2
Purchase price	$175,000	$150,000
Labor (Bill's)	4,000	4,000
Labor (other workers')	4,000	4,000
Supplies and materials	25,000	30,000
Total cost	$208,000	$188,000
Combined total for both units		$396,000

Bill estimates resale values for the properties once renovations are com-pleted. These values are after the deduction of any costs of sales, such as legal costs and sales fees, and built into the cost of labor, supplies, and materials are any other fees or interest he may have to pay. Wherever possible, Bill will take major steps not to interrupt any existing rent that is coming in. He may actually get a lot of cooperation in this respect from any existing tenants by offering them a preconstruction completion price on the new condominium units.

Resale Values Net to Bill After Work Is Completed

Property	*Resale Value*	*Less Total Cost*	*Net Profit*
Property 1	$275,000	$208,000	$ 67,000
Property 2	$255,000	$188,000	$ 67,000
Total net sale price	$530,000		
Total profit from sale of new units			$134,000

Bill is confident that his numbers are conservative and that he can do all that is necessary to make everything work.

Armed with his architect's drawings of how the finished buildings are going to look, he goes to the owner of the first property and makes an offer. Bill will take over the existing first mortgage and give the seller $25,000 in cash and a second mortgage on the second property in the amount of $50,000 plus the balance of the purchase price of $50,000 (plus interest) when the units are sold.

Recap of Bill's Offer on Property 1

Assume existing first mortgage	$ 50,000
Add cash to seller's pocket	25,000
Give seller second mortgage on property 2	50,000
Cash balance when units are sold	50,000
Total purchase price	$175,000

Bill then goes to the owner of property 2 and offers him a second mortgage on property 1 in the amount of $50,000, $50,000 in cash, and the balance of $50,000 when the units are sold.

The best way for Bill to close this deal would be for him to have the cash part of the fix-up in hand. That would be a total of $69,000 for the two properties. Keep in mind that $8,000 of that is Bill's own time at $40 per hour. If he did not have the full amount of cash needed to move forward on the deal he could seek a development loan from a local bank for the package deal. Based on an ultimate sellout, which would net $530,000, it would be likely that Bill would qualify for up to 70 percent of that amount, or $371,000 in new loans. If that was the case and he had some cash, he could choose a more conventional deal. However, the double exchange as shown would be the least costly route to follow, as there would be no loan origination costs with the institutional lender.

Show Me the Risk: The potential risk in any of the pyramid-type transactions is that the party making the exchange will become overextended with excessive debt and/or be unable to accomplish the level of improvements that generally go along with this kind of transaction. However, if you are negotiating with someone who is offering you a deal that looks like this kind of transaction, then pay close attention to the following. Ask the person what his or her record of accomplishment is and for references from other people he or she has dealt with in this kind of transaction. Now I know that might not be fair to the first-timer who is genuine and wants to do this kind of a transaction, but stick to your guns and either require a glowing past performance report or, if it is a first-time venture for the investor/developer, then expect that individual to put some cash into the deal, and ask for co-signers as well.

If you are trying to do this for the first time, make it as good a deal for the other party as you possibly can. You will build your reputation by being fair and honest with the people you do business with, and your good reputation will stay with you for the rest of your life.

Future Exchange

This exchange is a favorite with condominium developers. For example, Morris, who is a well-known condominium developer in Fort Lauderdale, has a good reputation in the community and is always on the lookout for good sites for new condominium developments.

He came to my office one day as the result of a conversation he had with one of his staff whom I knew very well and explained what he wanted. A few days later after making a few phone calls I stopped by his office and told him I had exactly what he wanted. I paused in my presentation and added, "But it will be a bit complicated as there is a land lease we have to buy out."

Morris smiled, as I thought he would. He loved a challenge, as I had been told, and he took pride in being able to put tough deals together. After all, he agreed with me, if it was easy, someone already would have bought the property.

The property was an oceanfront hotel right on the sand (as we say in Fort Lauderdale, where most of the "oceanfront" hotels are separated from the beach by a road). This hotel had changed hands many times over the 30 years of its life, and I personally brokered four of the previous five sales, so I was very familiar with the owners and the details of the land, which had been with the property since its original construction.

As it was, Hort, the trustee of his mother's estate, was in control of the land. It was easy to put him and Morris together, and nearly as quick as a hummingbird Morris made a deal that involved giving Hort his choice of several of the new condos (when they were built), plus $2,000,000 in cash when the building was 80 percent sold out.

The leasehold interest was held by other clients of mine to whom I had sold the hotel several years earlier. They owned another hotel in the same block, and had not been able to consolidate the management of the two hotels as they thought they could, and at a profit were ready sellers.

Scott's Condominium Exchange with Purvin: Purvin is both a good friend and a very good client. Over the past dozen or so years, Cummings Realty had brokered many millions of dollars in real estate sales and acquisitions for him and his family. Of them, we assembled three waterfront properties for him in a nice residential neighborhood that were zoned for multifamily apartments. There were 21 apartments spread between three buildings that had been owned by three separate owners before Purvin's acquisition. A year after the assemblage we brought a developer, Scott, to the property and suggested that he enter into a joint venture of sorts with Purvin and acquire the property. By the time the smoke cleared, Scott had tied up the property with an agreement to pay Purvin a profit that would turn out to be $2,000,000 over the $3,000,000 original purchase price. Of that profit, there was a bonus of $1,200,000 that was to be a percentage of the total sales amount of the units. Another future deal successfully concluded.

In his transaction, Morris was the buyer and he initiated the transaction. In Purvin's case, we, as his broker, structured a deal that made economic sense and I went out and found a developer who agreed. Scott was not the first developer I approached, but he quickly saw the advantage to the deal I brought to him.

The future exchange can be a very exciting approach for marketing developmental property. If you own a good development site a good approach to maximize your ultimate return on the sale of that site could well be to approach developers with the idea of a joint venture form of purchase. In both of the examples, I have shown the actual transaction was less of a joint venture and more of a sale with a minimum price and a bonus at the end when the condominium units reached a certain sales percentage.

It is important to respect the problems that most developers have to go through these days. While some communities are more development oriented and not only welcome the new addition to their tax base, but actually go out and seek developers to come to their community, other areas, like South Florida, are becoming a nightmare for the development world. Zoning laws are constantly changed and or in some sort of flux, which means they are being changed but we do not know to what extent yet. Because of these problems and delays in obtaining final permission to build or finding out exactly what you can build at that, sellers who will work with a developer give the developer the time it takes to get the approvals. These approvals, by the way, can cost hundreds of thousands of dollars even when developers are never sure they will get the approvals that will work economically.

Show Me the Risk: The risk in offering a seller a future interest in the new project to be built or remodeled is more for the buyer than for the seller. The seller generally has a minimum price that must be met, and the transaction is usually tied to a certain timetable. If the buyer (the developer) takes longer to get the approvals than the original timetable anticipated, the contract should contain extensions by additional payments made to the seller.

There are certain safeguards that the seller should insist on. First, if there is any debt on the property, that should receive the first priority to be paid off before the start of any development. Some principal should also be paid to the seller, and only the bonus part of the deal should be part of the future part of the deal. In essence, if the fair price of Purvin's three properties had been $3,800,000, then the bonus of $1,200,000 would be reasonable for the final payment to him when the sales reached the target amount.

Mixed Bag Exchange

This is an interesting kind of exchange that would be very difficult to attain except through an exchange organization. Basically, the mixed bag exchange consists of multiple properties and multiple owners coming together to structure the transaction. Expert broker assistance is critical in these transactions, because they will appear to be impossible and can frustrate even some experienced exchangers the first couple of times they attempt them.

These exchanges generally begin by a process that builds legs to the transaction. Remember, a leg is something that is offered in by a person who is a taker for the property that is available.

Mixed Bag: Example: Suppose you have eight F&C time-share weeks in Puerto Vallarta at one of the top resorts in Mexico. They may have originally sold for $20,000 each, which would give them an owner's value of $160,000 for the package. Wolf might offer you two 10-acre ranchettes in western Texas for the package of the eight weeks. Wolf would be quick to tell you (and anyone else listening) that he can replicate the offer as he has a total of 100 10-acre ranchettes remaining in his Texas development. So far, this is just the start of the leg-building process, which may occur during a zander session at the exchange organization or club.

The word *zander* is actually the common name for a type of pikeperch that is found in European waters. In the exchange group a moderator will select a property that will be at the center of a large board—say, your package of eight Puerto Vallarta weeks. The first step in the zander is a fishing expedition (ergo this could be why it is named after a fish) where the members of the exchange club are asked what they might put up in exchange to become a taker of the time-share weeks in the center of the board.

There might be many offers, some ridiculous, some absolutely outrageous. But some may actually be sincere and have merit. The moderator will cull out the ridiculous and outrageous proposals offered, and center on a core of up to 10 offers that he writes on the board around the center. Let's assume there are five offers and here is what they are:

Offers Made on the Center of the Board

1. A villa in Portugal that overlooks the Atlantic ocean, with 40 acres of land around it and a full operational wine-processing plant in the cellar. Value $400,000 and is F&C, balanced to the $160,000 time-share value with the owner holding a soft mortgage of $240,000 ($160,000 equity).

2. The two 10-acre ranchettes in western Texas, and more can be added ($160,000 equity).

3. A thousand acres of pasture land in Argentina, 200 miles west of Buenos Aires, valued at $660,000 that has a $500,000 first mortgage on it ($160,000 equity).

4. A condominium in Miami, with an owner's value of $280,000 and a first mortgage of $120,000 ($160,000 equity). Owner will balance with other equities from the taker.

5. A future condominium in a future development that has not started yet, up to $300,000 in value, credit given for the $160,000 time-share weeks.

The moderator will then ask the members if there is anything that they would like to offer on any of the five items that had been offered on the time-share weeks. The process continues and after those proposals are culled out by the moderator, assume that there are two offers on each of these five. They are:

Offers Made on the Second-Tier Properties

On item 1:
    A. A tract of F&C land in North Carolina worth $290,000 and a soft mortgage for the balance of $110,000.
    B. A deepwater home in Stuart, Florida, worth $1,000,000 for the Portuguese villa plus $600,000 cash back to balance the deal.

On item 2:

    C. A 200-acre farm in Georgia with house and barn and equipment, value $550,000 F&C for three 10-acre ranchettes ($240,000 value) plus $350,000 in cash.

    D. A selection of 15 different time-share resorts from a time-share developer, taker's choice up to $160,000 in value.

On item 3:

    E. Item B (above). However, the 1,000 acres must be F&C and the Stuart home will have a mortgage of only $340,000 on it.

    F. An amount of $500,000 cash, plus $200,000 selection from appraised gemstones (at retail value).

On item 4:

    G. A residential lot fronting on a golf course near Hilton Head, South Carolina. Owner's value is $300,000, will balance with $20,000 of a soft mortgage ($280,000 equity).

On item 5:

    H. A $1,500,000 F&C deepwater home in Fort Lauderdale, for equal value of F&C future condominiums.

    I. An amount of $100,000 cash, plus $300,000 in selection of lots in a North Carolina mountain subdivision.

Look back over the results of this zander. It should be obvious to you that the center of the board, the eight time-share weeks in Puerto Vallarta, controls everything that has gone up. Because of this, any element of the second tier of offerings (1 through 5) can also control the whole board if they move to the center. In that way, it is possible for multiple exchanges to occur.

For example, the outer layer of the board (A through I) can be exchanged without any direct connection to the center of the board, or involvement with the original eight time-shares in Mexico.

However, those owners who can replicate their offers, like the time-share developer who offered a selection from 100 different resorts, could deal with anyone who might want some of those weeks. Who would? Remember, each player in the zander has his or her own agenda to be served. F&C items, even time-share weeks, are often traded around much like currency. If you get a good deal on the weeks, you will discover a new realm of travel that you may not have experienced before. It is not the time-share that is bad; it is the value you pay for it that can be bad. By dealing with exchangers in exchange clubs, you will come across time-share weeks at some real bargain prices—if you are inclined to take them.

Show Me the Risk: Zanders function much like an auction. You can be caught up in the fast-paced action of the board. If the moderator is good, then many deals will be made and closed. Keep in mind that everything is based on the premise that each party to the zander exchange has the opportunity to make an inspection of the property. However, that inspection is limited to the honesty of the description of the property offered. In essence, if you are offered a sailboat and it is fully described to you as to its condition, age, color, type, and so on, you actually see a photograph, and you make the inspection that proves it to be exactly what it was described to be, and nevertheless you back out of the deal, then don't show up at the exchange club the next meeting.

Exchangers deal with people they learn to trust. Make one bad deal, one "this property is priced way below the market" statement that turns out to be a lot of baloney, then a moderator or fellow exchanger is apt to caution you. Make a misleading statement a second time and you will likely end your reputation as an exchanger in that circle at least. So, move to another town and start over.

Look, people are what they are. You have to try something to learn it. Everyone will forgive any mistake you make, even your first outright prefabrication. People do get fed up, sick to death, overly anxious, and distraught at some of the silliest things; they also get divorced, remarried, or ill, and some of them even get so disappointed with themselves that they just up and die.

People become incapable of paying off their debts or their monthly rent or car payments or alimony and they file for bankruptcy. Some people are able to make good sound snap decisions that stick, because they live by their good word and expect the same from other people. These people are often disappointed, but they never lose hope as they know it is better to expect more than some people can give because it encourages them to improve, to do better.

People act with a spontaneity of energy that can surprise or even shock you, or they loll around in an endless daze and are never quite sure where they parked their car, or what time of day it is, or even what day of the week it is. These people never quite grasp the point and rarely if ever make important decisions, but end up with decisions out of default because others have taken their chances away from them and they are left with the only option left, whatever it is.

People fall in love, hate, become consumed with jealousy, and try to hide their envy of others; often all these emotions can be directed to the same person. They can feel all these things because they are only human, which means they are full of faults and doubts and self-conscious about their actions, yet they can still feel pride, and not be ashamed at letting tears flow.

They are afraid of failure, and often fail because they do not make a decision at a time when any decision at all would have been sufficient. They are like you, and me.

When it comes to real estate investing, or investing in anything, you cannot depend on someone else making a mistake that turns your decision into a winner. Your profit or loss will not be a function of luck, although you might think that you are really lucky at having purchased something that turns out to be a big winner. Your profit or loss will simply depend on you doing what is necessary to get the facts, and to learn all you can about the real estate you want to buy, in the area you have chosen.

Sweat Equity Exchange

In a sweat equity exchange you use your labor, talent, or services as all or part of a transaction.

Sweat Equity Example: Rupert wants to purchase a fixer-upper duplex so that he can move his family into one side and rent out the other for income to help pay the mortgage he will likely have on the property. He finds one he likes that is on the market for $185,000. Rupert anticipates the work will cost him around 200 hours of his labor, which he values at $30 per hour or $6,000, plus an additional $20,000 for supplies and material. He knows that his best chance for financing will come once the property has been fixed up. Rupert makes a deal with the seller to allow him to tie up the property with a firm contract for $211,000 (the $185,000 plus the $20,000 of supplies and material and Rupert's $6,000 of labor). The closing will occur within six months, and Rupert agrees to complete all the work on the property within that time or forfeit the deal and lose the time, effort, and money he will have spent by that time.

The seller agrees, but insists that Rupert put the $20,000 into the closing agent's escrow, so it can be spent only toward the supplies and material that are earmarked for the property.

Show Me the Risk: If you are the seller and someone is offering you a down payment on your real estate that is tied to sweat equity, you need to protect yourself by not passing title until the sweat has been fully shed, and the work completed as promised. The biggest risk in any sweat equity deal is to have no guarantee that the work will be completed as promised on the timetable as outlined, and the quality of the work will be exactly as Leonardo da Vinci would have done it. Do not be such a trusting person that you let someone get ahead of you that way.

However, if you are offering your sweat equity in a deal, then do not underestimate the time it will take you, what you will have to spend for supplies and/or materials, and added labor when you get in over your head with a job that you cannot cope with.

For example, the electrician I hired to upgrade the electrical switches in my home recently was doing fine until he came to a three-way switch. A three-way switch is where two on/off switches in different locations (say upstairs and downstairs) will each turn on and off the same light. I got a clue that he was having trouble when he spent two hours going up and down the stairs working on those two switches. Except for that, he was great.

"No Sweat Off My Brow" Exchange

This is an advanced version of the sweat equity exchange. It could just as well be called the Tom Sawyer exchange, because although it involves sweat equity, the sweat comes from others and not you.

I have seen this exchange used many times in exchange clubs where there is easy access to labor for trade. I have also had this element play a role with several exchanges that I have closed for my own portfolio. It is very simple, as the example shows.

Chuck's Sweat, Bob's Equity Exchange: Bob belongs to a local exchange club in the Tampa, Florida, area. He wanted to remodel a couple of properties he owned, and had exchanged a vacant lot worth $30,000 he had in the Orlando area for construction work from a local builder. As it turned out, the builder, Chuck, was a general contractor who frequently had workmen sitting around for days on end with little to do, yet they were on his payroll, so anything that he could get in value for their lost time would be better than nothing.

Bob was in the process of negotiating an exchange that would enable him to lease the subject property (a 20-unit motel that he planned to convert to a wholesale/retail antiques center). He had previously locked up $30,000 of construction time with Chuck, which he was now going to cash in.

The deal with the seller was that Bob would give the owner of the motel rent for the next six months, based on the income that the owner had taken in the previous year for that same period less the operational expenses that the owner would not have. In essence, the owner could take the next six months off and make the same amount of money he did the previous year for that time. As it was the absolute bottom of the season, it turned out that the rent was going to be very reasonable.

In the end, Chuck's men were kept busy, and Bob did not have to front any cash other than the rent. Bob even let the workers use the motel over weekends; as long as they self-catered the units they could bring their families and use the pool, which many did.

Other forms of this technique would include a partial joint venture for the actual sweat equity in a deal. This would be where you have the ability to find good properties, and can negotiate deals with sellers where the down payment is the work that is going to turn the losing proposition into a winner. Once that is done, you introduce the deal to workers you know who can supply the sweat, and give them a bonus if they do the work and get paid later. Everyone wins.

Show Me the Risk: Look back at the risk statement for the sweat equity exchange. The only difference here is that the person you are dealing with is not the one who is going to do the actual work. This means you are one step further away from control over the work to which the sweat equity is tied. If you are attempting to do this kind of exchange, then be able to prove that you have already prepaid (either in cash or some other kind of exchange or trade transaction) for the work. Have the contractor or other party who is going to do the work give you a letter or some other pre-invoice that indicates exactly what work they are going to do, the timetable they have assigned to that project, and that the work has already been paid for. While this will not protect you from a real scam artist, it will cut your risk substantially. Always get references from the contractor or other person in charge of the work, no matter who is paying them.

Prepaid Rent Exchange

I have already shown you exchanges with prepaid rent as a part of the deal. Let's look at a couple of twists to this classic equity exchange. Anyone who has something for rent and it is vacant is losing the money it would bring in if it were rented. That we all understand. But at the same time, vacancy in just about any kind of property is a calculated item. For office buildings in any given market, it might run between 3 to 10 percent of the total space. In the long run, rental apartments for certain markets might be vacant, on the average 6 to 12 percent of the time. A lot of this has to do with the price range of the rents and the condition of the existing market.

Once you accept that fact, then why not try to cut that overall percentage by allowing for a certain percentage of your overall vacancy as prepaid exchange items? In essence, go out and offer the space in exchange for other things you may want or need, or that you can exchange for what you want or need.

Remember the term *legs*—things that were offered to you that you did not need and did not want, but which you knew you could exchange for other items you could use. Some people are very successful at turning part of their annual vacancy factor into value that works for them.

Sometimes the owner has to look in the far distance for the way to turn vacancy into use. For example, a hotel owner client of mine in the Miami area had an average of 40 percent vacancy in the slowest five months of the off-season. While these were summer months, Florida is still very active during that time (okay, sometimes with hurricanes), so this owner looked at the areas where the summer tourists were coming from, made up nice packages promoting a new barter program, and hired a young man to travel to those areas in the northern United States. He was offering one-week vacations to his hotel. He showed what the summer room rates were, threw in several hundred dollars of two-for-one restaurant deals that the restaurants normally offered in the local Saturday newspaper anyway, and guess what he was offered in exchange.

He was offered all the advertising he could use in those areas in local newspapers and radio; several nearly new vans, which he could use for his airport pickup and delivery; more free airline tickets than he thought he would ever use (but he did by trading them off for cleaning supplies); and other things. Many items he could not use or did not need, but everything ended up somewhere.

This kind of exchange works for businesses like hotels, motels, and restaurants where traffic generates more traffic. You are not convinced of this? Well, drive to a new town and start looking for a restaurant. Are you more likely to pull into the one with five cars outside (the cook and four waiters) or one that has only a few empty parking places in the lot?

Show Me the Risk: Prepaid rent is a great technique if you either have something for rent that is vacant or can exchange into prepaid rent from another transaction. The ability to go out and find what another person will take for what you want from them is a wonder of the exchange process. I have made exchanges with people around the world where I have not had what they wanted at the start of the exchange, but have found what they would take, then made an exchange to get it for them.

There is no real risk in a prepaid rental as long as it is completely documented and you have verified that you are dealing with the person who can make the decision and bind the lease that you think you are getting. A title check is always a good idea, even if there is every reason to believe that the manager of a property is actually qualified to sign a contract and bind the owner of the property.

Leaseback Exchange

A leaseback is a great investment tool when it suits the situation, no matter if it is used in a direct sale or as a part of an exchange. The basic way to use this tool is to give up the actual ownership of an asset, but not its use. Here is an example.

Jake's Leaseback Sale: Jake has a successful restaurant in Fort Lauderdale. It is in an old home that Jake purchased 20 years ago, and as the zoning allowed commercial use, he converted it into a very French-style restaurant. Now Jake wants to expand and open another similar facility in Palm Beach. He has found a historic mansion that will be perfect for the new restaurant. The only problem is Jake does not have the capital to buy and remodel the mansion. He has gone to several banks, but the lenders all shake their heads and say, "Restaurants are risky" (are they talking to that woman in California?).

But Jake has read one of my earlier books and knows all about a sale-leaseback. So, he puts his existing restaurant up for sale and writes a lease for himself as a part of the deal. Because he created a lease on his own property before he actually sold it, he can make the terms as reasonable as he wants. He has to keep in mind that the terms of the lease will affect the value he gets in the sale, but that is not that critical. All he needs to do is raise the money he will need to put a down payment on the Palm Beach mansion and cover the conversion into a restaurant.

Jake's Leaseback Exchange: In this instance, the mansion Jake has found is on a commercially zoned lot and on the market for $850,000. Jake knows that he can borrow up to 80 percent of its value as a residence, and later convert it into a restaurant. The conversion will cost around $350,000, with much of that going into the kitchen equipment, dining tables and chairs, and restaurant-type decorations. Here is how much of a dent that will make to Jake's pocketbook.

Purchase price of mansion	$850,000
Down payment (20%)	170,000
Conversion to a restaurant	350,000
Total cash to acquire and convert	$520,000

Jake isn't worried about the 80 percent to finance the Palm Beach mansion, but he knows that to finance the $520,000 will be next to impossible. So he goes to the owner and offers him his existing, and very famous, restaurant in Fort Lauderdale as an even swap, with a leaseback for 40 years at $70,000 a year with cost of living increases every two years. As Jake has an appraisal showing the property to be valued at over a million dollars, he also includes a buyback provision in the lease so that anytime after the fourth year of the lease, he can repurchase the restaurant at 10 times the annual lease at the time of the recapture.

The lease is triple net, which means that Jake continues to pay the taxes, insurance, and maintenance of the property, just as he has been doing all these years as owner. As he has owned the property for 20 years he would likely have a capital gain. But in this instance Jake has continued to add to the building, and has recently invested in a totally new kitchen. Those periodic reinvestments into his property would increase his tax basis to the point that at the sale price ($850,000), his capital gain is not a significant issue even if he were not doing a Section 1031 exchange. However, in this case he qualifies as he is moving from one investment to another. The fact that his business leases back a property he personally owned is not a disqualifying factor to Section 1031.

Show Me the Risk: There is risk for both sides of this deal. Jake is going to give up ownership of an asset he has built into a successful restaurant. The capital from that transaction (either sale or exchange) is going to be plowed back into a new restaurant. In the case of the exchange, Jake will get the Palm Beach mansion F&C of any debt, and he will then go to a bank and borrow up to 80 percent of its value to finance the conversion to his second restaurant. Now, from a banker's point of view this is a very risky situation for Jake. But then, what do bankers know about restaurants, except that they are very risky businesses to begin with? Jake isn't concerned about that, and he knows that once the new restaurant takes off, as he expects it will, he will be able to continue to expand into other locations. His plan is to have a dozen restaurants in the next 10 years, franchise the whole system, and retire a multimillionaire.

As for the seller of the Palm Beach mansion, he has cut about as risk-free a deal as could be had. The value of Jake's restaurant in Fort Lauderdale is easily verifiable, and as Jake was not trying to make a fortune on that sale, the leaseback terms were fair and would provide a nice economic return from the asset being exchanged. As the Palm Beach mansion was not the seller's residence, but a home he had been renting out for the past several years, it qualified for treatment under Section 1031.

Keys to Using a Leaseback: Both parties to a leaseback need to keep in mind a couple of factors:

1. The terms of the lease will reflect in resale value of the property given up. In this case, Jake's restaurant is now in the hands of the mansion seller. As Jake has a 40-year lease plus a recapture clause in his lease, the terms of the lease and the recapture provision will determine the ultimate resale value of the restaurant should the new owner choose to sell it prior to the termination of the lease, or before Jake recaptures it.

2. Any leaseback transaction should be examined very carefully by the person taking the property. The most important question to ask is: What if the tenant decides to sell the business? In this case, what if Jake sells his original restaurant? Restaurants tend to be good businesses when the business is good. Does this sound redundant? Well, what happens is it is generally the operator of the restaurant who makes the business a success. Along comes a retired stockbroker who knows more about operating a restaurant than Jake, and he offers Jake a ton of money to take over the restaurant (perhaps the second one, too), only to flop in the business. The restaurant now gets converted into a tarot card reader's den of fortune telling, and the best rent possible is $40,000 a year. The existing owner who anticipated a $70,000-a-year leaseback with increases along the way is not going to be a happy camper.

Personal Property Exchange

The personal property exchange is any exchange where you are giving up, or getting, something that is personal in nature. A diamond ring, 100 cases of wine, scrip worth $5,000 of your engineering services, $5,000 worth of dental work, a surgical operation (whether you need it or not), $5,000 of house painting credit, mechanic scrip, restaurant scrip, 200 hours of legal consultation (don't take it), vacation time, and so on—all items that do *not* qualify for Section 1031 treatment. But remember, even if those items are treated as boot and those values become part of the taxable element of the deal, the overall transaction may still qualify for Section 1031 tax-free treatment.

Suppose you want to sell your 50-unit motel. You price it at $2,500,000 and it is F&C. A buyer offers you $2,000,000 in cash (to be obtained from new financing) and a selection from a rather large portfolio of odds and ends. The list includes printing services, advertising time, airline tickets, cruise tickets, time-share weeks, gemstones, and so on—all of those items are personal property in nature, and will not qualify for Section 1031. But the bulk of the deal does qualify, and the $500,000 in personal property items will be considered boot.

Why would you take so much stuff? Well, you might have priced the hotel at $2,500,000 but would have been happy if you were able to get $2,200,000. So, guess what, you take the personal property stuff, which you think or hope you can either use, give to family for their birthdays and Christmas for the next 10 years, or trade off. After all, that $500,000 of stuff really cost you only $200,000.

Show Me the Risk: This is usually the least risky exchange of them all. Why? Because you get to see the personal property before you make the exchange. In essence it is like going to a store. You see what you are going to buy. If it does not fit, do not buy it. If you do not like the color, do not buy it. It is the same with personal property exchanges.

You do not get to take the merchandise back, however, as long as it was portrayed to you in an accurate and honest way and you took it home with you. Think of personal property exchanges like buying a popsicle.

Commission Exchange

Most real estate brokers who deal in exchanges will end up taking all or part of their fee in many transactions in the way of items offered in the exchange process. I know that from personal experience. What are some of the items I have ended up with as a part of my fee? Here is a partial list.

A pile of gemstones.

Odds and ends of jewelry.

A condo here and there.

Lots in North Carolina.

Lots in Port Saint Lucie, Florida.

Time-share weeks in Orlando.

Time-share weeks in Hollywood, Florida.

Rental time on yachts.

Airline tickets.

Rental time in charter aircraft.

Vacant tracts of land in Naples, Florida.

Hotel accommodations across the United States.

A hundred cases of prime California wine.

Second mortgage of $50,000 (that went way South).

Scrip for $80,000 of advertising time in a Northeastern newspaper.

Scrip in dozens of restaurants.

Scrip for massages.

Barter currency up to my ears.

Charter fishing boat time.

Dental work (suddenly more work than I had ever expected).

Limousine credit.

Two sailboats.

A 1950 Ford.

I could go on for several pages more, but you get the idea. To paraphrase someone, "Those who live by the exchange will survive by the exchange."

Show Me the Risk: The broker is the one who is taking any risk. But what risk is that? None.

Tenant-in-Common Exchange

This discussion is by Louis Rogers, an attorney in the Section 1031 field specializing in the syndication of tenant-in-common (TIC) interests as replacement property for 1031 exchanges. Rogers has overseen the syndication of more than 100 TIC properties with a market value exceeding $1 billion, including office buildings, shopping centers, industrial properties, and apartments throughout the country, formerly as head of the Real Estate Securities Practice Group at Hirschler Fleischer, Richmond, Virginia. On August 15, 2004, Rogers joined Triple Net Properties, LLC, the nation's leading sponsor of TIC properties. Triple Net is in the business of locating suitable TIC properties, negotiating the purchase agreements, conducting the necessary due diligence, obtaining financing, and closing the purchase with the 1031 exchangers as the owners of the property.

Introduction: A tenant-in-common (TIC) interest is an undivided fractional interest in a property where each co-owner owns an undivided portion of the property. The co-owners do not own a specified portion of the property, merely an undivided interest in the entire property.

A properly structured TIC interest in real estate is as like kind to fee simple real estate for the purposes of Section 1031. This means that properly structured TIC interests should qualify as replacement property in a typical Section 1031 real estate exchange.

TIC interests have been in existence for a long time and are fairly common in the estate context. For example, when a person dies leaving real estate to heirs, the heirs will own TIC interests in the real estate. In this classic sense, TIC interests are not very unusual. However, in the mid-1990s, Anthony W. Thompson, a real estate syndicator and founder of Triple Net Properties LLC, added an interesting twist by converting a traditional real estate syndication into a TIC syndication, with the TIC interests sold as securities through National Association of Securities Dealers (NASD) licensed broker-dealers. In this way, investors are able to acquire TIC interests as replacement property for their Section 1031 exchanges.

Key Tax Issues: The key to a properly structured TIC transaction for tax purposes is to avoid partnership or entity classification. In 1984, Congress added "interests in a partnership" to the items excluded from nonrecognition of gain or loss under Section 1031(a)(2). This means that a TIC interest will not qualify for Section 1031 treatment if the TIC structure constitutes a partnership or other non-TIC entity for federal income tax purposes.

The typical TIC structure has the co-owners on the title by each co-owner's name. Each co-owner has an undivided interest in the property. The co-owners typically enter into a Tenant-In-Common Agreement governing the management and operation of the property and to establish their status as co-owners and not partners. In most cases, the co-owners hire a property manager who is usually an affiliate of the sponsor.

Over the years, a number of alternative structures have been used. For example, in one structure, the co-owners own interests in a new partnership or limited liability company that elects not to be a tax partnership under Subchapter K of the Internal Revenue Code. Many tax attorneys now agree that this "election out" approach may not work, and its use is out of favor. Another alternative is to use a Delaware Statutory Trust (DST) as the title owner of the property, with the co-owners as the beneficiaries of the DST. This arrangement may qualify for nonrecognition of gain or loss under Section 1031 because the DST is a disregarded entity. However, the IRS recently issued Revenue Ruling 2004-68, which validates the use of DSTs—substantial restrictions and conditions that limit their use to very narrow circumstances—for example, where the real estate is net leased or master leased and the financing and master lease have the same term. These restrictions will make it very difficult to structure DST arrangements that conform to the revenue ruling. The most common structure is TICs on title, where the co-owners acquire fee simple title to the property as described earlier.

Many TIC interests are sold as securities through NASD licensed broker-dealers. Prior to issuance of Revenue Procedure 2002-22, there was some concern that TIC interests could be treated as securities for tax purposes (and not real estate) and disqualified from nonrecognition of gain or loss under Section 1031(a)(2)(C). However, it is clear under the revenue procedure clarified that TIC interests sold as securities should not be vulnerable under Section 1031(a)(2)(C).

Importantly, the revenue procedure 2002-22 confirms that properly structured TIC interests should qualify for nonrecognition under Section 1031. The revenue procedure is merely an advance ruling guideline, that is, it sets forth the conditions that must be satisfied to obtain an advance Private Letter ruling that a TIC structure is not a disqualified partnership or entity. However, the revenue procedure has become a litmus test for qualification under Section 1031. TIC programs that do not comply with the revenue procedure's requirements may still qualify but may later flounder in the market when compared to more compliant programs. This is true even though advance rulings are very rarely obtained for TIC programs.

Syndicated TIC programs have two basic structures—where the property is managed by an affiliate of the sponsor (property-managed programs) and where the property is master leased by an affiliate of the sponsor (master-leased programs). In the typical TIC program, an affiliate of the sponsor provides turnkey property management services under a Property Management Agreement. Alternately, and less frequently, the sponsor may master lease the entire property on a triple net basis. In a master lease structure, the co-owners lease the entire property to a master lessee, typically an affiliate of the sponsor. The master lessee is responsible for all operating expenses, taxes, insurance, and payment of debt service, and, in addition, pays the co-owners a stated rent. Master leases are commonly used for multifamily properties and a management contract is typically used for other classes of property. To comply with the revenue procedure, each co-owner must approve all sales, refinancings, leases and lease amendments, and the management agreement at least annually. The master lease structure solves a number of logistical problems raised by the revenue procedure. For example, in a multifamily property, there are many leases that need to be approved on a regular basis. It would be practically impossible to have each co-owner approve all such leases. By using the master lease structure, each co-owner approves a single master lease with the master lessee (an affiliate of the sponsor) on acquiring the TIC interest. The master lessee, as principal, enters into the subleases with the tenants, thereby alleviating the need for co-owner approval of each apartment lease. In the master lease structure, the co-owners typically do not enter into a management agreement; they simply enter into the master lease, thereby alleviating the need to approve the management agreement at least annually. For these reasons, the master lease is the preferred structure for multifamily properties.

According to Robert A. Stanger & Company, Inc. and Omni Brokerage, Inc., the syndicated TIC market is expected to approach $2 billion in TIC equity during 2004. (See Figure 9.1.) This is a dramatic increase over prior years. This trend is likely to continue barring anything unforeseen, such as a change in tax law or regulatory climate.

Why Are TIC Interests So Popular? TIC interests have become popular because they solve a number of problems for many property owners. First, the demographic of America is changing. As more property owners approach retirement, they tend to seek more passive replacement property that requires less active management. A TIC interest is fairly passive in terms of day-to-day management (however, under Revenue Procedure 2002-22, the co-owners retain ultimate control over the key

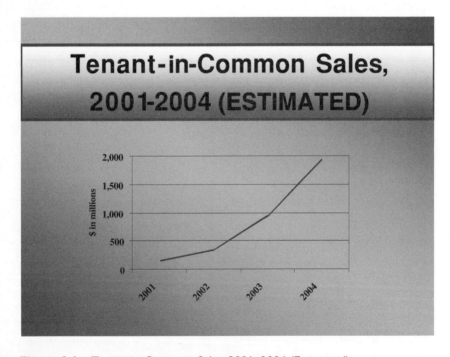

Figure 9.1 Tenant-in-Common Sales, 2001–2004 (Estimated)
Source: Robert A. Stanger & Company, Inc.; Omni Brokerage.

decisions). In addition, many taxpayers struggle with the 45-day identification period as imposed by Section 1031, being unable to locate suitable replacement property within such a short time frame. Syndicated TIC interests provide a bank of properties that are readily available to be identified quickly and acquired as 1031 replacement property. Additionally, many taxpayers do not have the expertise to find, conduct due diligence, negotiate purchase agreements, and obtain financing for replacement property. The sponsor of the TIC program takes care of all such matters, providing a turnkey replacement property solution. Finally, many taxpayers do not have sufficient funds from their exchange to acquire a 100% interest in a large property. TIC interests allow taxpayers to acquire a small percentage of a high-quality property that otherwise would be outside of their reach. For these reasons, TIC interests have become a popular replacement property option for taxpayers structuring exchanges.

Summary: TIC interests have evolved from a legal concept found mostly in the estate context to a syndicated security product sold through broker-dealers. Revenue Procedure 2002-22 validated the tax qualification of syndicated TIC interests. The market is booming with nearly $2 billion of TIC equity projected in calendar year 2004. With the aging of America, the proliferation of TIC interests is likely to continue and increase. Because TIC interests solve a number of problems facing taxpayers structuring exchanges and have been accepted for tax purposes, syndicated TIC interests are likely to continue to grow in popularity.

CHAPTER 10

Booby Traps That Await You in Exchanges

The goal of this chapter is:

To Introduce You to the Usual Pitfalls of Exchanges

Terms and Concepts You Need to Know

Your Investment Team
Real Estate Agents
Maps Galore
Important Elements You Must Double-Check Prior to Closing
It's Wonderful How Difficult It Really Is
Nine Booby Traps to Look Out for in Making Exchanges

Let's review these in detail.

Your Investment Team

Every real estate investor should have an investment team to back him or her up with the many details that are essential in a transaction. This aspect of the business makes me think of the credits that are displayed at the end of a film. They roll on and on, listing a mass of people, all of whom had a distinct task to perform to help make the film as good as possible. But then, that's filmmaking, and I guess we have grown to expect that kind of "cast of thousands" point of view. Then, just the other day I was listening to an award-winning talk show on public radio. There is such a wealth of thoughtful commentary that comes out of most of the shows I have heard on the public networks. I encourage you to tune in when you can. At the end of the hour-long talk show, during which there could not have been more than three people who called in, the host acknowledged the staff who put the show on the air. There were at least 30 names in the list.

Fortunately you will not have to generate a team of 30 people to deal with in the development of your team. Here is the team roster for your investment troop.

A Good Lawyer

You will need a lawyer who is familiar with the kind of real estate you are buying or selling. If you vary the types of real estate you deal with, you may need to have more than one lawyer that you can call on as needed. This might sound like an easy task, but I can assure you it is not. Just when you think you have achieved a good rapport with one lawyer, you discover that he or she is a lone wolf, great at what he or she does and glad not to be working in a big silk-stocking law firm. Only lone wolves tend to get busy with other clients, and may not be around or available when you need them. Then there is the great lawyer who works for a midsize office, whose only fault is that he wants to make your decisions for you.

Lawyers who want to make your decisions for you can be real deal breakers. They may tell you that they are *deal makers*, but that is their opinion and not what might be the reality. The word *makers* should be a clue. This kind of lawyer wants to take credit for making the deal come to the point of being a success, or they want to see the deal end because they have gotten emotionally into the transaction.

An Accountant

You will not have to use an accountant all that much, so get a good one who really knows and understands the elements of the type of real estate you deal with. If you are into hotels, then that accountant should be an expert in hotels. If you are a buyer and seller of retail strip mall stores, then your accountant should be experienced in that field as well. It is a good idea to have an in-between lawyer/accountant to whom you can reach out when there is a really sticky legal-tax problem that you need to check out. As anything to do with IRC Section 1031 is both legal and certainly a tax issue, this person will be someone you can hold in the background for those few times when you may need legal-tax expertise.

Title Insurance Company

Also called an escrow agent in some areas of the country, a title insurance company is an enterprise that performs the closing of title procedures and issues title insurance. Most lawyers can also perform this task, and there will be times when you might use your lawyer as the closing agent, and times when a title company will be more effective. I find that in uncomplicated transactions where everything has been going along smoothly, the title insurance company is a neutral space where your lawyer and the other party's lawyer can meet. Sometimes, when one lawyer is handling the closing, the other lawyer will be just a bit more picky about things and this can be a straw that will send the deal into a tailspin.

Inspection Teams

I use the plural of the word because not all inspection teams are qualified to inspect all kinds of real estate. The more complex the physical nature of the property, the more complex the inspections will be. Some inspection teams are great with single-family homes, but tend to leave some elements of other types of inspections undone. No single person, you will discover, is qualified to make a comprehensive inspection. It might be that your general contractor, if you have one, is qualified to pick other people who can inspect the myriad of elements of the subject property. Surely the same people would not inspect a major shopping mall as would inspect a high-rise office building. Never make the mistake of trying to save money on inspections. Once you close, it may be too late.

There are all kinds of inspections that must take place that many investors would never think of. One of the most critical is the audit of the many business documents that go with a business operation or the management of a shopping center or hotel. Leases, employment contracts, and inventory all take time and are essential to a smooth transition of ownership.

Section 1031 Facilitator

There are some great ones all around the United States. I have asked one of the best in the business to touch on the subject of what they do in the next chapter. I cannot understate the importance for you to be well represented by a qualified facilitator. Keep in mind that there are virtually no standards for this profession, no tests or state license laws that govern 1031 facilitators. For this reason it is critical that you meet with them and ask questions. Their job is not to give you legal advice, but they should have the experience to help the accountant and lawyer members of your team keep you ahead of any potential problems.

As with all the other professionals that you will tap for your investment team, you need to interview several of each category—lawyer, accountant, title company, inspection teams, and other experts that you may need for the deal in question. Get references, and call at least two of those references for each expert and check them out. In the next chapter (Chapter 11) I have asked Rochelle Stone, who is president and CEO of Starker Services, Inc., the oldest and largest independent qualified intermediary firm in the United States, to give us the insider look at the task of the facilitator in the handling of Section 1031 transactions.

Real Estate Agents

There are Realtors and non-Realtor real estate agents in great multitudes around the United States. They are usually segmented as either residential or commercial according to the category of real estate with which they prefer to deal. The two main categories can be further subdivided; for example, a residential agent may stick to single-family homes, while others gravitate to condominiums and co-ops. Commercial brokers and salespeople also spread out into industrial, restaurant/bar, general commercial, development sites, and vacant land.

The point I wish to make here is you need to be dealing with the agent who knows and understands the type of real estate you buy and sell. You will waste your time, and the agent's, if you take him or her out of the comfort zone of the kind of real estate they are comfortable with, and in which they specialize.

Maps Galore

I had a meeting with a Realtor who was giving me a presentation of several properties he represented for sale. In the meeting I asked him to get some aerial maps (which I said I would pay for) of the property he had presented and the surrounding several square miles. I even gave him the name, address, and phone number of the national company I use for these maps and aerials, trusting that he would be better put to order the maps because he knew the area, which was several hundred miles from my office, and would have the map coordinates necessary.

I noticed a pained look on his face as I pointed out an aerial map on the wall behind me. I told him that aerial was the kind we needed—one large photo that showed a total of nine square miles of property. His pain eased when I told him how reasonably priced these aerials were, and that if he would order them by tomorrow, we would likely have them within two days at the most. The price would be less than $30 per aerial.

In the old days, not all that long ago, I would have to hire a photographer to rent an airplane. The photographer would then take half a dozen or more photos, and I would pick the one or ones I wanted to have blown up into the same size as the one I had just pointed to on the wall of my office.

The cost? Easily $500 or more for a single aerial. If that example doesn't show you the declining cost of high-tech tools, I don't know what will.

Maps galore proliferate on the Internet. You can print them out on your own color printers, view them on your handheld devices, and accurately plot out the areas of town where you are working.

The county tax assessor's office has more maps and aerials that are available to you, some of them even less expensive than $30 per aerial. Surveys, at least those that are on file with the building departments and tax assessor's offices, can be copied at a nominal fee, often not more than a dollar or two each.

The point in all this is that there is no reason that any person should own a property that they have not fully documented, located, and measured, and then verified those measurements.

Because all this kind of documentation is available, and cheap at that, your investment team must be in tune with each other when it comes to the review and inspection of a specific property. Each of your investment team members is looking for certain elements of the transaction to make sure you are protected and that you don't overpay or get into a problem. The problem is that these members may not double-check facts for which other members are responsible. The lawyer checks the title based on the legal description, but is the address you went to the same property, or is it mistakenly the one next door, or down the block?

Because maps and all the other documentation are easy to come by, there is no reason for such mistakes, but they do happen. To ensure that you don't have a serious problem, like tearing down the wrong building or buying the wrong one, be especially careful with the following items.

Important Elements You Must Double-Check Prior to Closing

- **Legal description.** Is the legal description on the contract the one that the address (also on the contract) has defined?
- **Footprint of the building.** Does the footprint of the building that shows on the survey match the foot of the building that you think you are buying?

- **Square footage.** Is the total area of the property the same as the total area of the land under that office building you are about to close on?

- **Property lines and angles.** Are all the property lines and angles exactly as you have seen them in the building plans and survey?

- **Out parcels.** Have no out parcels been sold off that take away from the property you thought you were exchanging into?

You might be surprised to learn that the answer to all those questions has, on occasion, and in my personal experience, been no.

All the high-tech help in the world will not save you from a error made by a person who failed to double-check the simple factor: Is what it says what it is?

It's Wonderful How Difficult It Really Is

It is nice to come full circle sometimes. As you expand your experience in real estate investing, and especially in the exciting world of real estate exchanging, you will, at one point or another, begin to see how truly difficult it is to be successful in this business. Developers pull their hair out, contractors have sleepless nights, and bankers worry about every loan they underwrite.

Then you will pass into a full and complete understanding that this is the way it is supposed to be. It is the law of the jungle, isn't it, that only the most fit survive? As you expand your knowledge of the community where you plan to invest, and develop your comfort zone to the extent that you will become that expert in that area, your effort will begin to pay off. You will suddenly see the opportunities that had lain hidden behind the zoning you didn't understand, or the building setbacks that you can overcome.

And then you will smile.

Nine Booby Traps to Look Out For in Making Exchanges

1. Failure to report.
2. Violation of FIRPTA.

3. Greener Grass Syndrome.

4. Overpriced property.

5. Mortgages and leases of convenience.

6. The phantom.

7. Accountants and lawyers—yours and theirs.

8. Sloppy contracts.

9. Nonstandard standard-looking contract forms.

Let's review each in detail.

Failure to Report

Any exchange that you participate in must be reported in two documents. There are (1) IRS Form 4797, "Sales of Business Property," for any depreciable property (whether or not depreciation is taken), or Schedule D, "Capital Gains and Losses," for nondepreciable property, and (2) IRS Form 8824, "Like-Kind Exchanges," which was first required for any such transaction in 1991.

Failure to properly report any required action as deemed proper by the IRS in its codes may create a major problem for the taxpayer. To avoid this occurring, make sure that you properly report any exchange situation in the tax reporting for the year that it occurred.

Violation of FIRPTA

The Foreign Investment in Real Property Tax Act of 1980, commonly known as FIRPTA, is an act established by Congress to ensure that any foreign person who is a party to any of the elements that this act covers be properly reported. This is a requirement for both parties to any such transaction. In the general context of this provision, a foreign person is a nonresident alien individual, a foreign corporation, a foreign partnership, a foreign trust, or a foreign estate. Interestingly, a resident alien individual is not considered a foreign person under this act.

There are several dispositions that may mitigate the statement just made in the previous paragraph, and any situation that may have suggested that any of the above are ultimately included as foreign persons need to confer with their legal representatives to see if one or more of the mitigating circumstances will apply to them.

The importance of this act is substantially that any person who acquired a United States real interest from such a foreign person or foreign corporation on or after January 1, 1985, must withhold a tax in the amount equal to 10 percent of the sale price. This withholding is without respect to the actual amount of the *cash* paid by the transferee. Again, in keeping with the often confusing language of IRS-speak, there are also mitigating circumstances that can modify or remove these conditions.

The point is this: If you know you are a foreign person under the description just shown, or if you are dealing with anyone who is potentially covered by these restrictions, you must either be able to show that you are not required to submit to the penalty of the act, or on the other side of the coin, you must prove that you are exempt from the requirement of the act.

Failure to comply can result in a very unpleasant future.

Greener Grass Syndrome

I have spoken of the Greener Grass Syndrome in Chapter 8. I am especially called to reflect on this as the result of a conversation with a client I have mentioned earlier. He called me one afternoon and told me that he had just returned from an investor's trip to Oklahoma City. He said he could not believe how cheap the real estate is there, and how realistic the economics are in the way of investor returns versus investor risk.

I won't get into the balance of my conversation with him, other than to reflect on my own earlier Greener Grass Syndrome experiences in places like Switzerland, Bermuda, Jamaica, Hawaii, and Tulsa, Oklahoma, just to name a few of the places around the world where I have been tempted by the Greener Grass Syndrome.

Let me paint another picture that you might relate to more easily. Florida is the place where many people retire to from the Northeastern part of the United States. Also, south Florida has a great proliferation of service industries; most noted are restaurants, motels, and bars. Many of these retired folks from the Northeast believe they have a great deal of experience in these three businesses. Why? I would guess because they have eaten in a lot of restaurants, spent many nights in motels, and like to frequent bars. Suddenly they have time on their hands and some saved-up cash (their life savings), and they go out and buy one of these businesses.

Very few make it. Temptation by the green grass that grows on the other side of the fence can be powerful and very dangerous.

Overpriced Property

This is a chronic problem with any seller's market. There is always a seller's market in some category of real estate, just as there is nearly always a buyer's market in some category of real estate. The problem with this concept is that the same market—that is, buyers or sellers—is not always going on in every location of the United States at the same time. Real estate does not react that way, not at least like the stockbrokers think it should. Although real estate is an international commodity, it is truly very local in nature. Real estate does react similarly to national trends, such as a tight money market where mortgage rates are high everywhere, or an easy money market where interest rates for loans are low. However, the hot items or slow-to-move properties will vary depending on the local situation. Real estate trends in San Francisco may differ dramatically to those in Miami or Chicago as to what is hot, and what is not hot. Nonetheless, it is possible to apply the results of a trend that develops in one part of the country to another area if the reasons for the trend are seen developing in the new area. For example, if a county approaches or reaches its maximum cap of residences and prices for existing homes take a sudden jump and continue to rise, you can be sure the same situation will cause similar results in another part of the country as well. Consider Broward County (Fort Lauderdale and area). Broward is just about out of vacant land for new development and most cities in the county are close to their maximum population. The fact that the trend in Broward is that existing home prices are going through the roof has no effect on the more stable home prices of Tulsa, Oklahoma, which has lots of land around it for future development.

Mortgages and Leases of Convenience

Mortgages and leases of convenience are documents that are created by the seller in name only. These may be so created for negotiating purposes. For example, Martha may want to sell her strip mall store for $1,000,000. Assume for a moment that it is F&C, which would mean that she has $1,000,000 in equity in the property. A prospective buyer knows that he or she can negotiate any part of that $1,000,000. Martha may wish to limit the visible equity by offering her property at the $1,000,000 and report that there is $700,000 of financing on the property. Or she may offer the property for $500,000 and indicate that there is a $45,000-a-year land lease under the building. Each of these offerings reduces her visible equity. If Martha was proactive in trying to sell or exchange her property and she wanted to lease it back, then she would show the price with a leaseback situation. Here the full terms of the lease would be shown as if the lease was already in existence. To offer such a property and say, "Seller will lease back the property" and not disclose the terms leaves that whole situation up for negotiation as well.

Mortgages and leases of convenience can create problems, so a prospective buyer of such a property needs to ascertain as much information as possible in the following elements.

Terms of the Lease or Mortgage: If Martha says there is a $700,000 mortgage on the property that has a $3,000 a month payment over the next five years, that might look very attractive and entice a buyer to come along. But what if the mortgage interest rate is really 12 percent, and each month the difference between 1 percent of the outstanding loan and the $3,000 is added to the growing principal owed? Then the mortgage no longer looks so attractive. A lease that is executed by Martha's best friend with no security deposit and an option to purchase the property would not be an attractive lease for a new buyer to assume when purchasing the property, either. The full details of any lease or mortgage need to be carefully read and digested. Small "gotcha" provisions may look innocent, but carry a big bite. For example, a lease calls for an option to renew the lease for an additional 10 years at the average rent and terms of the initial lease. Exactly what does that mean? Would that tenant be able to have a 10-year lease at a fixed rent based on the average monthly rent over the past 10 years?

Other factors to question in mortgages and/or leases would be: What is the security to the mortgage or lease? Is there any subordination called for, and if so, what and how? A lease with an existing or future subordination provision could jeopardize the owner's equity by allowing the lessee the right to place financing on the leasehold interest ahead of the lessor's ownership.

Term, method of payment, adjustment in amounts of payment, cost of living, or other factors that could cause such adjustments in payments, right to renew or extend, penalty for default or prepayment, and so on are all important factors that need to be completely understood prior to starting any serious negotiation.

Review and Estoppel for All Leases and Mortgages: This can be a cumbersome job, and one that I would never personally tackle. Each separate document must be read and important elements tracked and listed. For example, if the property is a shopping center, every lease may be different. The critical elements are:

Important Elements of Leases

Tenant's name.

Who or what entity is responsible for the obligations of the lease.

List of what elements of the physical property the lessee is responsible for.

Description of the space rented.

Amount of square footage that is both inside and outside the building.

Start date of the lease.

Ending date of the lease.

Amount of the initial base rent.

Amount of security.

Terms of the security.

Terms of any options to renew.

Due date of the rent.

Penalty for late payment.

Statement of condition of the premises at date of occupancy of the tenant.

Use the tenant intends for the space leased.

Limitations to use.

Operating rules and regulations.

Common area maintenance details.

There are other terms and conditions that may be contained in a lease. Although every lease may end up being a duplication of the same terms, there might be some items that are different and that will haunt the new owner. Most closing agents will require estoppel letters signed by the tenants and mortgages. The existing lesser and lessee for leases, and the mortgagee and mortgagor for mortgages should execute the estoppel letter, usually attached to a copy of the lease or mortgage.

The estoppel letter will state that the parties agree that the document attached to the letter and that is described as a lease or a mortgage for the specific property is an accurate copy of the agreement between the parties and is the whole document. In situations where there are service and employment contracts that are inherited by the buyer, it is a good idea to also have estoppel letters verifying the true nature of the service or employment agreement.

The Phantom

I just love this person. In my many years as a broker and investor, I have run across more phantoms than you can imagine. Here are several examples of the form in which they appear.

The Yesterday Phantom: "You know, Mr. Cummings," the owner will tell me, "I had a buyer here yesterday and he says he is willing to offer me $200,000 more than you did just now."

"The Contract's Right Here" Phantom: "If you don't believe I have someone who has offered more than you, let me show you," at which moment the owner reaches back and picks up a document from the table behind him. He then produces what appears to be a standard purchase agreement. The owner fans the pages of the document and holds it too far from me to grab or read. He then shows me a signature page signed in what might be blood. "See," he says, obviously forgetting that he showed me the same pseudo-offer three years ago when I was dealing with him on another property.

The Foreign Phantom: The phone rings exactly 10 minutes after I walk into the seller's office to present my client's offer to buy his property. The seller at first pretends that the phone isn't ringing, then checks the caller identification pad and says, "It's from Saudi Arabia," and without even saying "Excuse me" he picks up the phone and begins a conversation in another language. However, every now and then he throws out words in English, words like, "not enough," and "five million" and then checking his calendar he taps on a date that looks as if it is next month with his fountain pen, says "Yah, Yah" and hangs up. He then leans back and smiles. "Those Arabs, aren't they crazy? Can you imagine? He says he will be in town in a few weeks and wants to know if I will take five million for the property (that is worth only $3,500,000.)"

My Partner the Phantom: This one is actually an invention by diplomats and is widely used in international negotiations of all kinds, and not just real estate transactions. Either the buyer or seller in any kind of transaction can use this phantom. The phantom does not exist at first. Only after an offer is made or a counteroffer tendered does this phantom appear. A seller's phantom is described this way: "Mister Cummings," the seller says, handing me the offer I had presented to him two days earlier, "I liked your offer. In fact if I didn't have a partner in this deal, we would be headed for the closing table right now. But my partner, who happens to be my brother, is adamant. He wants $5,000,000 and not a penny less."

The idea of using a surrogate who doesn't exist is very good technique and has been used by diplomats for thousands of years. In this way, the seller can act out both roles of the good guy/bad guy scenario. Although this can be cumbersome, you can't find fault with that. Still, typically the partner you never get to meet remains the obstacle that you face. Mind you, this is the best of all the phantoms to deal with; however, you must not let on that you know what is going on. Eventually, as long as the seller or buyer continues to pretend to want to do the deal, but needs to convince the phantom, you have a chance of being successful in the negotiations. You know you have made headway in the deal when the seller or buyer who has conjured up the phantom says, "I have an idea. I bet you that if you can modify your last offer this way . . . ," showing you on paper exactly what you could do to sweeten the deal, "that I could convince my sister-in-law's brother-in-law to accept the deal." Go figure that one out.

Keep in mind that the phantom can be either the good guy or the bad guy. This will depend on the real nature of the live person you deal with. The seller might use the phantom as the reason the property is for sale. ("My sister's family needs my help so I am moving to Chad to help them with the family sugar beet plantation there.") A buyer could use a phantom as a way to save face when his or her bluff didn't work. ("My father-in-law chewed me out last night when I told him I had rejected your last counter to my final offer. I guess he is right, too. Besides, my wife really likes the office building and I can't disappoint both my wife and my father-in-law, can I? So I guess you win, Mr. Seller. When can you close?")

Accountants and Lawyers—Yours and Theirs

Accountants and lawyers occupy an important position on your investment team as long as they serve you and help you safely and successfully achieve your goals. However, it is important that they understand what those goals are, and your timetable to attain them.

Discussing your goals with your accountant and lawyer may be difficult for some people, and if you wish to keep your goals a part of your business and not that of your own accountant or lawyer, then do so with this word of caution. Keeping essential details from someone who can help you is a calculated risk on your part. My recommendation is to review your goals by going over them in some detail. What are your target goals and their anticipated timetable to be reached? What are the interim steps you must take to get to those targets? Now, write down the reasons why you don't feel it essential or even prudent to discuss these steps with your advisers. My guess is that by doing this you will see there are no really good reasons for keeping silent on these elements.

The advisers on the other side of the fence are another story. The less they know about what you plan to do, the better. The only exceptions to that statement would be if you were attempting to do a joint venture or if the seller was going to hold a purchase money mortgage or land lease. In those situations the parties may require detailed information on what you plan for the property so some information about your goals may be divulged to the seller and his or her advisers.

There can be situations where your advisers and the other parties' advisers do not get along. Professional courtesy is one thing, but I have been in the midst of negotiations with buyers' and sellers' advisers who called each other names and pounded on tables, making threats to walk out and cut off the negotiation and end the transaction. I have been a party to sales where the buyer's advisers were not responsive to requests for documents that the contract called for them to deliver: lawyers who did not return phone calls, accountants who suddenly went on vacation when they were supposed to be drafting the year-end statement essential to proceed in the closing, clearly and deliberately stonewalling a deal.

If it is your advisers who are part of the irritation to the situation, take them aside and explain to them that you will be very upset if this transaction fails because of the conflict between the parties. If they pass the buck to the other side of the table ("Well, they started it"), then suggest that they leave if they cannot act diplomatically and make the deal rather than help it self-destruct.

Usually it is not a situation of one side being the sole cause of the conflict. Sometimes it is the buyer or seller who really is the source of the problems and he or she is using advisers much like they would use a phantom. I have found that one of the best approaches is to take the other principal aside. Explain that you are not the cause of whatever it is that is creating a conflict in this transaction and perhaps the two of you can get better control of the deal and your respective advisers. If that doesn't work, then move on. It is easy to waste a lot of time with buyers or sellers who cannot control their advisers, or who don't want to admit that they don't want to spend the money to hire good ones.

Sloppy Contracts

One of the most dangerous things that can happen in the negotiation of a transaction is that the contract itself can become either totally or at least partially unreadable: handwritten words added, then scratched out, initials on top of initials with no real way to tell when they were added or what they were meant to indicate. Memories of the parties dim, or take on an entirely new significance as to what the intent was and whether that word that looks like "no" really means "now."

Technology can play a role in the proliferation of sloppy, unreadable contracts when they are faxed from one place to another, alterations made, and that copy faxed back for the other party to review, execute or change and initial, and so on. Because, historically, all legal documents were in an $8\frac{1}{2} \times 14$ inch size (U.S. contracts at least), fax machines had a problem sending or receiving this size of document when there was only $8\frac{1}{2} \times 11$ inch letter-sized paper in the machine. The manufacturers of these machines had a brilliant idea. Why not let the fax machine shrink the $8\frac{1}{2} \times 14$ inch document so that it will fit on the letter-sized paper? In fact, why not just routinely shrink the size of a fax?

What happens is that each successive fax tends to get smaller, the words darker, and after a couple of back-and-forth faxes the document is totally wasted. But wait. There is a solution that may not show up in the index of the user guide to your fax machine under "totally unreadable fax copies" but it will show up under the term "resolution."

I have yet to find a fax machine that did not have a way to improve the resolution of the fax. Most machines will fax in these modes: standard, fine, and superfine. Some may also have color modes and photo modes for their resolution quality. Generally fine is sufficient to ensure that the fax will be nearly as good as the original. Superfine might be overkill for a long document because as you improve the resolution you also slow down the transmission of the fax.

As most residential and many commercial real estate purchase agreements are generated by a software program that the real estate agent or your lawyer is using, the tendency to fill in the blank or put the "x" in the appropriate box is the extent of the maker's effort in drawing up the offer. These catchall forms may work well some of the time, but in an attempt to force them to deal with some of the more complex matters that are unique to a specific property the agreement may contain an addendum, sometimes handwritten, and generally difficult to read and understand. These addendums sometimes are completely rewritten in a counteroffer, and then are not properly identified as to which one came first. Sloppy to be sure, but more important, full of potential legal problems that can be costly.

The key to saving you from a sloppy contract is to insist that fresh documents be drawn anytime there has been more than one pass at the addition of anything to a contract that is different from its printed or written words.

You might say, "The few words that I have added to this document are okay and all the seller and I have to do is initial them, with the date of those initials clearly shown on the faxed pages." The dates, by the way, will be printed when a fax is sent by a fax machine programmed to add the date (sometimes the name of the sender and other data as well). But did you know that the programmer can fudge the date and time and send faxes that are dated as the year 1492? It is a good idea to start putting dates on documents and do not rely on the fax machine to do it for you.

Professional advice as to the business merit of a decision that you have made or are about to make should be tethered to the benefits you need and the benefits offered. Too often the professional will look at the situation from a different perspective, which can cause the advice to be correct, but from the wrong point of view. Let me give you an example of what I mean. The transaction at hand is this. You have a motel that you and your wife have been personally operating for 15 years. Little by little you have grown tired of this management-intensive business and eventually have put the property on the market for sale. No one has made you an offer anywhere close to your asking price, and it has been on the market for eight months. Along comes a prospective buyer who has an inn that he inherited from his parents, who passed away a year ago. The property is in a ski resort area near Lake Placid, New York. It actually has two distinct seasons, a winter and a summer, and often closes down for two months between each season. The owner of this property lives in the area near your motel, and wants to move his equity from the New York area to his hometown. You fly up to Lake Placid and spend a week doing some homework about the property, the business community, and the nature of this kind of business operation.

You and your wife like what you see and decide to go through with the deal. The elements of the exchange require that you take the New York property free and clear of any debt, and that you hold a $2,000,000 mortgage on your motel. The mortgage is to be interest at 5 percent per annum for the first two years, then prime plus 2 points after that, interest only for a total of 12 years. The mortgage will balloon at that time.

You work out the basics of the deal and ask your accountant and lawyer for their respective input on the deal. It would not be unusual for each of them to play devil's advocate with you and try to scare you or talk you out of the deal. Their point of view on the arguments they may use would be directed to what I call "third party" point of view. By this I mean they are likely to examine the deal from the point of view that you are not a seller of the motel, but a lender asked to make a loan on the terms stated earlier. They may also not see the merits of the exchange, but look at the acquisition of the New York property as though you are making a direct purchase. Worse still, they may not consider that no one has been willing to come close to your price for eight months and that your primary goal of the whole "let's get rid of the motel" was exactly that, to get rid of the motel. If the mortgage at the terms offered will help you do that, and the chance to inject something new and exciting into your life in the form of a Lake Placid ski lodge excites you, then you need to tell your advisers that. You can, if you think it is important, leave out the fact that your wife has threatened to kill you if you didn't get rid of the motel by the end of the year.

Nonstandard Standard-Looking Contract Forms

In this modern world of computers, the ability to draw documents that look like they are preprinted forms means it is possible that a contract that looks exactly like the standard form you may be used to may not be standard after all.

As I have mentioned before, it doesn't take much in the way of wording for an agreement to switch from being in your favor to being a disaster for you.

How do you protect yourself? Make sure you and your advisers treat every document as though it *is not* a standard form document. This means that every term needs to be read carefully each time the document is presented. If there have been counteroffers, double-check the document when it is returned to you for your approval of the counter. This means check even pages that do not have pen changes on them. They could have been retyped in the computer and words like "buyer" changed to "seller" or other provisions altered to further modify the agreement.

One good way to double-check such alterations to a preread document would be to hold the original pages (which you had read very carefully) one at a time under the new returned page, and hold them up to a bright light. You should be able to match the pages exactly so that the words fit perfectly over each other. Any modification tends to stand out as the changed words block the original ones, or lengthen the line ever so slightly that the change stands out like a sore thumb.

I was testifying in a trial recently and was handed a document by the lawyer of one of the plaintiffs in the case. She asked me if I recognized the letter, saying that it was, in fact, an identical letter to the one that I had just testified to as having drafted myself. I looked at the long letter she had just handed me, and slid the already approved letter under the one the lawyer had just handed me. To everyone's surprise I lifted them up to the lights of the courtroom and announced that they were not identical.

Try it sometime. It does work.

Okay, what do you do when you find that the other side is pulling this kind of stuff on you? My suggestion is that you insert the original correct page back into the contract, make your modifications or approvals to the counteroffer sent to you, and return the document, which you have restored to good health.

CHAPTER 11

Closing Section 1031 Exchanges: The Qualified Intermediary's Point of View

The goal of this chapter is:

To Provide You with the Qualified Intermediary's Point of View of Section 1031 Closings

Acknowledgment of Contribution for This Section

I want to thank Rochelle Stone, CES, and David Kuns, CES, who co-authored the following chapter. Rochelle Stone is the president and CEO of Starker Services, Inc. and Mr. Kuns is vice president of Starker Services, Inc. Both are Certified Exchange Specialists. As president of Starker Services, Rochelle Stone is responsible for the fine service for which Starker Services, Inc., is well known. In addition to his duties as vice president of Starker, Mr. Kuns sits on the board of the Federation of Exchange Accommodators, which is the largest national trade association representing exchange professionals. Additional thanks go to Doug Watanabe, senior exchange counselor at Starker, and Holly Fruehling, who is the marketing manager for Starker, for their editing and graphics used in this chapter.

Starker Services, Inc. is the nation's oldest, largest, and most experienced independent qualified intermediary firm and successfully completes thousands of exchanges each year. Starker remains committed to unparalleled service and maintains ongoing education for Realtors, CPAs, and attorneys as to the ever-evolving Internal Revenue Code that governs IRC Section 1031 exchanges.

Introduction

The definition of real estate dates back to the time when only royalty was allowed to own real property. Fortunately, real property is no longer an asset held only by an elite few. In fact, as many millionaires have been created through the ownership of property as with any other form of investment. But owning or building wealth is not the only challenge. Preserving wealth is every bit as important as creating wealth for effective estate planning. To further complicate the planning for investors, the tax code has changed significantly over the past 30 years. In some cases, the changes have forced investors to adapt their estate planning dramatically to avoid unnecessary taxes.

Although favorable tax treatment for exchanges has been in existence since 1921, until fairly recently it was unclear how a transaction could qualify unless performed as a direct swap or simultaneous transfer of assets. Simultaneity and the inherent problems of direct swaps made the very process of tax deferral untenable for the average investor. In a series of court cases from 1975 through 1979, a taxpayer named T. J. Starker challenged this need for simultaneity. The resulting tax court decision in his favor began a new way of performing exchanges in the states governed by the Ninth Circuit.

The rest of the country remained unclear as to how the *Starker* decision affected them. Many of the lingering questions were answered on May 16, 1990, by the publication of the proposed regulations that interpreted previous amendments to IRC Section 1031. These regulations supported the Starker or delayed exchange format and sought both to clarify the issues arising out of deferred exchange transactions and to govern their tax treatment. The proposed regulations were finalized by Treasury Decision 8346 and were released to the public on April 25, 1991. In September 2000, the IRS enacted Revenue Procedure 2000-37 (published in October as IRS Bulletin 2000-47) establishing safe-harbor guidelines for the reverse exchange as well.

Prior to the *Starker* court decision of 1979, investors who wanted to exchange their real estate were faced with having to simultaneously acquire their replacement property. In many cases this was difficult to coordinate. However, after the changes to the tax code allowing for the delayed or Starker exchange, a new world of opportunity opened to owners of property who wished to change their investment property. The rules for tax deferment changed dramatically for owners of real estate. The changes under Section 1031, including the creation of the role of the qualified intermediary in a delayed exchange, are now some of the most powerful investment techniques to help with the protection of wealth.

Throughout this chapter we seek to describe the steps necessary to structure exchange transactions in order to meet the rules and safe harbors provided in the tax code, while also identifying successful strategies to assist in effecting a qualified transaction. We seek to help the investor understand the role of the qualified intermediary in the exchange process, describe what benefits the use of the intermediary brings to the transaction, and explain how to search for and choose a competent intermediary.

The Qualified Intermediary

This form of safe harbor provides that the exchanger may use an outside party who becomes a part of the transaction to prevent the taxpayer from constructive receipt of cash. The taxpayer who uses a qualified intermediary is not in constructive receipt of cash held by the intermediary, even if the intermediary otherwise would be treated as the agent. A qualified intermediary is a person other than the exchanger or a person related to the exchanger who, for a fee, acts to facilitate the exchange by acquiring the relinquished property from the exchanger and acquiring the replacement property and subsequently transferring it to the exchanger.

This safe harbor is by far the most common form of safe harbor. The use of an exchange intermediary allows tremendous flexibility, while avoiding concerns regarding agency and constructive receipt.

Disqualified Parties

The Treasury regulations also clearly specify who cannot function in the capacity of an intermediary. A disqualified person is defined as:

i. any person who is an agent of the taxpayer at the time of the transaction or any person who has acted as the taxpayer's employee, attorney, accountant, investment banker or broker, or real estate agent or broker within the 2-year period ending on the date of the transfer of the first of the relinquished properties;

ii. any person who is related to the taxpayer including any family members;

iii. any individual, partner or corporation where a related party owns more than 10% of capital or profit interest or stock value, or;

iv. two corporations in a controlled group, a grantor and fiduciary in a trust, or any other entity that would appear to be an agent under local law.

v. an intermediary cannot be an agent of the exchanger, nor can they have any fiduciary responsibility to the exchanger if the exchange is to be tax-deferred. Any person or entity having had a fiduciary relationship to the exchanger within the two years prior to the transfer of the relinquished property, including real estate agents, attorneys, escrow holders, bankers, accountants, etc. is disqualified as an intermediary.

Any entity construed as a related party to the exchanger can also be disqualified as an intermediary. A family member is obviously considered a related party. A corporation or other entity owned 10 percent or more by a related party or agent of the exchanger will not qualify as an intermediary. This arm's-length treatment ensures the exchanger *never* has control over proceeds from the sale of property. If the intermediary is an agent of the exchanger, or can be shown to have a fiduciary responsibility to the exchanger outside of the exchange transaction, the exchanger will be viewed as having constructive receipt of the sale proceeds and the exchange would be disallowed.

Using Principals as the Intermediary

There are several ways to use an intermediary as part of the exchange transaction without using a disqualified party. Prior to the Starker decision, the most common was for the seller of a property (the taxpayer) to use either the buyer of the property or the seller of the replacement property. In other words, one of the principals in the transaction acted as the accommodating grantor. Depending on the form, either the seller (Baird exchange) or the buyer (Alderson exchange) can be used to accommodate the exchange for the exchanger.

Baird Exchange—The Seller as the Accommodator

The Baird exchange (*J. H. Baird Publishing Co. v. Commissioner* [1962] 39 TC 608) is a form of simultaneous exchange in which the seller of the replacement property (property B) acts as the accommodator. The seller/accommodator and exchanger trade their properties (property A for property B). (See Figure 11.1.)

The seller/accommodator completes the transaction by selling the exchanger's property A to a third-party buyer for cash. In this format, the seller/accommodator assumes the additional liability as the seller of the exchanger's property. It is extremely important for the seller/accommodator in a Baird exchange to be fully aware of the liability of acting as an accommodating grantor. Any future problems with property A could result in the seller being sued as the seller of property A.

Alderson Exchange—The Buyer as the Accommodator

In the Alderson exchange (*Alderson v. Commissioner* [9th Circuit 1963] 317 F2d 290), the buyer wishing to purchase the exchanger's

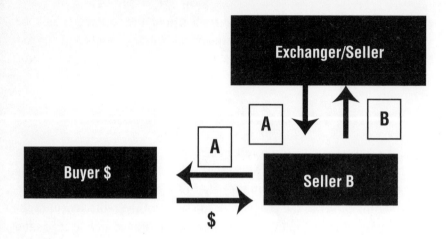

Figure 11.1   Baird Exchange

property becomes the accommodator. Instead of purchasing the exchanger's property (property A), the cash buyer/accommodator uses the cash to purchase the property the exchanger wishes to own (property B) and subsequently trades it for the exchanger's property A. (See Figure 11.2.)

The buyer now assumes the liability for acting in the capacity of both an exchanger and a buyer. This basic exchange is exactly the same as the Baird format other than which party acts as the accommodator. As

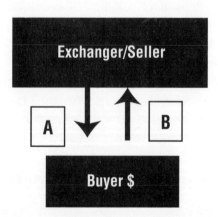

Figure 11.2   Alderson Exchange

with the Baird, there are three transfers of property (property B from seller to cash buyer/accommodator, transfer of replacement property B to exchanger, and exchange of exchanger's property A to cash buyer/accommodator). Again, the buyer must be willing to accept full liability as the accommodator.

Alderson or Baird Exchanges

The potential problems of using the buyer or seller as the accommodating party are similar. For purposes of discussion, we will highlight the difficulty of the use of the buyer as accommodator. Using the buyer as an intermediary, as occurred in the *Starker* case, is undesirable both from the point of view of the exchanger and the buyer. The exchanger should be concerned about using the buyer since the buyer's cooperation after transferring title to the relinquished property, while contractual, may depend on circumstances completely uncontrolled by the exchanger. What if the buyer is not financially able to acquire the replacement property due to an unexpected personal financial change? What if the buyer becomes incapacitated or even dies during the exchange period? The exchanger may have funds tied up for lengthy periods, making the exchange impossible to complete.

Conversely, the buyer may not want to accommodate the transaction due to the inescapable liability inherent in owning property in which the buyer has no real interest. Should the buyer agree to participate by acquiring replacement property for the exchanger, whether going on title and subsequently deeding immediately to the exchanger or never being on title, the buyer becomes a part of the transaction. At the worst, the buyer is now forever a part of the title history of the property; at the least, the buyer is a part of the transference of ownership. Any future dispute concerning title or condition of the property, including toxic waste, title problems, or material defects, may result in litigation that could involve the buyer as an interested party.

While the buyer may demand and receive indemnities from the exchanger, enforcing those indemnities could mean a costly legal battle. Few attorneys would advise their clients to act as an accommodator. The presence of a professional intermediary in the exchange means the buyer is responsible only for performing as the buyer without assuming further exposure as accommodating grantor.

The Professional Intermediary

The intermediary exchange involves a fourth-party principal, the intermediary, who is brought into the exchange solely for the purpose of passing ownership rights and cash to the proper parties while insulating the exchanger from constructive receipt. The intermediary becomes the accommodator and assumes the liability of the accommodating grantor. The intermediary assumes the role of seller, exchanger, and buyer while protecting all parties to the transaction.

Obviously, professional intermediaries charge a fee. Financial benefit to the intermediary is derived only from participation in the exchange, not from any involvement typically associated with agency. They exist to perform a service, pursuant to a written agreement; acting to dispose of the relinquished property and acquire replacement property for the taxpayer/exchanger. The intermediary becomes the principal in the exchange transaction, acting only on its own behalf.

When to Use an Intermediary

Whenever using Section 1031 exchange provisions, it is highly recommended that you use a qualified intermediary to help safeguard your benefits. Review the following comments as they apply to simultaneous and delayed exchanges.

Simultaneous Exchanges

The 1991 Treasury regulations do not clarify whether the buyer or seller can act as an intermediary (Baird and Alderson formats), nor were they mentioned in the safe harbor definitions; however, most tax authorities agree they can be used in a simultaneous exchange if all the parties agree. However, under the 1991 Treasury regulations, the *only* safe harbor available to an exchanger in a simultaneous exchange is the use of a qualified intermediary. The IRS has further stated it will "scrutinize closely" any simultaneous exchange performed without a qualified intermediary.

Delayed Exchanges

Most investors do not care to use the buyer or seller in a delayed (or Starker) exchange because of the obvious issues of control, liability, and survivorship. If one of the parties is used as the intermediary in a delayed exchange, there is a chance something may happen to that person making him or her incapable of finishing the exchange. Any problems, personal or financial, that involve the individual acting as the intermediary attach themselves to the exchanger's transaction, possibly disrupting or even ruining the exchange.

Structuring the Delayed or Starker Exchange: The delayed or nonsimultaneous exchange using an intermediary is handled in two phases. In phase 1 the exchanger transfers ownership of the relinquished property A to the intermediary. This is done by the exchanger assigning his or her contractual rights to the intermediary and the closer following the exchange instructions to make the intermediary a part of the closing. (See Figure 11.3.)

The intermediary immediately transfers the relinquished property A to the buyer and receives the cash sales proceeds. Phase 1 is complete.

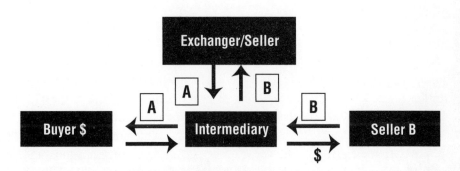

Figure 11.3   Starker or Delayed Exchange

The exchange proceeds will remain with the intermediary until such time as they are needed for the purchase (phase 2). Phase 2 occurs later when the intermediary acquires the replacement property B using the exchange proceeds and transfers ownership of the replacement property to the exchanger to complete the exchange.

During the entire process the intermediary will be available to answer questions from closers, agents, and their clients, and they will also be reviewing documentation to look for inconsistencies or problems with the exchange. The following examples represent only a few of thousands of similar situations in which the intermediary provided essential assistance.

Problem: An exchanger wishes to acquire California property valued at $400,000. He also wants to sell his $600,000 one-half ownership interest in property in New York; however, the purchase of the replacement property would precede the sale of the exchanger's New York property by several months.

Solution: The closer in New York uses a process commonly called a "reverse exchange." In a reverse exchange the intermediary can be utilized to close on the replacement property up to 180 days prior to the sale of the relinquished property.

Problem: The closer for an exchanger's replacement property forwards title work to the intermediary to prepare the buy side exchange instructions. The intermediary notices that the proposed insured is a corporation yet the exchanger and his wife are on title as joint tenants on the relinquished property.

Solution: The intermediary contacts the exchanger to notify him that he cannot change ownership during an exchange and that the corporation is a separate taxpayer from the exchanger and his wife. There are other forms of ownership that may offer more protection than individual ownership without disallowing the exchange that he may want to consider.

Problem: The exchanger has sold a rental property and the intermediary is holding exchange proceeds in the amount of $200,000. The closer for the replacement property requests the funds to be wired for the purchase. After reviewing the settlement statement the intermediary sees funds in the amount of $20,000 being refunded to the exchanger at closing. There is also a new mortgage for $128,000. (See Figure 11.4.)

Solution: The intermediary will instruct the closer to do a principal pay-down on the new loan to prevent the exchanger from receiving the $20,000 in cash in the middle of the exchange. This will save the exchanger capital gains on the $20,000. (See Figure 11.5.)

Responsibilities of Intermediary

Potential problems with exchanges can be avoided by thorough and complete documentation. This documentation provided by the intermediary must follow the guidelines of the Treasury regulations and place significant restrictions on the taxpayer according to those regulations. A qualified intermediary usually provides several documents in order to leave a clear paper trail for the defensibility of the exchange:

Exchange Agreement

The exchange agreement outlines the intermediary's relationship to the transaction. It also substantiates important elements of the exchange such as:

- Motive and intent.
- Interdependence.
- Disbursement of sale proceeds.
- Requirements for replacement property.

Note: A deposit receipt containing language referencing an exchange and the nontransfer of sale proceeds to the exchanger at the closing *will not* constitute a valid exchange agreement, even if the closing instructions also reflect the intent to exchange.

A.	
U.S. DEPARTMENT OF HOUSING & URBAN DEVELOPMENT	1. ☐ FHA 2. ☐ FmHA
SETTLEMENT STATEMENT	6. FILE NUMBER:
	8. MORTGAGE INS CASE NUMBER:

C. NOTE: *This form is furnished to give you a statement of actual settlement costs. Amounts paid for Items marked "[POC]" were paid outside the closing; they are shown here for information only.*

D. NAME AND ADDRESS OF BORROWER: **COMPANY NAME** Intermediary for Tom Smith, Exchanger	E. NAME AND ADDRESS OF SELLER:
G. PROPERTY LOCATION: **1400 Main Street**	H. SETTLEMENT AGENT: PLACE OF SETTLEMENT

J. SUMMARY OF BORROWER'S TRANSACTION	
100. GROSS AMOUNT DUE FROM BORROWER:	
101. Contract Sales Price	300,000.00
102. Personal Property	
103. Settlement Charges to Borrower (Line 1400)	8,000.00
120. GROSS AMOUNT DUE FROM BORROWER	308,000.00
200. AMOUNTS PAID BY OR IN BEHALF OF BORROWER:	
201. Deposit/earnest money $50,000.00 RETURNED	
202. Principal Amount of New Loan(s)	128,000.00
203. Existing loan(s) taken subject to	
204.	
205. Exchange Proceeds	200,000.00
206.	
220. TOTAL PAID BY/FOR BORROWER	
300. CASH AT SETTLEMENT FROM/TO BORROWER:	
301. Gross Amount Due From Borrower (Line 120)	
302. Less Amount Paid By/For Borrower (Line 220)	( )
303. CASH (FROM)(X TO) BORROWER	*20,000.00 ←

*This cash to borrower would be taxable boot

Figure 11.4   Sample Settlement Statement (HUD) with Taxable Boot

A.		
U.S. DEPARTMENT OF HOUSING & URBAN DEVELOPMENT	1. ☐ FHA 2. ☐ FmHA	
SETTLEMENT STATEMENT	6. FILE NUMBER:	
	8. MORTGAGE INS CASE NUMBER:	

C. NOTE: *This form is furnished to give you a statement of actual settlement costs. Amounts paid for Items marked "[POC]" were paid outside the closing; they are shown here for information only.*

D. NAME AND ADDRESS OF BORROWER: **COMPANY NAME** Intermediary for Tom Smith, Exchanger	E. NAME AND ADDRESS OF SELLER:
G. PROPERTY LOCATION: **1400 Main Street**	H. SETTLEMENT AGENT:
	PLACE OF SETTLEMENT

J. SUMMARY OF BORROWER'S TRANSACTION	
100. GROSS AMOUNT DUE FROM BORROWER:	
101. Contract Sales Price	300,000.00
102. Personal Property	
103. Settlement Charges to Borrower (Line 1400)	8,000.00
104. Paydown Principal Loan	20,000.00
120. GROSS AMOUNT DUE FROM BORROWER	308,000.00
200. AMOUNTS PAID BY OR IN BEHALF OF BORROWER:	
201. Deposit/earnest money $50,000.00 RETURNED	
202. Principal Amount of New Loan(s)	128,000.00
203. Existing loan(s) taken subject to	
204.	
205. Exchange Proceeds	200,000.00
206.	
220. TOTAL PAID BY/FOR BORROWER	
300. CASH AT SETTLEMENT FROM/TO BORROWER:	
301. Gross Amount Due From Borrower (Line 120)	
302. Less Amount Paid By/For Borrower (Line 220)	( )
303. CASH (FROM)/(X TO) BORROWER	0.00

Figure 11.5   Sample Settlement Statement (HUD) with Principal Paydown

Assignment Agreement

The assignment agreement assigns the contractual obligations from the exchanger to the intermediary. This document is necessary for the intermediary to become a party to the closing.

Exchange Closing Instructions

Detailed instructions for the closing agent provide guidelines to structure the exchange closing properly. These often include requirements for the handling of funds, as well as review of documentation by the intermediary for format prior to closing.

Step by Step—How Does This Look?

When a client contacts a qualified intermediary, the first thing a professional intermediary will do is attempt to understand what the client is trying to accomplish by asking questions about the proposed transaction. It is important to know the intentions of the prospective client to determine whether a valid exchange is even possible. In many instances, once all the important facts are ascertained, it becomes apparent that the proposed transaction will not allow for tax deferral. Some examples of exchanges that won't work are: (1) the client wishes to exchange a rental house for a principal residence (not like-kind property); (2) the intended replacement property is of substantially less value than the one being sold (the taxable boot may exceed the gain recognized); and (3) the property to be acquired will not be available for purchase until well after the expiration of the 180-day replacement period allowed for under Section 1031 (180 days is the maximum period of time allowed under the code).

Once the qualified intermediary determines an exchange transaction is possible, the intermediary will ask certain questions in order to properly draft the exchange documents and set up a defensible exchange. Questions such as who owns the property, the address or legal description of the property, who the real estate agent is (if any), and who the closing agent is must be addressed in order to set up the exchange. An improperly structured exchange will result in disqualification by the IRS and payment of capital gains tax together with penalties and interest.

Upon developing a client profile, the intermediary will begin by first contacting the real estate agent for a copy of the purchase and sale agreement. If no real estate agent is being used, the client will be required to provide a copy. It is important for the intermediary to review the purchase and sale agreement in order to verify who the seller is as listed in the contract. In some instances, the client contacting the intermediary to facilitate the exchange is not listed as the seller under the real estate contract. Clients may forget they have held the property in a limited liability company or living trust, or that their ex-spouse may still be on title to the property. Since the seller's rights under the purchase and sale agreement must be assigned to the intermediary at closing, it is essential to verify the seller's identity by reviewing the contract to avoid delays or problems at closing.

The next step to creating a tax-deferred exchange requires the intermediary to contact the closing agent. The closing agent is the company employed to draft the closing documents, including the settlement statement and deed. The closing agent also pays off any liens on the subject property and receives the buyer's purchase funds. In most Western states, the closing agent is a title or escrow company. The East Coast and parts of the South normally use closing attorneys to perform this function.

The intermediary will find out which closing attorney or escrow officer is responsible for closing the client's specific exchange transaction. The intermediary will need to obtain a copy of the title report (commitment) in order to draft the exchange agreement. The title report contains the legal description of the property, which can be used to describe the property in the exchange agreement if there is no street address for the property being exchanged. The report will also show the vested property owner. Since a tax-deferred exchange requires the taxpayer who sold the relinquished property to be the same taxpayer who buys the replacement property, it is essential that all exchange documents are drafted to reflect correct ownership.

Once the intermediary obtains a copy of the title report, exchange documents can be produced, usually consisting of an exchange agreement and an assignment agreement. Treasury regulations require the taxpayer to execute an exchange agreement with an intermediary, restricting the client's access to the exchange proceeds during the 180-day replacement period. As stated earlier, the purchase and sale agreement needs to be assigned by the exchanger/seller to the intermediary with the buyer being notified in writing of this assignment. The assignment serves the purpose of both giving written notification to the buyer of the exchange and allowing direct deeding of the property being relinquished from the exchanger to the buyer.

Together with closing instructions, the exchange documents will be forwarded by the intermediary to the closing agent for execution at closing. Copies of the documents are provided to the exchanger and the real estate agent.

How to Work with Your Closers

When the closing finally arrives, the closing agent will contact the client to come into the agent's office to sign all closing documents. These documents will include such items as escrow instructions (when applicable), the settlement statement, a warranty or grant deed, transfer tax documents, and, of course, the exchange documents. It is the closing agent's responsibility to make sure the exchange agreement and assignment agreement are signed, dated on or before the close of escrow, and returned to the intermediary after closing. Adherence to this step is essential as these documents will likely be required in an IRS audit. Without appropriately executed exchange documents, an exchange would most certainly fail.

The closing instructions provided by the intermediary are meant to assist the closing agent when drafting the settlement statement and other ancillary documents. The instructions should require that the intermediary's name be listed as the seller on the settlement statement. Another method of depicting the fact that a closing is an exchange transaction is to list the exchange company's name "as intermediary for" the exchanger.

In either case, the reason for doing this is to establish for the taxpayer's accountant, and in some instances an IRS auditor, that this was an exchange closing and not an outright sale.

Exchange instructions should request that the settlement statement be forwarded to the intermediary for review and signing prior to the close. This further bolsters the premise that this was in fact an exchange closing and not a typical sale transaction. It also provides the intermediary with an opportunity to review the settlement statement for errors or for items that could potentially be taxable to the exchanger or cause the exchange to fail. The intermediary will also look for items that may cause taxable boot or problems in an audit.

Many taxpayers and closing agents alike do not realize that prorated rents and security deposits on a settlement statement will cause taxable boot to the exchanger. It is standard practice for closing agents to credit the buyer for security deposits and rents currently in possession of the exchanger/seller. However, by providing for only a paper credit, the actual funds remain in possession of the exchanger. After the closing, this money is now the unfettered property of the exchanger and subject to tax. Properly constructed exchange closing instructions will address this problem prior to settlement and request that security deposits and prorated rents be handled between the parties outside of closing. An alternate approach is to have the exchanger deposit these funds with the settlement agent so that they may be properly credited to the buyer.

Other issues addressed in the exchange closing instructions include the proper method to complete the 1099-S form and various disclosure and transfer tax forms. Even when a closing is subject to a tax-deferred exchange on behalf of a seller, the 1099-S form and transfer tax documents should still be completed in the exchanger's name. This is because these forms are forwarded to the IRS (in the case of the 1099-S) and local taxing authority (in the case of transfer tax forms).

The exchange closing instructions provide for the immediate delivery of all exchange proceeds and signed exchange documents to the intermediary after closing. The exchange proceeds are usually sent to the intermediary either by a bank wire or by overnight delivery.

Once the intermediary receives the exchange proceeds, it should notify the exchanger of the amount received, as well as the final settlement date. This date is important, as the 45-day identification period, as well as the 180-day replacement period, both start from the settlement date of the relinquished property.

Once the replacement property is located and a closing is scheduled, the exchanger will need to notify the intermediary who will prepare the buy side exchange paperwork. The intermediary will contact the agent and closer for the buy side property and make arrangements to wire the exchange proceeds to the closing when the purchase is scheduled. The intermediary will review the closing paperwork, including the settlement statement, to assure the procedures for a defensible exchange have been followed and there are no items of taxable boot for the exchanger.

After closing, the intermediary will usually maintain a complete file for some period of time in case the accountant for the exchanger has some questions or needs copies of documents for the filing of the tax return.

Finding the Right Closer

While local custom usually governs which party to a real estate transaction selects the closing agent, it is a negotiable aspect of any real estate transaction. When considering an exchange of real estate, it is always advisable to discuss with one's real estate agent who might be best suited to facilitate the settlement process. Delayed exchanges have been around in their current form since 1991, so most established closing agents have been involved with an exchange closing at one time or another. It will be a less trying settlement if a closing agent is selected with experience in handling tax-deferred exchanges.

When selecting a closing agent, a simple approach is to interview several local closing companies in advance of entering into an agreement to sell the relinquished property. Asking them whether they have settlement agents on staff familiar with tax-deferred exchanges and their relative experience level will certainly make for a smoother closing process.

Sometimes it becomes necessary to use a closing company that might not have a closing agent on staff familiar with tax-deferred exchanges. If this is the case, working with an experienced intermediary will help to stabilize the settlement process. An experienced intermediary can speak with the closer and assist with any questions or concerns the closer may have. After working through one or two exchanges with a knowledgeable intermediary, a once inexperienced settlement agent should now be able to join the ranks of those settlement agents who can competently close exchange transactions.

How to Select
an Intermediary

The intermediary should be carefully chosen to ensure an exchange is defensible. As a quasi-principal in the transaction, the intermediary will have as much responsibility as the exchanger for performance of contractual obligations in the selling and buying of property. The real estate agent for the exchanger will become the real estate agent for the intermediary and, if the agent is unfamiliar with exchanging, it may be the intermediary's responsibility to ensure that the transaction is conducted properly.

An intermediary with experience in negotiation, contract law, taxation, investment analysis, closing, and real estate practice is extremely valuable should problems arise. Exchange problems frequently require knowledge of all of these areas in order to arrive at a solution. The intermediary should also have the finest legal and tax counsel available to assist when a problem requires specialized knowledge. An intermediary is a valuable resource to the investor, to the real estate agent, and to the investor's tax and legal counsel. A properly trained intermediary will identify problems *before* they threaten an exchange.

Given the availability of professional qualified intermediaries who are clearly not agents or fiduciaries outside of any exchange transaction, there is no reason to risk disallowance of an exchange by using the exchanger's attorney, real estate agent, or any other party who can be construed as having an agency relationship.

Currently the exchange industry has little regulation. In an unregulated industry there is a wide variance in the quality and services provided. Any individual or company can hold themselves out to be an intermediary. This results in little protection for the unwary investor. There are questions the exchanger should *always* ask before becoming involved with anyone offering services as a qualified intermediary.

A significant issue that should be addressed during selection is whether the intermediary is a member of the Federation of Exchange Accommodators (FEA) and has a Certified Exchange Specialist (CES) on staff. The FEA is the nation's largest trade organization comprised primarily of professional tax-deferred exchange accommodators specializing in aiding property owners to defer capital gains tax through an IRC Section 1031 exchange. With close to 300 member companies located in every state, the FEA has served its members for over a decade in such capacities as governmental advocate and liaison, educational resource, and ethics administrator. The CES designee possesses a certification that demonstrates to exchangers and their professional advisers that they have attained a superior professional standard of competency and knowledge in the exchange facilitation field. A CES designee must both meet a work experience standard and pass a comprehensive written test on exchange rules and regulations as well as industry practice and standards.

Just as when one selects an attorney, accountant, or real estate agent, it's important to review the credentials of any professional adviser prior to beginning a relationship with them. An exchange professional who has the CES designation will have demonstrated a high level of proficiency in dealing with tax-deferred exchanges.

Other questions that should be asked are:

1. **Who initially referred the intermediary?** Maybe the exchanger's accountant, attorney, title company, or real estate agent has previously worked with the intermediary. Personal referrals from other professionals always give a greater degree of comfort to the exchanger.

2. **What are the intermediary's professional references?** Most intermediaries will not release the names of clients as a matter of their clients' rights to privacy, but they should have a list of professional references to provide.

3. **How long has the intermediary been in business?** Obviously, it is far better to do business with a company established many years ago as an indicator of both the stability of the firm, as well as the experience level of the staff.

Accomplishing a tax-deferred exchange would be virtually impossible without the services of a professional qualified intermediary. The intermediary plays an integral part of the transaction as an adviser not only to the exchanger and closing agent, but also to legal and tax counsel. The intermediary also prepares the exchange documents, which under the Treasury regulations are crucial to a defensible exchange. Such significant responsibilities mean it is important to select an established intermediary with a reputation for thoroughness and expertise. With so much at stake, selecting the right intermediary will make the exchange process less confusing and provide peace of mind that the exchange was performed properly.

CHAPTER 12

Putting It Together for Successful Transactions

The goal of this chapter is:

To Illustrate the Importance of Positive Steps That Yield Positive Gains

Summary

Accept that exchanging can create benefits.

- Exchanges work to save you the payment of capital gains taxes when the properties involved qualify for Section 1031 treatment.

- Not all tax-free exchanges are completely free of tax.

- The exchange can be a proactive approach to help you sell a property when the market has not produced a buyer.

- The exchange can be a way out of a difficult situation as well as help you reach your goals.

- An exchange can open opportunities other than those you might have considered.

- An exchange does not have to save you money to take you closer to your ultimate goal.

Remember, the achievement of your goals is the most important element that you must direct your attention. This means, however, that in the absence of a clear direction offered to you that will take you closer to your goal, do not close doors on solutions that at least stop you from being taken farther away from your goal. Success in real estate investing is governed by targeting worthwhile goals, then establishing the interim goals that will carry you there.

As part of your periodic readjustment of your goals, there will be times that you must accept the fact that something did not work out as you had hoped it would. It is not important whether it was the plan that was wrong, or that mistakes were made, or that other circumstances over which you had no control were the cause. What is important is that you do not prolong the agony once you see the handwriting on the wall. In any investing there may come a time to cut your losses. All the tools available to you should be called into play during that time, and one of the best could well be an exchange. Why? Because what you see as a downward spiral someone else may see as an opportunity to start at the base of the hill and go up.

WYSIWYG

What you see is what you get. Word processing is this way, and so is your investment career if you open your eyes. By this I mean that your perception of what success means to you will govern how and at what level you set your priorities. This will, in logical projection, direct where and how much energy you plug into the effort to attain those goals. When you set those goals they must have an ultimate connection to happiness. The path to success and happiness may need to allow room for a balance of compromise and sacrifice. If either compromise or sacrifice is not preaccepted in your plan, then the need to do either will be a shock to the plan. This can cause you to be confused and you will be frustrated in the achievement of all your goals. Because of this, you need to define success in your own terms as it relates to your concept of happiness. If you target a success-oriented goal and encounter a need to sacrifice things such as a new home, a new car, or vacations and you and/or your partner in life begin to hate those sacrifices, then you need to readjust either your goal or your attitude about those sacrifices. A compromise may help you mitigate the sacrifice and can be a way to use teamwork to get through the tough times rather than simply to give up or reduce your goal levels.

Most people view their success from someone else's point of view. I have called this the "third-person point of view." This comes about partially from the peer pressure we experience. We listen to our friends and family and other people around us and sometimes secretly look for role models. We tend to believe or at least envy what those role models say and do. It is easy to believe that we should follow in their footsteps and emulate how they have attained their status in life. If we target that way of life without questioning whether those people consider themselves happy, then we may be on the wrong path ourselves. It is too easy to see ourselves in someone else's shoes without understanding what sacrifices or compromises they may have dealt with to get there and whether they are truly happy.

So often, the method people choose to select their goals and target the future is not based on a careful review of what they genuinely want to be or do. The usual tendency is to reach for the moon, without the understanding that going to the top of the hill is a far more realistic goal that can be easily attained, and will lead to the attainment of even higher aspirations. After all, when you go to the top of the hill you have a grander view of everything around you.

Yet, the pressure to succeed comes at us from every quadrant. It is easy to set the wrong priority under such pressure. The urgent tends to be treated as the most important, where in reality what we need to do is tackle the important long before it becomes urgent. If it isn't a family member shoving us along, it will be a friend, or worse still, our own inner explosion of embarrassment at having remained stagnant while our friends and acquaintances seem to be sailing along happily toward success. It is important to be careful about such circumstances. Without being willing to admit it, it is easy to become your own worst enemy. The self becomes a very destructive force when frustration and disappointment enter the picture. It is easy to become miserable and bitter and even fear everything without acknowledging that it is the self that is keeping us in the miserable state we are in. It is the self that can actually refuse to accept this self-imprisonment, and given half a chance, the self will blame everything and/or everyone while at the same time exonerating itself in a defensive manuever.

Many people ramble about their life with no clear purpose. They have either never learned the power of goal making or for that matter even what a real goal is. They either give up or wander through life never finding a job they like. They move from one job to another or they stick with a job they grow to hate and eventually blame everyone around them for being stuck in that situation. Sometimes they fail to make a move, no matter how great their hate and frustration, because they are afraid to move away from the familiarity of their surroundings. Or they wake up, perhaps tomorrow morning, and realize that there is a way out of that rut and frustration. It is what I call waking up to becoming a superperson.

A superperson is someone who recognizes that he or she can control his or her own motivation force and can take positive steps to energize this force. Once the force is energized, then the steps to change the way you think, act, and tackle the future will begin to alter your perspective of everything around you. You will become a proactive person who will focus on all the positive aspects of your life and of those around you. It will not be a sudden move from frustration to pure bliss, but you will see and feel the change almost immediately.

The first thing a superperson must do is to renounce everything negative around them. This means both negative thoughts and negative people. As a positive-thinking person, you will begin to attract a different kind of person to you. These different people are other positive people who understand the negative force of negative thinking. Together you and these other positive-minded people will reinforce each other, and before long you will discover that some of the most negative people you had known in your past are either gone or converted into positive thinkers, just as you have changed.

A superperson discovers rather quickly that the path to success and happiness in life is dependent on this force being kept alive. The negative thoughts and actions that are around you may start to seep back into your life, and you must continue to build positive bridges to lead you away from them. In time, the simple elements of negativity will disappear. No longer will you need to ask, "How can I overcome my weaknesses?" because you will focus on building on your strengths. The drive to attain a true inner happiness in harmony with success is now within your grasp.

Health is the ultimate goal that should be at the core of your target goals. Yet many people fail to understand that and abuse their bodies. It is never too late to start anew on the path to better health. As a newly formed superperson you can accept the simple effort it takes to improve on your health and to encourage those around you to follow your example. There is a grand benefit from having a clear mind and a healthy body, not just because these are positive elements that will shine as a beacon to others, but because you feel good about having achieved one of the most important aspects of life.

Looking around you, you have seen truly happy people. You have even envied their smiles and laughter and felt good as you watched clearly happy families share that laughter in loving situations, even though you knew that those people did not have as much as you do, or have the same opportunities that you might have. Yet, most truly happy people do not live in a utopia. They have their times when the positive dam leaks and some negative thoughts slip in, and there is pain and frustration, but positive people are able to pull through this and come out on top every time. You see, a superperson recognizes and accepts that there can be no ultimate success without an occasional failure. The key to overcoming this is to learn that failure is not the opposite of success.

Failing to achieve a goal is a signal that a new approach to the same goal must be considered, or a new goal must be targeted. A quick review of what happened in not reaching a goal you had been working for might point out that the interim steps were either passed over prior to attaining them, or that the goal was still just a little out of reach and perhaps the timetable needs to be adjusted. Sometimes failing to reach a goal is the inner self telling you that you are going down the wrong path. Be careful with when you get this feeling. The subconscious can be so protective that it will not want you to fail and will convince you that sometimes the best way not to fail is not to try to succeed. I have had many salespeople hate to fail so strongly (both consciously and subconsciously) that they would pick tasks to take them so far away from failure that they never had to confront the potential of success. Instead of calling a prospective client and asking if they could come over to discuss the sale of the prospect's property, they would drive across town to look at some other broker's open house. Or they would get in the habit of developing a migraine whenever there was the slightest possibility that they would be asked to do something at which they could fail. Always listen to your thoughts, but do not be too quick to follow their suggestions.

Deal Out the Negative

If you are able to deal out everything negative that touches your life, your tomorrow will be brighter and clearer, and your future destined to be a happier one. If you take a pass on everything negative you automatically let in everything positive. Your vision of yourself and of other people around you improves. You begin to see more of the positive in other people because you are closing out the negative. It doesn't matter if the negative is still there, as long as you shut it out. You stop making excuses for yourself and for those around you and begin to focus on your own inner strength. Never again is there any reason to dwell on "Why didn't I do something different?" as you now focus on "What do I need to do right?"

How Positive Thoughts Are Connected to Real Estate Investing

If you are wondering what in the world does any of this have to do with success in real estate investing or real estate exchanging, then you are in for a surprise. It has everything to do with real estate investing, and for that matter, everything you do that is in any way connected with your vision of success and happiness.

The Electrical Energy of Success

Nothing is better for your self-conscious than a good dose of success. So, build a pattern of success. Start your day with a series of things, baby steps you will do, that guarantee you will attain each one. Make them positive steps, and if you want to get an added bonus out of the effort, let them involve other people. For example, if you are married and have a family, then in the morning, no matter how well you slept or what problems are on your mind, have a routine that includes doing something positive for your health. Try to give your kids a big hug, tell your spouse how much you love her or him, and compliment at least two people on something they accomplished recently. Start saying nice things about other people; acknowledge that you notice they have changed their hair style, and how attractive it is that way. Read your immediate interim goals and remind yourself that those are goals you chose, and that they are designed to take you to your target goal.

You will be nurturing an electrical energy force that will flow through your body. You will stop complaining, and you will become more patient with genuine problems. You will focus on what is important, and never let things drift into the urgent column. Charged with this positive flow, you will change from a follower to a leader and you will feel good about yourself. You will be able to see a total picture while at the same time you will understand that to paint any picture requires more than one brush-stroke. You will begin to adjust your life from trying to get everywhere in leaps and bounds to the solid success of simple steps, each directed toward that target goal, and none of them so important in their own way that if they prove to be a misdirection you cannot quickly and positively change them into steps in the right direction.

The dynamics of this process are so wonderful that once you attain this state of mind you will never be the same person again. The irony is that although this state is simply gained, it is rarely found because most people are frightened at the prospect that their success will depend on no one but themselves. Some people are scared to death that if left to their own devices they will fail, and that failure is a measure of worthlessness. To fail is to be a loser. But in that thought, it is the negative that is sliding through the positive defenses. They are wrong. To fail is not a step in the direction of being a loser. Losers rarely fail because they have stopped trying to succeed. Failure is not a measure of worthlessness. Failure is the sweetener of success.

The fear of failure is what puts the butterflies in your stomach, and what injects that little bit of extra energy to push harder to succeed.

Failure is a trial run that allows you to remove the negative from your attitude and presentation and to build on the positive. Never fear failure, but embrace it. Put your arms around it and learn all you can when it happens. Get as much of all the failure you will ever experience behind you as quickly as possible; after all, it is only practice anyway.

Accept that to succeed, the only person you have to outdo is yourself.

Master List of Terms
and Concepts
You Need to Know

Chapter 1

Pretax Investment Value

Boot Paid or Received

Tax Basis

Net Operating Income

Amortization

Balloon Mortgage

Estate Taxes

Planning and Zoning

Comfort Zone

Chapter 2

Easy Access to Information

Toxic Sources of Pollution

Finding the Owner of a Specific Property

Offers to Exchange

Balance Exchange Equities

Date the 1031 Clock Should Start

Constructive Receipt

FIRPTA

Chapter 6

State Laws versus Federal Laws

Foreign Property

Chapter 7

Value versus Marketability

Dual Values

Justifying Value

Tax Appraisal Value

Lender's Appraisal

Common Area Maintenance (CAM)

Chapter 8

Importance of Timely and Effective Due Diligence

Outside the Comfort Box

Greener Grass Syndrome

Expanding Your Horizons and Options with Exchanges

Eight Motivations of Exchanges

Chapter 9

Creative Financing

Tenant-in-Common Interests

Chapter 10

Your Investment Team

Real Estate Agents

Maps Galore

Important Elements You Must Double-Check Prior to Closing

It's Wonderful How Difficult It Really Is

Nine Booby Traps to Look Out for in Making Exchanges